MEDIEVAL LITERATURE AND ANTIQUITIES

Studies in honour of Basil Cottle

For out of olde feldes, as men seyth,
Cometh al this newe corn from yer to yere,
And out of olde bokes, in good feyth,
Cometh al this newe science that men lere.

MEDIEVAL LITERATURE
AND ANTIQUITIES

*Studies in honour of
Basil Cottle*

EDITED BY

MYRA STOKES AND T. L. BURTON

D. S. BREWER

First published 1987 by D. S. Brewer
240 Hills Road, Cambridge
an imprint of Boydell & Brewer Ltd
PO Box 9, Woodbridge, Suffolk IP12 3DF
and Wolfeboro, New Hampshire 03894–2069, USA

ISBN 0 85991 237 X

British Library Cataloguing in Publication Data

Medieval literature and antiquities:
  studies in honour of Basil Cottle.
  1. Anglo-Saxon literature—History and
  criticism   2. English literature—Middle
  English, 1100–1500—History and criticism
  I. Stokes, Myra   II. Burton, T. L.
  III. Cottle, Basil
  820.9′001   PR176
  ISBN 0-85991-237-X

Library of Congress Cataloging in Publication Data

Medieval literature and antiquities.
  1. English literature—Middle English, 1100–1500—
  History and criticism   2. English philology   3. Cottle,
  Basil   I. Stokes, Myra   II. Burton, T. L.
  III. Cottle, Basil
  PR260.M44 1987   820′.9′001   86-24521
  ISBN 0-85991-237-X

Photoset in Great Britain by Galleon Photosetting, Ipswich
and printed in Great Britain by St Edmundsbury Press, Bury St Edmunds

Contents

Lexicography and Semantic History

List of Plates

The cover illustration shows the arms of the Cottle family.

THE CONTRIBUTORS

IAN BISHOP: Reader in English at the University of Bristol.

J. A. BURROW: Winterstoke Professor of English at the University of Bristol.

T. L. BURTON: Senior Lecturer in English Language and Literature at the University of Adelaide.

ÉAMONN Ó CARRAGÁIN: Professor of Old and Middle English at University College Cork.

RACHEL CRABTREE: Postgraduate student in the Centre for Medieval Studies at the University of York.

J. E. CROSS: Baines Professor of English Language at the University of Liverpool.

MARGARET E. GOLDSMITH: formerly Reader in English at the University of Bristol.

RUTH KENNEDY: Postgraduate student in the Department of English at the University of Bristol.

NICOLAS JACOBS: Fellow of Jesus College Oxford and University Lecturer in English.

PAT ROGERS: DeBartolo Professor of the Liberal Arts at the University of South Florida.

NIALL RUDD: Professor of Latin at the University of Bristol.

JOHN SCATTERGOOD: Professor of Medieval and Renaissance English at Trinity College Dublin.

MYRA STOKES: Lecturer in English at the University of Bristol.

HANNEKE WIRTJES: Temporary Lecturer in English at the University of Bristol.

ABBREVIATIONS

BL	British Library
CCSL	Corpus Christianorum, Series Latina (Turnhout, 1953–)
EETS	Early English Text Society (London, 1864–); ES: Extra Series; OS: Original Series; SS: Supplementary Series
JEGP	*Journal of English and Germanic Philology*
MED	*Middle English Dictionary* (Ann Arbor, Michigan, 1952–)
MLN	*Modern Language Notes*
MLQ	*Modern Language Quarterly*
NM	*Neuphilologische Mitteilungen*
OED	*The Oxford English Dictionary*
PL	Patrologiae Cursus Completus, Series Latina, ed. J. P. Migne (Paris, 1844–64)
PMLA	*Publications of the Modern Language Association of America*
RES	*Review of English Studies*; NS: New Series
RS	Rolls Series (London, 1858–)
TLS	*The Times Literary Supplement*

ACKNOWLEDGEMENTS

This volume could not have been published without the generous financial assistance which the Publications Committee of Bristol University gave to the project. The secretarial assistance of Jan Tarling and Tracy James, who run the Office of the English Department at Bristol, was almost equally invaluable.

We would also like to supplement the acknowledgements made by the individual contributors by expressing our thanks to the following institutions for providing photographs which they have kindly permitted us to use as illustrations: the Bodleian Library; the British Library; and the Dean and Chapter of St Paul's Cathedral (copyright in the case of the relevant MS residing with the Guildhall Library, London).

M.S.
T.L.B.

MA, PhD, Fellow of the Society of Antiquaries,
Reader in Medieval Studies at the University of Bristol

Expertise is a noun which the English, true to their inveterate habit of distorting French, have wrenched from its original signification ('survey', 'assessment', 'valuation'); and it is one which sounds awkward in the plural. But, though no one would in the normal course of things plead Basil Cottle in excuse for solecism, the compounded infelicity of *expertises* is one he would virtually force on his biographer. Primarily a specialist in Middle English Language and Literature, he also has degrees in Latin and Greek, and in the early 1950s gave lecture courses on the Greek Lyric for the Classics Department; he is familiar with numerous other languages; and, a Welshman by birth, he has a particular interest in all things Keltic. He has also considerable talent in the less august ingenuities of *homo loquens*, such as anagrams and limericks. During the war he was employed by HMG as a professional cryptanalyst: he was a member of the 'Enigma' team at Bletchley Park; and in 1946 he wrote an Albanian Grammar and Syntax for internal use by the Foreign Office. His published writings range over the entire history of the English language and its literature, from its pre-Conquest beginnings to the present day, from Cædmon to David Jones, from classics such as Chaucer, Shakespeare and Jane Austen to eccentrics such as 'Baron Corvo' and Thomas Chatterton. Besides languages and literatures and nomenclature, architecture, archaeology, palaeography and heraldry are all subjects on which he is expert, and on which he holds classes for undergraduates and postgraduates, inside and outside the English Department. His contributions to the study of archaeology are particularly notable: he has for some time given lecture courses both on Anglo-Saxon and on Early Christian Irish Archaeology in the Subdepartment of Classical Archaeology; he is president of the Council of the Bristol and Gloucestershire Archaeological Society; and he represented the University on the Camelot Research Committee for the excavation of South Cadbury, and at the 1975 Arthurian Congress at Exeter.

He is a devout Anglican (he has been Churchwarden at four churches in Bristol), and an especial interest in the Christian Church is perhaps the most common factor discernible in his many and disparate scholarly pursuits: an interest that extends from the structure of its buildings and the glass in its windows to the wording of its services and the lives of its early saints. One of the research projects on which he is currently engaged is the revision and rewriting of Miss Rotha M. Clay's *Hermits and Anchorites of England*.

His academic services to the University have been considerable. Before he retired in 1980, his formidable teaching commitments often amounted to over twenty hours a week (and not one hour has ever been lost through illness); and his contributions since retirement have continued only somewhat less remarkable, though much less well remunerated. He was also for twenty-four years Subwarden of Burwalls Hall of Residence. Despite this busy professional schedule, he has always taken an active interest in the city itself, its churches and its literary heritage. This interest is reflected in his contributions to the literature on the city, but it has also bequeathed to the community even more tangible benefits: he has at his own expense saved from export a number of MS letters of Coleridge, Wordsworth, Southey, Crabbe and lesser literary figures; and in 1967 he commissioned the sculpting of the Chatterton tablet now on the wall of the south transept in St Mary Redcliffe.

In the English Department, where he has taught for forty-one years, his wit, clarity and personality have succeeded in making Anglo-Saxon and Middle English accessible and fun to many generations of students, including the present editors. His lectures on Anglo-Saxon art have often been felt by them to provide the only irrigation in otherwise very dry terrain; and when he ran the Advanced Middle English course ('advanced muddle', as he termed it) it proved to be amongst the most popular of the options on offer. He has performed the same popularizing service to his subjects outside the University. He speaks willingly and frequently on very varied subjects to very varied audiences, has been on television and radio, and writes books which give proof positive that it is not necessary to be difficult or boring in order to be scholarly and informative. He does not write to preach only to the converted; he intends to be (and is) as intelligible and interesting to the layman as to the academic: few of us could boast, as he can, of a fan-letter from a Japanese businessman.

It was Tom Burton's idea that his seventieth birthday (he was born on St Patrick's Day, 1917) should be marked by way of this volume of essays, contributed by past and present colleagues and by former students. To represent the full range of his interests and abilities would have been impossible, if only because the resultant collection would have constituted a cataloguing nightmare for librarians. But we have tried to take account of his interest in art and archaeology and in the language and literature of all periods. We would all beg him 'To vouchen sauf, ther nede is, to correcte', for we cannot hope he will not detect the errors and infelicities that have escaped our united efforts at purgation.

The list of his published works that follows gives but an imperfect idea of the variety of his true output, and the generous enthusiasm with which he puts his talents at the disposal of all kinds of projects, in earnest or in game, for solace or sentence. It does not include, for instance, the verse prologue which he composed and delivered for the opening of the Studio Theatre in the Wills Memorial Building of the University in 1951; the two verse addresses of welcome to HRH Princess Marina, Duchess of Kent, at the opening of the Vandyck Theatre in 1968; the words he composed for the anthem performed in Waltham Abbey in 1966 to commemorate the nine-hundredth anniversary of the burial there of King Harold II Godwinson; the edition he prepared in 1970 of Chatterton's play *Ælla* for its first-ever performance at Chatterton's old school (Colston's, Bristol); the sermon he gave in Bristol Cathedral in 1972 to commemorate the bicentenary of the birth of Coleridge; or the coats of arms he has devised. Nor does it record that large body of compositions which are among his most talented and engaging, but which are necessarily of a fugitive and occasional nature: the many limericks, anagrams and comic verses with which he has entertained his colleagues and pupils for many years; and the witty scripts he wrote for staff pantomimes bearing such titles as 'The Babes in the Sacred Wood' and 'Snow White and the Seven Deadly Types of Ambiguity'.

Myra Stokes

Published Works

Books

The Life of a University (Bristol: Arrowsmith, 1951; 2nd edn, 1959): with J. W. Sherborne, pp. 116; 2nd edn 147.

St Mary Redcliffe, Bristol: Church Guide (Bristol: Mardon, 1957), pp. 32.

Metaphor and Symbol: Proceedings of the Twelfth Symposium of the Colston Research Society (London: Butterworths, 1960): ed. with L. C. Knights, pp. xi, 150.

The Penguin Dictionary of Surnames (Harmondsworth: Penguin, 1967; 2nd edn, 1969), pp. 334; 2nd edn 444.

The Triumph of English 1350–1400 (London: Blandford, 1969), pp. 318.

The Plight of English: Ambiguities, Cacophonies and Other Violations of Our Language (Newton Abbot: David & Charles, 1975), pp. 159.

Names (London: Thames and Hudson, 1983), pp. 224.

The Language of Literature: English Grammar in Action (London: Macmillan, 1985), pp. 176.

Articles and Pamphlets

'Early Christian Keltic Art in Ireland and Wales (1)', *Cymry'r Groes* 1 (September, 1945) 14–16.

'Early Christian Keltic Art in Ireland and Wales (2)', *Cymry'r Groes* 1 (Christmas, 1945) 20–4.

'The Arts in Bristol since 1800', in *Bristol and its Adjoining Counties*, ed. C. M. MacInnes and W. F. Whittard (Bristol, 1955), pp. 243–53; revised and reprinted (Wakefield, 1973), pp. 243–53 and 348–9.

'The City of Bristol', *Proceedings of the Chemical Society* (1958) 41–3.

'The City of Bristol', in *Bristol: A Booklet to Commemorate the Seventy-Ninth Annual Meeting of the Society of Chemical Industry* (Bristol, 1960), pp. 9–18.

Thomas Chatterton (Bristol Branch of the Historical Association, 1963); 15 pages; revised and reprinted in *Bristol in the Eighteenth Century*, ed. P. V. McGrath (Newton Abbot, 1972), pp. 89–108.

'Thomas Chatterton', *Encyclopaedia Britannica*, 14th edn (1963), v. 348–50; (1967), v. 348–50.

'Westbury's Part in Literature', in *1250 Years at Westbury-on-Trym* (Bristol, 1966), pp. 26–7.

'The University', in *The Visitors' Guide to the City and County of Bristol* (Constaple, 1966), p. 47.

'Ermitas de Santiago', in E. la O. Miracle, *Santiago en America y en Inglaterra y Escocia* (Madrid, 1970), p. 93.

'Wordsworth and his Portraits: Two Unpublished Letters', *Notes and Queries* 218 (1973) 285–6.

'Bristol Writers' in *The Redcliffe Press Guide to Children's Bristol* (Bristol, 1976) 66–9.

'Popular Reading and our Public Libraries: the Abjured Prescription', *Library Review* 27 (1978) 222–7.

'The English of Series 3 Holy Communion', *PN Review* (13) 6 (1979–80) 18–19.

'Names', in *The State of the Language*, ed. Leonard Michaels and Christopher Ricks (Berkeley, California, 1980) 98–107.

Robert Southey and Bristol (Bristol Branch of the Historical Association, 1980); 20 pages.

'The Significance of St Woolos (Cathedral, Newport)', *Friends of St Woolos, First Annual Report* (1980) 5–15.

'The Cult of Saints in Mediaeval Bristol', *Avon Past* 5 (Autumn, 1981) 5–13.

Reviews

Chaucer: Contes de Cantorbéry, Contes Choisis, ed. Joseph Delcourt: *Modern Language Review* 43 (1948) 129.

Haldeen Braddy, *Chaucer and the French Poet Graunson*: *RES* 24 (1948) 150–1.

Margaret Adlum Gist, *Love and War in the Middle English Romances*: *RES* 25 (1949) 351–2.

Bernard Martin, *The Ancient Mariner and the Authentic Narrative*; and Herbert Read, *Coleridge as Critic*: *The Charles Lamb Society Bulletin* (1949; July, No. 90).

Fernand Mossé, *Manuel de l'Anglais du Moyen Âge, II: Moyen-Anglais*: *RES* NS 2 (1951) 65–7.

W. H. G. Armytage, *Civic Universities: Aspects of a British Tradition*: *The Universities Review* 28 (1955) 29.

An Exposition of 'Qui Habitat' and 'Bonum Est' in English, ed. Björn Wallner: *RES* NS 6 (1955) 192–3.

R. M. Lumiansky, *Of Sondry Folk: The Dramatic Principle in the Canterbury Tales*: *JEGP* 55 (1956) 292–3.

Joseph T. Shipley, *Dictionary of Early English*: *JEGP* 55 (1956) 499–501.

Eleanor Shipley Duckett, *Alfred the Great*: *JEGP* 56 (1957) 468–9.

A. W. Wade-Evans, *The Emergence of England and Wales*: *JEGP* 56 (1957) 469–70.

The Ancrene Riwle, trans. M. B. Salu: *JEGP* 57 (1958) 117–19.

The Benedictine Office: An Old English Text, ed. James M. Ure: *JEGP* 57 (1958) 333–4.

The Complaint Against Hope: An Edition, ed. Kenneth G. Wilson: *JEGP* 57 (1958) 334–5.

The Works of Geoffrey Chaucer, ed. F. N. Robinson, 2nd edn: *JEGP* 57 (1958) 531–3.

Paston Letters, selected and ed. Norman Davis: *JEGP* 58 (1959) 289–90.

Paull F. Baum, *Chaucer: A Critical Appreciation*: *JEGP* 58 (1959) 676–8.

MS. Bodley 959 (Vol. I: Genesis and Exodus), ed. Conrad Lindberg: *JEGP* 59 (1960) 565.

The Parlement of the Thre Ages, ed. M. Y. Offord; and *The South English Legendary* (Vol. III), ed. Charlotte D'Evelyn and Anna J. Mill: *JEGP* 59 (1960) 727–8.

Eilert Ekwall, *The Concise Oxford Dictionary of English Place-Names*, 4th edn: *JEGP* 60 (1961) 160–2.

A Deuout Treatyse Called the Tree and XII. Frutes of the Holy Goost, ed. J. J. Vaissier: *RES* NS 12 (1961) 182–3.

H. C. Dent, *Universities in Transition*: *Universities Quarterly* 15 (1961) 408–11.

MS. Bodley 959 (Vol. II: Leviticus–Judges 7. 13), ed. Conrad Lindberg: *JEGP* 61 (1962) 372–3.

Pe Liflade ant te Passiun of Seinte Iuliene, ed. S. R. T. O. d'Ardenne: *JEGP* 61 (1962) 634–5.

Hans Schnyder, *Sir Gawain and the Green Knight: An Essay in Interpretation*: *JEGP* 61 (1962) 913–15.

A Selection of English Carols, ed. Richard Leighton Greene: *RES* NS 14 (1963) 277–9.

Marguerite-Marie Dubois, *La Littérature Anglaise du Moyen Âge (500–1500)*: *JEGP* 62 (1963) 201–2.

Elizabeth Salter, *'Piers Plowman': An Introduction*: *JEGP* 62 (1963) 213–14.

Marie Borroff, *Sir Gawain and the Green Knight: A Stylistic and Metrical Study*: *JEGP* 62 (1963) 364–5.

The Oxford Illustrated Dictionary, ed. J. Coulson, C. T. Carr, Lucy Hutchinson, Dorothy Eagle: *RES* NS 15 (1964) 112–13.

The English Text of the 'Ancrene Riwle': 'Ancrene Wisse', ed. from MS. Corpus Christi College Cambridge 402 by J. R. R. Tolkien: *JEGP* 63 (1964) 330–1.

MS. Bodley 959 (Vol. III: Judges 7. 13–II Paralipomenon), ed. Conrad Lindberg: *JEGP* 63 (1964) 331–2.

Harold Orton and Eugen Dieth, *Survey of English Dialects* (Introduction and Vol. I, Parts I and II): *JEGP* 63 (1964) 479–80.

Laȝamon: Brut (Vol. I), ed. G. L. Brook and R. F. Leslie: *JEGP* 63 (1964) 484–5.

Three Middle English Religious Poems, ed. R. H. Bowers: *JEGP* 63 (1964) 485–7.

The English Text of the 'Ancrene Riwle', ed. from Cotton MS. Titus D. XVIII by Frances M. Mack; together with *The Lanhydrock Fragment*, ed. from Bodleian MS. Eng. th. c. 70 by A. Zettersten: *JEGP* 63 (1964) 761–2.

Medieval English Lyrics: A Critical Anthology, ed. R. T. Davies: *JEGP* 63 (1964) 763–7.

G. L. Brook, *English Dialects*: *JEGP* 63 (1964) 835–7.

The Bodley Version of Mandeville's Travels, ed. from Bodleian MS. e Musaeo 116 by M. C. Seymour: *JEGP* 64 (1965) 161–3.

Beverly Boyd, *The Middle English Miracles of the Virgin*: *JEGP* 64 (1965) 286–7.

H. Steen Sørensen, *The Meaning of Proper Names*: *RES* NS 16 (1965) 224.

A. H. Smith, *The Place-Names of Gloucestershire*: *RES* NS 17 (1966) 75–7.

H. W. Fowler, *A Dictionary of Modern English Usage*, 2nd edn rev. Sir Ernest Gowers: *RES* NS 17 (1966) 185–8.

A. F. Scott, *Current Literary Terms: A Concise Dictionary*: *RES* NS 17 (1966) 422–3.

Stella Brook, *The Language of the Book of Common Prayer*: *JEGP* 65 (1966) 331–2.

Sir Eglamour of Artois, ed. Frances E. Richardson: *JEGP* 65 (1966) 578–9.

Bror Danielsson, *John Hart's Works on English Orthography and Pronunciation* (Part II: Phonology): *JEGP* 65 (1966) 589–90.

MS. Bodley 959 (Vol. IV: I Esdras-Ecclesiasticus 48. 6), ed. Conrad Lindberg: *JEGP* 65 (1966) 708–9.

A. J. Bliss, *A Dictionary of Foreign Words and Phrases in Current English*: *RES* NS 18 (1967) 441–2.

Arne Zettersten, *Studies in the Dialect and Vocabulary of the 'Ancrene Riwle'*: *JEGP* 66 (1967) 116–18.

The Oxford Dictionary of English Etymology, ed. C. T. Onions with the assistance of G. W. S. Friedrichsen and R. W. Burchfield: *JEGP* 66 (1967) 282–6.

Hans Aarsleff, *The Study of Language in England, 1780–1860*: *JEGP* 66 (1967) 562–3.

The Orcherd of Syon (Vol. I), ed. Phyllis Hodgson and Gabriel M. Liegey: *JEGP* 66 (1967) 563–6.

A. H. Smith, *The Place-Names of Westmorland*: *RES* NS 19 (1968) 182–3.

Sir Paul Harvey, *The Oxford Companion to English Literature*, 4th edn rev. Dorothy Eagle: *RES* NS 19 (1968) 303–7.

Early Middle English Verse and Prose, ed. J. A. W. Bennett and G. V. Smithers: *JEGP* 67 (1968) 140–4.

Eduard Kolb, *Phonological Atlas of the Northern Region: The Six Northern Counties, North Lincolnshire and the Isle of Man*: *JEGP* 67 (1968) 179–80.

Walter Hilton's Eight Chapters on Perfection, ed. Fumio Kuriyagawa: *JEGP* 67 (1968) 297–8.

Gillis Kristensson, *A Survey of Middle English Dialects 1290–1350: The Six Northern Counties and Lincolnshire*: *JEGP* 67 (1968) 694–5.

Guy of Warwick, ed. William B. Todd: *JEGP* 68 (1969) 281–3.

A Dialogue Between Reason and Adversity: A Late Middle English Version of Petrarch's 'De Remediis', ed. F. N. M. Diekstra: *JEGP* 68 (1969) 283–5.

Arthur O. Sandved, *Studies in the Language of Caxton's Malory and that of the Winchester Manuscript*: *JEGP* 68 (1969) 289–90.

Derek Pearsall, *John Lydgate*: *The Times Educational Supplement*, 30 October 1970, p. 24.

The Middle English 'Genesis and Exodus', ed. Olaf Arngart: *JEGP* 69 (1970) 163–5.

Mortimer J. Donovan, *The Breton Lay: A Guide to Varieties*: *JEGP* 69 (1970) 304–6.

Jerome Mitchell, *Thomas Hoccleve: A Study in Early Fifteenth-Century English Poetic*: *JEGP* 69 (1970) 306–7.

MS. Bodley 959 (Vol. v: Ecclesiasticus 48. 6–Baruch 3. 20), ed. Conrad Lindberg: *JEGP* 69 (1970) 515–17.

George Sampson, *The Concise Cambridge History of English Literature*, 3rd edn rev. R. C. Churchill: *RES* NS 22 (1971) 174–8.

J. McN. Dodgson, *The Place-Names of Cheshire* (Parts II and III): *RES* NS 22 (1971) 463–5.

Edward Peters, *The Shadow King: 'Rex Inutilis' in Medieval Law and Literature, 751–1327*: *JEGP* 71 (1972) 111–12.

Judson Boyce Allen, *The Friar as Critic: Literary Attitudes in the Later Middle Ages*: *JEGP* 71 (1972) 116–18.

The Penguin Companion to Literature: Britain and the Commonwealth, ed. David Daiches: *RES* NS 23 (1972) 321–5.

J. McN. Dodgson, *The Place-Names of Cheshire* (Part IV): *RES* NS 24 (1973) 193–4.

John Field, *English Field Names: A Dictionary*: *RES* NS 24 (1973) 317–19.

Norman Fruman, *Coleridge, the Damaged Archangel*: *Essays in Criticism* 23 (1973) 413–19.

The English Text of the 'Ancrene Riwle', ed. from B.M. Cotton MS. Cleopatra C. VI by E. J. Dobson: *JEGP* 73 (1974) 239–40.

Margaret Gelling, *The Place-Names of Berkshire* (Part I): *RES* NS 25 (1974) 187–8.

The Oxford Anthology of English Literature (2 vols), ed. Frank Kermode and John Hollander: *RES* NS 25 (1974) 318–23.

Thomas H. Bestul, *Satire and Allegory in 'Wynnere and Wastoure'*: *JEGP* 74 (1975) 221–3.

Harry Blamires, *A Short History of English Literature*: *RES* NS 26 (1975) 452–4.

P. H. Reaney, *A Dictionary of British Surnames*, 2nd edn, rev. R. M. Wilson: *The Times Higher Education Supplement*, 26 March 1976, p. 17.

E. J. Dobson, *Moralities on the Gospels: A New Source of 'Ancrene Wisse'*: *JEGP* 75 (1976) 401–2.

Piers Plowman: The B Version, ed. George Kane and E. Talbot Donaldson: *JEGP* 75 (1976) 589–92.

Martyn F. Wakelin, *Language and History in Cornwall*: *RES* NS 28 (1977) 61–2.

The English Text of the 'Ancrene Riwle', ed. from Magdalene College, Cambridge MS. Pepys 2498 by A. Zettersten: *JEGP* 76 (1977) 541–2.

The Concise Oxford Dictionary, 6th edn, ed. J. B. Sykes: *RES* NS 28 (1977) 314–16.

Dorothy Eagle and Hilary Carnell, *The Oxford Literary Guide to the British Isles*: *RES* NS 29 (1978) 244–6.

Margaret Gelling, *Signposts to the Past: Place-Names and the History of England*: *British Book News* (July, 1978) 584.

Richard Cavendish, *King Arthur and the Grail: The Arthurian Legends and their Meaning*: *British Book News* (October, 1978) 810.

Secretum Secretorum: Nine English Versions (Vol. I), ed. M. A. Manzalaoui: *JEGP* 77 (1978) 586–7.

Andor Gomme, Michael Jenner and Bryan Little, *Bristol: An Architectural History*: *British Book News* (May, 1979) 372–3.

Priscilla Martin, *'Piers Plowman': The Field and the Tower*: *British Book News* (December, 1979) 1028.

Paul Procter *et al.*, *Longman Dictionary of Contemporary English*: *RES* NS 30 (1979) 195–6.

Jean Branford, *A Dictionary of South African English*: *RES* NS 30 (1979) 323–4.

A. J. Gilbert, *Literary Language from Chaucer to Johnson*: *TLS*, 14 March 1980, p. 300.

Terry Jones, *Chaucer's Knight: The Portrait of a Medieval Mercenary*: *Country Life*, 27 March 1980, pp. 968–9.

Norman Davis, Douglas Gray, Patricia Ingham and Anne Wallace-Hadrill, *A Chaucer Glossary*: *RES* NS 31 (1980) 445–6.

J. D. Burnley, *Chaucer's Language and the Philosophers' Tradition*: *British Book News* (February, 1980) 115.

Arthurian Legends: An Illustrated Anthology, selected and introduced by Richard Barber: *British Book News* (March, 1980) 158.

Nigel Wilkins, *Music in the Age of Chaucer*: *British Book News* (May, 1980) 306.

Records of Early English Drama: Chester, ed. Lawrence M. Clopper: *British Book News* (June, 1980) 367.

Essays on 'Troilus and Criseyde', ed. Mary Salu: *British Book News* (June, 1980) 369–70.

Nigel Wilkins, *Chaucer Songs*: *British Book News* (July, 1980), 432.

Jürgen Schäfer, *Documentation in the O.E.D.: Shakespeare and Nashe as Test Cases*: *British Book News* (August, 1980) 475.

C. David Benson, *The History of Troy in Middle English Literature: Guido delle Colonne's 'Historia Destructionis Troiae' in Medieval England*: *British Book News* (August, 1980) 496–7.

The Franklin's Tale, ed. Gerald Morgan: *British Book News* (August, 1980) 497.

T. P. Dunning, *'Piers Plowman': An Interpretation of the A Text*, 2nd edn rev. T. P. Dolan: *British Book News* (November, 1980) 688.

Old English Literature in Context: Ten Essays, ed. John D. Niles: *British Book News* (December, 1980) 761–2.

Peter Beal, *Index of English Literary Manuscripts* (Vol. I: 1450–1625): *British Book News* (January, 1981), 14–15.

T. E. McNeill, *Anglo-Norman Ulster: The History and Archaeology of an Irish Barony*: *British Book News* (January, 1981) 59.

Derek Brewer, *Symbolic Stories: Traditional Narratives of the Family Drama in English Literature*: *British Book News* (February, 1981) 113.

Klaus Forster, *A Pronouncing Dictionary of English Place-Names Including Standard Local and Archaic Variants*: *British Book News* (August, 1981) 505–6.

Aspects of Malory, ed. Toshiyuki Takamiya and Derek Brewer; and *The Alliterative Morte Arthure: A Reassessment of the Poem*, ed. Karl Heinze Göller: *British Book News* (September, 1981) 564–5.

Susan M. Pearce, *The Archaeology of South West Britain*: *British Book News* (November, 1981) 697.

Jan Jönsjö, *Studies on Middle English Nicknames: I. Compounds*: *RES* NS 33 (1982) 68–9.

Thomas Pyles, *Selected Essays on English Usage*, ed. John Algeo: *RES* NS 33 (1982) 190–1.

T. H. Long *et al.*, *Longman Dictionary of English Idioms*: *RES* NS 33 (1982) 303–4.

Josefa Heifetz Byrne, *Mrs. Byrne's Dictionary of Unusual, Obscure, and Preposterous Words*: *RES* NS 33 (1982) 445–6.

M. Sue Hetherington, *The Beginnings of Old English Lexicography*: *RES* NS 33 (1982) 446–7.

H. Patrick Montague, *The Saints and Martyrs of Ireland*: *British Book News* (April, 1982) 217.

Arthurian Literature 1, ed. Richard Barber; and *The Arthurian Bibliography 1*, ed. Cedric E. Pickford, Rex Last, Christine R. Barker: *British Book News* (April, 1982) 229.

G. H. Roscow, *Syntax and Style in Chaucer's Poetry*: *British Book News* (May, 1982) 316–17.

Brian de Breffny, *In the Steps of St Patrick*: *British Book News* (July, 1982) 408–9.

Chambers Universal Learners' Dictionary, ed. E. M. Kirkpatrick: *RES* NS 34 (1983) 196–7.

A. D. Mills, *The Place-Names of Dorset* (Part II): *RES* NS 34 (1983) 316–17.

Seinte Katerine, re-ed. from MS. Bodley 34 and the other manuscripts by S. R. T. O. d'Ardenne and E. J. Dobson: *JEGP* 82 (1983) 222–4.

The Late Medieval Religious Plays of Bodleian MSS. Digby 133 and E Museo 160, ed. Donald C. Baker *et al.*: *JEGP* 82 (1983) 439–40.

C. H. Sisson, *Anglican Essays*: *British Book News* (September, 1983) 544.

Leslie Alan Dunkling, *The Guinness Book of Names*: *Nomina* 7 (1983) 134–6.

Eugene Ehrlich *et al.*, *Oxford American Dictionary*: *RES* NS 35 (1984) 74.

Kurt Rydland, *Vowel Systems and Lexical-Phonemic Patterns in South-East Cumbria: A Study in Structural Dialectology*: *RES* NS 35 (1984) 433.

A Supplement to the Oxford English Dictionary (Vol. III: O–Scz), ed. R. W. Burchfield: *RES* NS 35 (1984) 517–18.

Glanville Price, *The Languages of Britain*: *TLS*, 11 May 1984, p. 527.

Manuscripts and Readers in Fifteenth-Century England: The Literary Implications of Manuscript Study, ed. Derek Pearsall: *TLS*, 13 July 1984, p. 795.

Louis Heller, Alexander Humez and Malcah Dror, *The Private Lives of English Words*: *TLS*, 20 July 1984, p. 807.

The Arthurian Bibliography 2: Subject Index, ed. Cedric E. Pickford, Rex Last, Christine R. Barker: *British Book News* (January, 1984) 12.

Francis Wormald, Collected Writings I: Studies in Medieval Art from the Sixth to the Twelfth Centuries, ed. J. J. G. Alexander *et al.*: *British Book News* (July, 1984) 420.

Margaret Gelling, *Place-Names in the Landscape*: *British Book News* (October, 1984) 631.

Muriel Whitaker, *Arthur's Kingdom of Adventure: The World of Malory's 'Morte Darthur'*: *British Book News* (November, 1984) 693–4.

English Today: The International Review of the English Language (Preview Issue): *British Book News* (December, 1984) 917.

Tirant Lo Blanc, trans. David H. Rosenthal: *Country Life*, 27 December 1984, pp. 2018–19.

Caxton's Malory: A New Edition of Sir Thomas Malory's 'Le Morte Darthur', Based on the Pierpoint Morgan Copy of William Caxton's Edition of 1485 (2 vols), ed. James W. Spisak and W. Matthews: *JEGP* 84 (1985) 252–3.

The Court of Sapience, ed. E. Ruth Harvey: *JEGP* 84 (1985) 417–18.

Hali Meiðhad, ed. Bella Millett: *Medium Aevum* 54 (1985) 136–7.

Five Hundred Years of Words and Sounds: A Festschrift for Eric Dobson, ed. E. G. Stanley and Douglas Gray: *RES* NS 36 (1985) 545–6.

Michael Stapleton, *The Cambridge Guide to English Literature*: *RES* NS 36 (1985) 617–21.

Classics

Towers and Citadels in the Aeneid

NIALL RUDD

To A.B.C. for much enjoyable talk

In Roman writers cities are characterized by their walls, their buildings, and their citadel or *arx*. So, strictly, *arx* represents only a part of the whole. It is, however, the most vital part, for reasons which will be discussed below. In addition, the plural *arces* is often used, by Virgil at least, for a city's high buildings; and sometimes, by an easy extension, *arx* or *arces* means a mountain height.

Throughout the *Aeneid* hill-towns provide a series of focal points. One thinks immediately of Troy, Carthage, and Pallanteum (the future Rome); but there are others too. Obviously some places occur because they have already figured in the Aeneas legend.[1] Yet Virgil's imagination gives them an imposing character which in certain cases is found in neither Homer nor history. In *Iliad* xx. 216 ff. we read:

> Not yet was sacred Ilium built on the plain as a city of articulate men, but they still lived on the slopes of many-fountained Ida.

Speaking of the same period, Anchises says,

> nondum Ilium et arces
> Pergameae steterant; habitabant uallibus imis.   (III. 109–10)

> [Not yet had Ilium and the towers of Troy been built; people lived in the bottom of the valleys.]

Virgil has not only abandoned Homer's 'formulaic' epithets; he has modified the topography so as to contrast the hill of Troy with the low valleys. Earlier in the poem, when the town was blazing, Hector's ghost had cried 'ruit alto a culmine Troia' (II. 290) ['Troy is crashing down from its high pinnacle']—a striking picture, yet Troy VIIa rose less than a hundred feet above the plain.[2] Later,

---

[1] Versions of the legend describing Aeneas' journey to Italy were given by several writers, Greek and Roman, before Virgil's day. See R. D. Williams's edition of *Aeneid III* (Oxford, 1962), pp. 7–12.

[2] See A. J. B. Wace and F. H. Stubbings, *A Companion to Homer* (London, 1962), pp. 365 and 386.

when the Trojans in the course of their wanderings approach Buthrotum in Epirus, Aeneas says, 'We enter the . . . harbour and approach the lofty city of Buthrotum' (III. 292–3). By ordinary prosaic standards Buthrotum is not lofty. As N. G. L. Hammond says, 'It stands on a low hill of limestone formation'.[3]

As for Carthage (founded, according to tradition, in 814 BC), archaeologists believe that its development was a very gradual process. The eighth-century settlement is thought to have extended 'along the coast from Salammbo to the Bordj Djedid bay'; 'the need for a citadel only arose later, when the colony began to dominate the neighbouring folk and there was danger of an attack by land.'[4] Yet Virgil speaks more than once of buildings going up on the citadel fairly soon after the Carthaginians' arrival (I. 366, 424); and that is where he situates Dido's palace (IV. 410, 586). The hill which he had in mind was doubtless the Byrsa, a two hundred foot eminence now known as the Hill of St Louis. It was about three-quarters of a mile from the harbour. On level ground, much nearer to the harbour, stood the so-called sanctuary of Tanit. Since Tanit was a fertility goddess, it is unlikely that she acquired major importance until the fifth century or later, when Punic agriculture developed. Then, as protectress of the city, she became identified with the Roman Juno. This time-scale was probably unknown to Virgil, and in any case it would not have suited his purpose. For him Juno was in control of Carthage from the beginning; she cherished it in the hope that it would eventually become mistress of the world. So in the *Aeneid* her temple, a huge building, stands in the centre of the city (I. 441–9).

As a final example of history's being adjusted to poetry, we may take VI. 830–1, where Anchises is prophesying civil war:

> aggeribus socer Alpinis atque arce Monoeci
> descendens, gener aduersis instructus Eois.

[The father-in-law [Caesar] coming down from the ramparts of the Alps and Monoecus' citadel, the son-in-law [Pompey] arrayed against him with the armies of the East.]

Butler's note says: 'The statement that [Caesar's troops] descended from the Alps is untrue. He was himself south of the Alps . . . when the final rupture took place, and the legions which he summoned to his assistance must have come by the coast route in the dead of winter.'[5] So the idea of legions pouring down from the heights above Monaco seems to have been brought in for pictorial or dramatic effect.

In other passages a similar effect is produced without any distortion of

[3] *Epirus* (Oxford, 1967), p. 99.
[4] D. B. Harden, 'The Topography of Punic Carthage', *Greece and Rome* 9 (1939) 6 and 5.
[5] *The Sixth Book of the Aeneid*, ed. H. E. Butler (Oxford, 1920), p. 254.

history. Early in Book II, when the Trojans are wrangling about what to do with the horse, Laocoon rushes down from the citadel (41). Conceivably, as Austin says, we are to infer that he has been on the look-out.[6] But surely the main reason for putting him there was to let him make this exciting entrance. Much later, Virgil describes how Amata and the other matrons rode up to the temple of Pallas on the citadel of Laurentum to pray for the destruction of Aeneas (XI. 477–85). Then Turnus (leader of the anti-Trojan forces in Italy) put on his armour, which included a flashing breastplate and greaves of gold. He buckled on his sword, 'and he glittered as he rushed down all golden from the high citadel':

> fulgebatque alta decurrens aureus arce.   (490; cf. XII. 698)

Finally, a rather different kind of example: Aeneas is on Delos, praying to Apollo:

> da propriam Thymbraee domum; da moenia fessis
> et genus et mansuram urbem; serua altera Troiae
> Pergama, reliquias Danaum atque immitis Achilli.
> > (III. 85–7; cf. VIII. 36–7)

[Grant us, o Lord of Thymbra, an abiding home; grant us in our weariness walls, descendants, and a city that will endure; preserve Troy's other citadel, the remnant left by the Greeks and the cruel Achilles.]

The new Troy of the future is thought of as potentially existing in the persons of those who are to inhabit it—a metaphor which shows once again how prominent a place the citadel held in Virgil's imagination.

But why did it hold that place? First, we should probably think of the citadel as an image with historic associations. A famous line of the *Georgics* speaks of

> tot congesta manu praeruptis oppida saxis   (II. 156)

[so many towns set by men's hands upon steep crags].

The hill-town is a piece of handiwork testifying to man's struggle against wild nature. Immediately after, we hear of

> fluminaque antiquos subterlabentia muros

[and rivers gliding beneath ancient walls].

Here too, in the idea of continuity, we have something very close to Virgil's heart. When he looked at the citadel of Cumae (not far from Naples), he pictured first of all the settlers who had come from Chalcis in Euboea nearly seven hundred years before he was born; then his thoughts went back beyond

---

[6] *Aeneidos: Liber Secundus*, with a commentary by R. G. Austin (Oxford, 1964), p. 45.

them to misty traditions about Daedalus who, after escaping from Crete, 'floated to the cool north by a route never taken before' and finally alighted on the Chalcidian citadel (VI. 16–17).

Again, the *arx* is a fastness built to defy an enemy. In epic, war is part of the hero's life; it is a theatre for the display of *uirtus* and the winning of *gloria*. Cruelty and pain are certainly involved, but one hears nothing about squalor and degradation. Such reminders would detract from the dignity of the genre. Heroes do not suffer from lice or dysentery, and we are told very little about the common man. In the same way, there are no low buildings on the citadel; they are all soaring pinnacles.

As the hero represents man's nearest approach to deity, the citadel is the site for the temples of the gods. Athena has Troy, Juno Carthage, Apollo Cumae. The religious aura of such buildings can be seen in the description of King Latinus' palace at Laurentum:

> August and huge, rising upwards with a hundred columns, his house stood on the city's highest point, once the palace of Laurentian Picus, made awesome by its grove and by the holiness of former generations.   (VII. 170–2)

As Camps remarks, 'The king himself receives [the Trojan envoys] in a vast pillared building which is both temple and council chamber, scene also of ritual banquets, set high on a hill, with statues of former kings before the doors; a description of which every detail is applicable to the great temple of Jupiter on the Capitol at Rome.'[7]

Beauty, antiquity, warlike strength, and piety—all are related to the citadel's height, and this blends easily into the notion of epic sublimity. In those lines mentioned earlier, where Amata offers prayers and Turnus prepares for battle (XI. 482–97), the word *altus* occurs four times in the space of sixteen lines. The average for the *Aeneid* as a whole is over twenty instances per book—a frequency even greater than that of the notorious *ingens*. A similar emphasis is found in passages of Milton; for example:

> High on a throne of royal state, which far
> Outshone the wealth of Ormus and of Ind,
> Or where the gorgeous East, with richest hand,
> Showers on her kings barbaric pearl and gold,
> Satan exalted sat, by merit rais'd
> To that bad eminence: and from despair
> Thus high uplifted beyond hope, aspires
> Beyond thus high.   (*Paradise Lost*, II. 1–8)

So far we have been examining ways in which the *arx* functions in single

---

[7] W. A. Camps, *An Introduction to Virgil's Aeneid* (Oxford, 1969), p. 18; cf. p. 153, n. 14.

passages. It can also on occasion form part of a major theme. In the struggle for Troy in Book II the citadel is a military objective. To study what happens we must begin with the horse. Built 'by the divine art of Pallas' (15), it has ribs (16), beams (112), and a *cauerna* (19)—a word used for a ship's hold. After Laocoon's horrible death the Trojans put rollers under the horse and drag it inside the city with ropes (235–7). These details connect the horse with the ships of the Greek fleet. There is also another sort of connection, namely juxtaposition. After describing the horse in 15–20, Virgil begins the next line with the words 'est in conspectu Tenedos' [in sight there is Tenedos], the island where the Greek fleet is hiding. Later, when Sinon the spy has given a false explanation of the horse, we read:

> But lo from Tenedos across the calm deep (I shudder as I relate it)
> twin serpents with endless coils are leaning on the sea and making
> side by side for the shore.   (203–5)

The two serpents prefigure the brothers Agamemnon and Menelaus, who are in command of the Greek fleet.[8] Finally, when the horse has been pulled in and the Trojans are sleeping after their delirious celebrations, the fleet itself sets out from Tenedos (254–5). Horse, serpents, and ships are therefore related by metaphor and juxtaposition.

They are also related in a larger structural sense, in that all of them converge on the citadel. After removing Laocoon, the two snakes glide up to the citadel (226), where they conceal themselves beneath the shield of Pallas. As Austin says, 'the serpents return to the protection of the goddess who sent them' (p. 108). Terrified by what has happened to Laocoon, who tried to destroy the horse, the Trojans not only bring it inside the walls; they haul it up to the citadel: 'et monstrum infelix sacrata sistimus arce' (245). One recalls that the horse was made 'by the divine art of Pallas' (15). So the monstrous creation fulfils its purpose by joining the goddess who presided over its construction. The parallel with the snakes is obvious. As for the Greek forces, they slowly fight their way to the citadel, spreading fire and destruction as they go. The first soldier to break into Priam's palace is, appropriately, Achilles' son Pyrrhus ('Fiery'); on his arrival he is compared to a snake which has sloughed its skin (471–5). Aeneas hurries back to his father's house, but is stopped by Venus, who shows him the dreadful vision of the gods wrecking Troy. Neptune and Juno are both at work, but for us the important lines are:

> iam summas arces Tritonidis, respice, Pallas
> insedit nimbo effulgens et Gorgone saeua.   (615–16)

> [See, Tritonian Pallas has now taken over the topmost towers,
> shining against a dark cloud and fierce with her Gorgon shield.]

---

[8] The connections were first pointed out by B. Knox, 'The Serpent and the Flame', *American Journal of Philology* 71 (1950) 379–400.

7

Here, in the phrase *Gorgone saeua*, we find the culmination of the snake motif, at least in its destructive form.[9] Eventually Aeneas and his family leave the house, but on reaching the rallying point outside the walls they suddenly miss Aeneas' wife, Creusa. Aeneas plunges back into the inferno, making his way for the last time to Priam's palace on the citadel: 'procedo et Priami sedes arcemque reuiso' (760). There, the struggle is over; the plunder is being collected; and the women and children stand shivering in a long line. It is appropriate that the last mention of fire in this extraordinary book should come in the picture of the burning temples on the *arx* (764).

In Book III the citadel functions as an object of nostalgia. On escaping from Troy, the exiles first land in Thrace (north-eastern Aegean), but the area turns out to be under religious pollution. So they sail south to Delos to consult Apollo. (We have already noted Aeneas' prayer on Delos: 'Preserve Troy's other citadel'.) Apollo tells them to seek their motherland, which they mistakenly interpret as Crete. Aeneas describes his activities on landing there:

> ergo auidus muros optatae molior urbis
> Pergameamque uoco, et laetam cognomine gentem
> hortor amare focos arcemque attollere tectis. (132–4)

[So I eagerly set to work on the walls of my longed-for city. I call it Trojan, and my people rejoice at the old name. I urge them to cherish their hearth and to raise buildings on the citadel.]

But again their hopes are dashed, this time by a plague, and they have to sail westward towards Italy. It is clear from these details that psychologically the exiles are still prisoners of the past. Visualizing their new city as a reproduction of the old Troy, they expect simply to continue the life they have left off.

On their journey to Italy the wanderers sail up the west coast of Greece and put in at Buthrotum, the home of Helenus (a son of Priam) and Andromache, who was once married to Hector. Andromache, whose role seems to be an invention of Virgil's, is first seen making offerings at Hector's cenotaph. On seeing the Trojans she faints, and on coming to asks dazedly 'Where is Hector?'. When she explains how she has come to be in Buthrotum, she begins by envying the fate of Priam's daughter, the murdered Polyxena (321); and later, when Aeneas is leaving, she loads his son Ascanius with presents and likens him to her own son Astyanax who died at the sack of Troy (489–91). So she is deliberately presented as a pathetic figure who lives in the past.

But that is not all. It transpires that these patriotic exiles in Buthrotum have kept the old Troy alive by the names given to their new home. The plains are

---

[9] A vivid representation of Athena using her aegis in attack is to be found on a black-figure amphora (*Denkmäler*, ed. A. Baumeister, 3 vols (Munich, 1884–8), I. 220). The goddess lunges at the giant Enceladus; the aegis, placed over her left arm, is fringed with writhing snakes.

called Chaonian, and the whole district Chaonia, after Chaon of Troy. One local river is the Simois, another the Xanthus. There is a Scaean Gate, and the whole town is a miniature Troy, complete with citadel (336). So Helenus and Andromache have done what Aeneas so passionately wished to do; they have rebuilt Troy.[10] It is ironic that by the time Aeneas has reached Buthrotum he has learnt enough about his mission to know that he cannot stay there. But he is not yet aware that the city which he is destined to found will be something quite different in kind.

In Books I and IV the citadel represents a rival plan for the course of world history.[11] Juno had heard vaguely that some nation was supposed to overthrow the Punic towers (I. 20), but she had not, it seems, enquired any further, or been informed about the intentions of Jupiter and fate. She was determined that *Carthage* would become the foremost power; and her people had made an energetic start. When Aeneas arrived, he saw not only the huge walls and the buildings going up on the citadel (I. 365–6) but also paved streets, a harbour, and a theatre (I. 420–9). He envies the people's stability and confidence: 'How fortunate are those whose walls are already rising!' Soon after, when this longing for permanence is intensified by Dido's passion, he forgets the idea of founding his own community; he adopts Punic dress and joins in the work of building Carthage's towers (IV. 260). Juno, we are told, assents to this situation: presumably in due course Aeneas can be eliminated; at any rate no rival power will be established anywhere else. But already Aeneas' behaviour has been brought to Jupiter's attention, and Mercury is sent down to remind him of his duty—especially his duty to his son: does he, asks Jupiter indignantly, begrudge Ascanius the towers of Rome (*Romanas arces*)? Those towers are the Trojans' true objective. Aeneas' conscience is stirred, and he decides he must leave. As he tries to defend himself to Dido he says: 'If you, a Phoenician, are firmly attached to the towers of Carthage and to the sight of a Libyan city, why grudge the Trojans the right to settle in the land of Italy?' (IV. 347–50.) So he leaves, and poor Dido takes her own life.

In Book VIII the citadel is a double symbol: of Rome's past and of its present. In that book Aeneas, who has now landed in Italy, seeks help from King Evander, an Arcadian immigrant who lives with his fellow-Greeks in Pallanteum, the site which will eventually be Rome. As Aeneas and his comrades make their way up the Tiber, 'they see in the distance the walls and

[10] The last manifestation of the nostalgic dream (apart from Venus' words in X. 55–62) comes towards the end of Book V. The women, who long for a settled home, are stirred up by Juno's emissary: 'Will there never be walls named after Troy? Shall I never see a Xanthus and a Simois, Hector's rivers?' In a frenzy they set fire to the ships. Eventually the older men and women, and also the unfit, are left behind with some kinsmen in Sicily. The others press on to Italy.

[11] Silius Italicus, whose *Punica* owed much to Virgil, has the sentence 'It was long in doubt on which citadel Fortune would establish the capital of the world' (I. 7–8).

citadel and the scattered roofs of houses which have now been raised to the sky by Rome's power but were then the humble property of Evander' (98–100). Then and now. So, too, the Capitol is said to be 'golden now, once rough with woody thickets' (348). But there is continuity as well as contrast. The caves on the Aventine are the same; so are historic names like the Argiletum. And the ceremony in honour of Hercules, which was in progress when Aeneas arrived, was still held in Virgil's day. At two points, in order to convey the impression that 'then' and 'now' somehow coexist, Virgil employs deliberate ana-chronisms. Thus when Evander takes Aeneas to his house on the Palatine, 'they see cattle all round, lowing in the Roman Forum and the expensive Carinae [an exclusive shopping centre]'. And when Evander begins his account of early Latium and the golden age of Saturn, he is called (313) 'the founder of Rome's citadel' [Romanae conditor arcis]. So, though Rome's glorious present may have been in the forefront of the Augustan reader's mind, he was nevertheless not allowed to forget the wistful picture of its Arcadian past. After all, Virgil was also the poet of the *Eclogues*.

'The towers of Rome': we will finish by considering what the phrase implied in the context of the *Aeneid*. To do so we must go back to Book I. There, when the refugees are shipwrecked on the coast of Africa, Venus tearfully reminds Jupiter of an earlier promise. He had said, it seems, that from the Trojans the Romans would arise and eventually rule the world (234–7). Reassuring her, Jupiter now indicates how one race will emerge from the other: by Mars, Ilia ('Trojan lady', a distant descendant of Aeneas) will become the mother of Romulus (274). But though the reader overhears this conversation in heaven, the Trojans know nothing of it. Only gradually are they told of their destination: to sail across the deep (II. 295); to seek Hesperia, the western land (II. 781); to make for the kingdom of Italy (III. 185); to avoid the east coast of Italy (III. 396); to go round Sicily (III. 412); and to land at Cumae (III. 441). And what kind of destiny awaits them in their new country? They will found a great city (Hector's ghost in II. 294–5); Aeneas will have a kingdom by the Tiber and a royal wife (Creusa's ghost in II. 781–4); the house of Aeneas will rule over all lands (Apollo in III. 97); his descendants will be exalted to the stars and his city will hold sway (the Penates in III. 158–9); he is to raise mighty Troy to the heavens (Helenus in III. 462). This is the faith that inspires Aeneas' famous speech to his shipwrecked comrades in Book I: 'Through various perils and so many crises we are pressing on to Latium. . . . There it is granted that the kingdom of Troy will rise again' (204–6). So as they struggle westwards Aeneas and his followers believe that in Italy they will form a dominant community which will eventually rule over a Trojan empire. They have never heard of Rome.[12] At the end of Book V, in Sicily, Anchises appears

[12] The phrase *Romanaque tellus*, used by Mercury to Aeneas in IV. 275, should have been incomprehensible to the listener. It is best regarded as a slip which might have been corrected had Virgil lived to revise the work.

in a dream and summons Aeneas to meet him in the underworld. 'Then you will learn all about your descendants and hear what kind of city is assigned to you' (737). In the underworld, as Anchises begins his last and climactic speech, it becomes clear that a resurgent Troy, in the sense in which Aeneas and his followers have understood it, is something of an illusion. 'Come now, and I shall explain what glory will attend the Dardanian [i.e. Trojan] line, what descendants of Italian stock are to come' (VI. 756–7). So Aeneas' posterity will be *Itala de gente*. From his Italian wife Lavinia, now named for the first time, will come a long line of kings who will reign in Alba Longa. The last of these will have a daughter, who from her union with Mars will give birth to Romulus. Under his auspices Rome, here explained for the first time, will enclose her seven pinnacles (*arces*) with a wall (783) and will exercise dominion over the world.

Eventually, of course, Virgil had to bring in the Italian element and the story of Romulus. But again he made a virtue of a necessity. He could, after all, have allowed Aeneas to know everything from the start. Instead of talking vaguely about a royal wife beside the Tiber, Creusa's ghost could have described the future settlement in detail. What a disaster that would have been! Not only would a gradual discovery have been ruled out; psychological credibility would also have been destroyed, for it is doubtful whether the exiles could have been persuaded to strive for such a future. One can argue that only a narrow patriotic vision of a Trojan empire could have kept them together and sustained them through their weary odyssey.

In his state of reverence and wonder Aeneas never questions Anchises' revelation; he accepts it joyfully. His reorientation is seen in Book XII when he commits himself to the idea of a partnership with the Italians: 'I shall not ask the Italians to accept Trojan rule, nor do I seek the kingdom for myself. Let both peoples, undefeated, make a treaty for all time on equal terms' (189–91). Even now Aeneas does not know the full extent of the sacrifice which will be required of the Trojans; and in fact the poem ends before he finds out. The reader, however, does know, because he is present at the final negotiations on Olympus. There Juno, who has championed Turnus against Aeneas, abandons her opposition provided (1) the Latins keep their name and do not become Trojans; (2) they retain their language; (3) they keep their national dress. Then, for good measure, she adds:

> Let Latium stand; let the Alban kings continue through the ages;
> let the Roman stock flourish, strong in its Italian valour. Troy is
> fallen; grant that she stay fallen, name and all.

To anyone who has followed the Trojans' fortunes, that last verse must sound astonishing: 'occidit, occideritque sinas cum nomine Troia' (828). Yet Jupiter, so far from making objections, gives her everything she asks for. He even adds a further concession: that the Italians shall keep their traditional way of life

11

(*mores*). Apart from the blood of their royal house, transmitted through the female line, the Trojans' only contribution will lie in the field of religion, where their worship will be combined with Italian rites. For the rest, they will simply be absorbed: 'subsident Teucri' (836). We are told that 'Juno gave her assent to these terms and gladly reversed her attitude'. And well she might.

When it came, then, after all the bitterness and bloodshed, the new order was one which nobody had expected. A modern reader may call to mind some words from Eliot's *Little Gidding*:

> Either you had no purpose
> or the purpose is beyond the end you figured
> and is altered in fulfilment.

That is what Aeneas discovered. And for us, who lack the certainties of the Victorian reader, perhaps his most impressive quality is the combination of steadiness and adaptability which enabled him to enter a new age without wholly betraying the past.

Anglo-Saxon Art

A Liturgical Interpretation of the Bewcastle Cross

ÉAMONN Ó CARRAGÁIN

The present paper argues that the Northumbrian liturgy of the late seventh and early eighth centuries provides contexts within which the coherence of the Bewcastle Cross can begin to be appreciated. The Bewcastle monument is remarkable in its unstrained beauty. Compared with it, the Ruthwell Cross (erected by the same school of sculptors some thirty miles to the west) seems somewhat crowded, as though its designer wished to use every inch of surface to elaborate the theological ideas which preoccupied him.[1] The primary impression the Bewcastle Cross makes is one of balance: balance between the design of the two broad sides; between the two narrow sides (based on a different design principle from that of the broad sides); and between the three related figural panels on the broad west side.

I THE WEST SIDE

At present four panels survive on the west face of the Bewcastle monument (Plate 1). The lowest panel is separated from the two other figural panels by a panel of runic inscriptions, now almost all illegible. The inscription seems to have been commemorative and perhaps funerary, though it is not possible to identify with certainty the persons whose names have been preserved.[2] Above the runic panel we have two figural panels. It is likely that the designer of the

---

[1] I assume, following Professor Rosemary Cramp in her discussion of Bewcastle in Vol. II of the *Corpus of Anglo-Saxon Stone Sculpture* (forthcoming), that the Bewcastle monument was originally a cross, not a stele: the existence of a dowel for a (now lost) cross-piece has been recorded. I am grateful to Professor Cramp for allowing me to consult at proof stage what will be the standard account of the Bewcastle Cross; and I rely on its descriptions and judgements at several points in this article. I am also grateful to Professor Cramp for permission to print the plates, from photographs taken by Mr Tom Middlemass of the Department of Archaeology, Durham University. Dr David Howlett read this article in typescript and saved me from several errors.

[2] R. I. Page, 'The Bewcastle Cross', *Nottingham Medieval Studies* 4 (1960) 36–57; Professor Page also discusses and transcribes the runes in Cramp, *Corpus*, forthcoming.

cross intended these to be seen as a pair: the close analogues for both which occur on the Ruthwell Cross were there given the same relationship to each other as at Bewcastle (I here assume that when the Ruthwell Cross was reconstructed in the nineteenth century the large upper stone was correctly fitted to the lower stone).

Each of the three figural panels at Bewcastle contains a standing human figure. Of these, only one (the figure of Christ in the second panel from the top) is nimbed. Each of the two standing figures without a nimbus bears a creature: a lamb (in the upper panel) and a bird (in the lower). The lamb in the upper panel is provided with a nimbus. It would seem that the only figures to be provided with a nimbus are figures of Christ, who is represented as the Agnus Dei in the top panel and as a majestic human figure in the panel immediately below. Between these two panels, the words '+ gessus kristtus' have been inscribed in runic letters: a title which could refer to either panel or to both.[3] All three panels combine human figures with non-human creatures. In the panels at top and bottom, the human figures bear the creatures, and by their gestures invite the onlooker to concentrate his attention on these creatures. In the top panel, the human figure points across his body with his right hand at the Lamb of God whom he cradles in his left forearm; in the bottom panel, the human figure stands in profile, with the upper part of the body turned back towards the onlooker so as to attract the viewer's attention to the bird which perches on his left forearm. In his right hand, this human figure bears a rod. In contrast, the two animals at the foot of the central panel bear aloft the figure of Christ, whose feet are planted firmly on their heads. These animals are anonymous: they cannot be identified with any particular species, and they have not been differentiated from each other; they form a pair. There seems to be no opposition or enmity between them and the figure of Christ. His right hand is raised in blessing. Whom or what does he bless? Perhaps the onlooker; or the animals who bear him aloft; or the closed scroll just below (his left hand holds the scroll close to the blessing right hand); and also perhaps the names inscribed in the panel immediately underneath. He is dressed in a cloak and (ecclesiastical?) pallium, not in the armour of a warrior. The outer paw of each animal points upwards towards the figure of Christ, presumably in reverent recognition. The inner paws (now damaged and worn) are crossed: enough remains to make it probable that they (like the inner paws of the beasts at Ruthwell) originally formed an 'X' pattern. As it occurs immediately below the feet of a figure which has the (runic) inscription 'Gessus Kristtus' just above its head, the 'X' pattern does not seem random. It provides a title for the human figure: the pair of animals are engaged in the

---

[3] É. Ó Carragáin, 'Liturgical Innovations Associated with Pope Sergius and the Iconography of the Ruthwell and Bewcastle Crosses' in *Bede and Anglo-Saxon England*, ed. R. T. Farrell, British Archaeological Reports 46 (Oxford, 1978), pp. 131–47, at p. 135.

act of recognizing Jesus as 'kristtus', the anointed one. The letter *Chi* was a major symbolic motif in insular art, and in closely similar visual puns 'X' patterns denote the title 'Christus' on two of the (ninth-century?) Irish high crosses at Kells (a Columban monastery, with strong connections with Iona).[4] At Ruthwell, a Latin inscription makes clear how the 'Christ over the beasts' panel was understood there: '+ IHS X[PS] IVD[E]X [: A]EQV[IT]A[TI]S : BESTIAE : ET : DRACON[ES] : COGNOUERVNT : IN DE : SERTO : SALVA[TO]REM : MVNDI :' ['[+] Jesus Christ the judge of equity. The animals and the serpents recognized the Saviour of the world in the desert'].[5] But even before this inscription was added to the panel, the crossed paws of the Ruthwell animals indicated that they recognized 'the Saviour of the world' as 'XPS', the anointed one. At Bewcastle, the juxtaposition of a panel in which a human figure points at the Agnus Dei and one in which beasts point at '+ gessus kristtus' suggests that the designer was interested in the symbolic and human forms under which Christ was to be recognized.

The most likely context for an interest in the recognition of Christ in symbolic and in bodily form is the Eucharist. Perhaps the oldest Christian liturgical theme preserved to us is that of Christ 'recognized in the breaking of bread'.[6] The figure who points to the lamb in the upper panel is usually identified as John the Baptist. The pointing hand is clearly designed, like the

---

[4] On the *Chi* and *Chi Rho* symbols in early insular art, see Suzanne Lewis, 'Sacred Calligraphy: the Chi Rho Page in the Book of Kells', *Traditio* 36 (1980) 139–59; also G. H. R. Horsley and E. R. Waterhouse, 'The Greek *Nomen Sacrum* XP- in Some Latin and Old English Manuscripts', *Scriptorium* 38 (1984) 211–30. It is likely that the name 'Christ' was understood in Northumbria in the eighth century to mean 'the anointed one'. During the ceremony on Holy Thursday of the blessing of the oil of chrism, the priest prayed publicly that the oil should be blessed by God through the power of Christ 'a cuius sancto nomine ch[r]isma nomen accepit': see the Gelasian Sacramentary, *Liber Sacramentorum Romanae Aeclesiae Ordinis Anni Circuli*, ed. Leo Cunibert Mohlberg (Rome, 1960), par. 388, p. 62; also the Sacramentary of Gellone, *Liber Sacramentorum Gellonensis*, ed. A. Dumas, 2 vols, CCSL 159 and 159A, Vol. 159, par. 623, p. 84. See further below, pp. 29–30. On 'X'-puns on the Kells crosses, see É. Ó Carragáin, 'The Meeting of St. Paul and St. Anthony: Visual and Literary uses of a Eucharistic Motif' in *Keimelia: Studies in Archaeology and History in Honour of Tom Delaney*, ed. Gearoid Mac Niocaill and Patrick Wallace (Galway, 1987), pp. 1–61 (at pp. 18 and 25).
[5] Text and translation adapted from E. Okasha, *Hand-List of Anglo-Saxon Non-Runic Inscriptions* (Cambridge, 1971), p. 110.
[6] See the Emmaus episode, Luke 24: 35; and St Paul's account of the Eucharist in 1 Cor. 11: 24. That the recognition of the real presence of Christ in the Eucharistic species was a matter of concern at Whitby in the late seventh century is made clear by the occurrence of the earliest version of the 'Miracle of St Gregory' in *The Earliest Life of Gregory the Great*, ed. Bertram Colgrave (Cambridge, 1985), Chapter 20, pp. 104–9. See also X. Le Bachelet, 'Le vénérable Bède témoin de la foi eucharistique dans l'église anglo-saxonne', *Proceedings of the Nineteenth International Eucharistic Congress* (London, 1909), pp. 311–26.

crossed paws of the animals in the panel below, as a visual pun. It recalls a famous scriptural phrase: the thrice-repeated 'Ecce' ('behold') with which the Baptist recognizes Christ as the Lamb of God in St John's gospel (1: 29, 36): '*Ecce* Agnus Dei'. This visual pun had strong patristic authority. St Augustine emphasized that the word 'Ecce' implied the gesture of pointing, and saw in the implied gesture a sign that John the Baptist was uniquely close to Christ, and greater than all the prophets: 'to the prophets who went before, it was given to announce beforehand the things that were to come to pass concerning Christ; but to this man it was given to point him out with his finger' ['prophetis praecedentibus praenuntiare de Christo futura concessum est; huic autem digito ostendere'].[7]

I have argued elsewhere that there was a particular reason why John the Baptist, pointing to the Agnus Dei, should be given prominence on a Northumbrian cross at this period. A chant based on John 1: 29, 'Agnus Dei, qui tollis peccata mundi, miserere nobis', had recently been introduced into the Roman liturgy of the Mass. It was sung by both clergy and people as the bread was broken for communion.[8] The breaking of bread was usually interpreted as a re-enactment of the breaking of Christ's body by the nails and spear on the Cross.[9] Liturgical readings for the ninth hour on Good Friday (the moment of Christ's death) included both Old and New Testament references to the Paschal Lamb (Exodus 12: 1–11; John 19: 36); and the Roman 'station' for Good Friday (i.e. the symbolically appropriate basilica at which the ceremonies of that day were enacted) was Holy Cross in Jerusalem.[10] The Bewcastle Cross therefore invites the onlooker to recognize Christ both in Eucharistic terms (in the words of the 'Agnus Dei' chant) and as sacrificed on the Holy Cross on Calvary (i.e. broken for men at Mass under the appearance of bread, as he had been sacrificed as the Paschal Lamb on the Holy Cross in Jerusalem).

The 'Christ over the Beasts' panel derives iconographically from Psalm

[7] *Augustinus: In Iohannis Evangelium Tractatus CXXIV*, Tractatus IV, par. 1; ed. R. Willems, CCSL 36, p. 31.

[8] É. Ó Carragáin, 'Liturgical Innovations', pp. 134–7; see also Ó Carragáin, 'Christ over the Beasts and the Agnus Dei: Two Multivalent Panels on the Ruthwell and Bewcastle Crosses', *Sources of Anglo-Saxon Culture*, ed. Paul E. Szarmach (Kalamazoo, 1986), pp. 377–403, at pp. 391–9.

[9] See J. A. Jungmann, *The Mass of the Roman Rite*, 2 vols (New York, 1951–5), II. 301–3; and the Irish commentary on the Mass in the Stowe Missal, in *Thesaurus Palaeohibernicus*, ed. Whitley Stokes and John Strachan, 2 vols (Cambridge, 1901–3), II. 253, pars 11 and 12.

[10] See Michel Andrieu, *Les Ordines Romani du haut moyen âge*, 5 vols, Spicilegium Sacrum Lovaniense, Vols 11, 23, 24, 28 and 29 (Louvain, 1931–61), Ordo XXIII, Nos 11–12 (III. 270–1); and G. G. Willis, 'The Roman Stational Liturgy' in *Further Studies in Early Roman Liturgy*, Alcuin Club Collections 50 (London, 1968), pp. 1–88, at p. 46. The implications for Ruthwell of the Roman stational liturgy are worked out in É. Ó Carragáin, 'The Roman Liturgy and the Ruthwell Cross', forthcoming.

90: 13 (Vulgate numbering): 'Thou shalt walk upon the asp and the basilisk: and thou shalt trample under foot the lion and the dragon'. But the role of the beasts has in this panel (and in that at Ruthwell) been transformed: they appear not as images of evil but as images of conversion. As I have argued elsewhere, both panels seem designed to recall at once both Psalm 90: 13 and the Old Latin text of the Canticle of Habbakuk, where it is prophesied of Christ that 'you will be known in the midst of two animals' ['in medio duorum animalium innotesceris']. This canticle was sung every Friday at Lauds. Thus, for Bede, the canticle above all prophesied Christ's Passion, and he interpreted 'you will be known in the midst of two animals' as referring to the way in which both the divinity and the humanity of Christ could be recognized in the signs which occurred when he hung on the Cross between two thieves. But in the Old Roman liturgy of the early eighth century, the opening verses of the Canticle of Habbakuk were sung on Good Friday at the ninth hour, as the responsory after the first reading at Holy Cross in Jerusalem; and Psalm 90 was sung after the second reading. This panel then, like the panel above, invites the onlooker to recognize the union of humanity and divinity in Christ; and to remember that his majesty was paradoxically revealed to men as his body was raised up on the Holy Cross on Good Friday.[11]

It has been disputed whether the bottom panel (Plate 2) is secular or religious: it is the only figural panel of the three in which no nimbus occurs, and the costume of the standing human figure (calf-length robes and a large ruff-like collar) may possibly denote secular rather than ecclesiastical fashions.[12] In her extremely important forthcoming discussion of the problem, Professor Cramp comes cautiously to the following conclusion: 'on the whole, it seems more prudent to suppose that the figure is one of St John the Evangelist with his symbol the eagle, despite the lack of halo and the unorthodox posture'. I shall proceed on the hypothesis that the figure is John the Evangelist; its posture, though original, is relevant to what was known of that saint.[13] As Professor Cramp remarks (forthcoming), 'the man has long curling hair but the details of his face are difficult to distinguish and may have been recut. The eyes are very deeply hollowed but may not be in their original form.' Whatever the details of his face, his stance is remarkable. The feet and lower body are in full profile, facing right; the upper body turns outward, so that although the figure presents his right shoulder towards us he seems to gaze out past the bird directly at the onlooker. Professor Cramp's

[11] This paragraph summarizes the argument of O Carragáin, 'Multivalent Panels', pp. 383–90.
[12] These points are made by Cramp, forthcoming.
[13] John and the other evangelists are normally represented seated, writing their respective gospels; or, as in the case of St John in the Lindisfarne Gospels, displaying a scroll: see Janet Backhouse, *The Lindisfarne Gospels* (Oxford, 1981), p. 54.

remark that the figure is presented 'as though in arrested movement' is the key to understanding the panel. The figure is represented in the act of turning either from the bird (which he has, so to speak, been contemplating) to the onlooker or from the onlooker to the bird. On either interpretation, the man's turning stance can reasonably be construed as inviting the onlooker to gaze at the bird he holds. The importance of the bird is increased by making the body of the bird face outwards (the head of the bird is so worn that it is not clear whether it faced the onlooker or was turned towards the man). The way in which the stance of the human figure directs the onlooker's gaze to the bird seems theologically significant. Of the four evangelists, John was the great contemplative, who wrote of that 'which we have seen with our eyes, which we have diligently looked upon and our hands have handled' (1 John 1: 1–3).[14] The importance of seeing and contemplation is central to John's theology.[15] Images of seeing occur, for example, in the great Christological prologue with which his gospel opens, a passage in which the evangelist presents his namesake the Baptist as the first to proclaim Christ's eternal divinity in words:

> And the word was made flesh and dwelt amongst us; and we saw his glory, the glory of the only begotten of the Father, full of grace and truth. John beareth witness of him and crieth out, saying: 'This was he of whom I spoke: He that shall come after me is preferred before me; because he was before me.'   (John 1: 14–15)

The contrast between the way John the Baptist stands, squarely facing the onlooker as though to confront him with the Agnus Dei, and the way the lower figure turns, directing the onlooker's gaze towards the bird, may imply a contrast between word ('ecce') and silent act ('seeing'), and so between the complementary roles of preaching and contemplation in bringing about conversion (*conversatio morum* was the second of the three solemn vows prescribed in the Benedictine Rule[16]). It was John the Evangelist who wrote 'My little children, let us not love in word nor in tongue, but in deed and in truth' ['Filioli mei, non diligamus verbo neque lingua, sed opere et veritate'] (1 John 3: 18).

The eighth-century Roman liturgy suggests a reason why John the Evangelist might be representd in isolation from his synoptic fellows, and why such centrality might be given to his symbolic eagle. Alone of the four evangelist-symbols, the eagle was seen to symbolize the new life promised to

---

[14] In the first of Augustine's sermons on John there is an extended account of John as contemplative: CCSL 36, pp. 1–6. (Biblical quotations in English are from the Douay Bible.)

[15] See *Dictionnaire de Spiritualité* (Paris, 1937–   ), VIII, cols 192–247, under 'S. Jean l'Évangéliste', at cols 217–20.

[16] *The Rule of St. Benedict*, Chapter 58; ed. Justin McCann (London, 1952), p. 130.

the Christian. In the eighth-century liturgy, the catechumens preparing for baptism and the Eucharist (the sacraments they would normally receive during the vigil of Easter) participated, on an unspecified day during the fourth week of Lent, in an important ceremony in which the chief documents of the faith (the Our Father, the Creed, and the Four Gospels) were handed on to them. Homilies explaining these documents were prescribed: so important were these homilies considered that their text is preserved, not merely in the relevant Roman *ordines*, but also in eighth-century sacramentaries, the altar-books which preserved the canon, prefaces and variable prayers for Mass.[17]

We can be sure that the ceremony of the giving of the gospels ('traditio evangeliorum') was performed in Northumbria in the eighth century: Bede provides us with the two earliest unambiguous descriptions of the ceremony to survive from any source.[18] The ceremony was a dramatic event. In solemn procession, preceded by two candle-bearers and clerics bearing incense in thuribles, four deacons proceeded from the sacristy, each carrying a gospel book open at the beginning of a different gospel. Each gospel book was placed at a different corner of the altar, so that the congregation could gaze on them: the magnificent evangelist portraits and carpet pages which precede each gospel in early insular gospel books may thus have had a practical liturgical and catechetic function.[19] The beginning of each gospel was then read by the deacon to whom that gospel had been assigned. After each reading, the presiding priest read (and/or paraphrased in the vernacular?) the homily preserved in the sacramentaries. This taught the catechumens how the iconography of the appropriate beast illuminated the qualities of the gospel just read. The richness of the explanation of the final symbol, John's eagle, is particularly striking:

> Ioannes habet similitudinem aquilae, eo quod nimis alta petierit; ait enim: In principio erat Verbum et Verbum erat apud Deum et Deus erat Verbum. Hoc erat in principio apud Deum. Et David dicit de

---

[17] See Andrieu, Ordo XI: Vol. II, Nos 45–72, pp. 428–41; the Gelasian Sacramentary, ed. Mohlberg, pars 299–328, pp. 46–53; the Sacramentary of Gellone, ed. Dumas, CCSL 159, pars 534–64, pp. 65–73 and (another redaction of the homilies) pars 2262–98, pp. 321–30. These homilies are discussed by Pierre de Puniet, 'Les trois homélies catéchétiques du sacramentaire gélasien pour la tradition des évangiles, du symbole et de l'oraison dominicale', *Révue d'Histoire Ecclésiastique* 5 (1904) 505–21, 755–86; 6 (1905) 15–32, 304–18. See also de Puniet's article 'Apertio Aurium', in *Dictionnaire d'archéologie chrétienne et de liturgie [DACL]* (Paris, 1907–53), I, Part 2 (1924), cols 2523–37.

[18] *Bedae Venerabilis Opera, Pars II, Opera Exegetica*, Vol. 2A: *De Tabernaculo, De Templo, In Esram et Nehemiam*, ed. H. Hurst, CCSL 119A, p. 89 (*De Tabernaculo*, II, lines 1846–55); and pp. 310–11 (*In Ezram et Nehemiam*, II, lines 924–7).

[19] As suggested by Patrick Simms-Williams in his review of Kathleen Hughes, *Celtic Britain in the Middle Ages*, in *Journal of Ecclesiastical History* 36 (1985) 306–9 (at p. 308).

persona Christi: Renovabitur sicut aquilae juventus tua, id est Iesu Christi Domini nostri, qui, resurgens a mortuis, ascendit in caelos. Unde iam vobis conceptis praegnans gloriatur Ecclesia omni festivitate votorum ad nova tendere christianae legis exordia: ut, adveniente die venerabilis Paschae, lavacro baptismatis renascentes, sicut sancti omnes mereamini fidele munus infantiae a Christo Domino nostro percipere. Qui vivit et regnat in saecula saeculorum.[20]

[John the evangelist has the likeness of an eagle, because he sought out very elevated things. For he affirms: 'In the beginning was the Word and the Word was with God and the Word was God. He was in the beginning with God.' And David says of the person of Christ: 'Your youth will be renewed like the eagle's' (Ps. 102: 5), that is, like that of Jesus Christ our Lord, who rising from the dead ascended into heaven. Whence, now that you have been conceived, the pregnant Church rejoices on each festival of vows to strive forward [*tendere*: perhaps 'to strain, stretch' (as in childbirth); or 'to bring (you) forward'] to the new beginnings of the Christian law, so that, when the solemn Passover day comes, you, born to new life from the laver of baptism, may be worthy to receive, like all the saints, the faithful gift/responsibility of a [new] childhood from Christ our Lord, who lives and reigns for ever and ever. Amen.]

The progression of ideas in this paragraph is of the greatest interest. The eagle, who of all birds flies highest, is first seen as an appropriate symbol of the sublimity of John's gospel, the only gospel to trace back the existence of Christ the Word to the beginning of time, and to explore in detail the relations of God the Father and his Word. Then the eagle is associated with Christ himself, who rose from the dead to new life in heaven. But the point of the comparison between the eagle and the resurrected Christ is to emphasize that the catechumen will also rise to new life. The homily uses the striking and beautiful image of gestation to link the two ways in which the catechumens are promised new life. The Church is seen as joyfully pregnant, awaiting the birth of the catechumens from the baptismal font in a few weeks' time, at the Easter vigil. The reference to 'omni festivitate votorum' presumably refers to the various ceremonies of the Lenten catechumenate, such as the ceremony at which this passage was read. It could perhaps be paraphrased 'on each festival on which you make your vows'. These festivals formed, as it were, stages in the gestation of the catechumens in the womb of the Church; the catechumens, transformed into neophytes, would be spiritually reborn from the virginal font of baptism during the Easter vigil.[21] The homilist's stress on the new birth given to 'all the saints', in the immediate context of the standard

---

[20] I quote the critical text of de Puniet, *RHE* 5 (1904) 515–16.
[21] See Michel Dujarier, 'Le catéchuménat et la maternité de l'église', *La Maison-Dieu* 71 (1962) 78–93.

closing 'Qui vivit' formula with its reference to Christ living and reigning for eternity, suggests that he identifies the life given at Easter with the eternal life already given to the saints: for him the baptismal rebirth of the catechumens during the vigil of Easter Sunday looks forward to the final rebirth of all the Church into the eternal Sabbath of the Heavenly Jerusalem. The homilist had strong patristic authority for such a view: both Augustine and Cassiodorus in their commentaries on Psalm 102: 5 also identify the renewed life of the eagle with life after death and the Eucharistic banquet which prefigures that life.[22]

As interpreted for the catechumens and the congregation in the *Traditio Evangeliorum* ceremony, St John's eagle was much more significant than any of the other evangelist beasts. Those who planned the Bewcastle Cross could have found the homily in the most authoritative liturgical documents available to them: Gelasian sacramentaries (which they very probably used), or Roman *ordines* for the catechumenate.[23] Sculptors and designers would surely have found it striking that the Lenten liturgy included a discussion of the evangelist symbols. The Bewcastle designer was correct not to provide the eagle with a nimbus: that would have destroyed the symbolic multivalence of the image. At Bewcastle the bird can stand as a symbol for the evangelist and his insights; for eternal life; for the catechumen awaiting baptism; and for the Christian longing for eternal life—as well as for Christ himself, the first-born of those that sleep. The most remarkable fact about this multivalence is that the various perspectives of the image do not contradict each other in any way, but enrich each other. The evangelist's turning stance invites the onlooker to concentrate on a profoundly rich image of the 'very elevated things' ['nimis alta'] to be found in his gospel, and promised by the Church in her liturgy.

The rod held by St John the Evangelist is symbolically interesting. The image of the rod [*virga*] was an important image in the psalms for the discipline which led to Christ's kingdom ('the rod of thy kingdom is a straight rod' ['virga recta est, virga regni tui'], Ps. 44: 7;[24] 'thy rod and thy staff: they

---

[22] See below, p. 25. Augustine, *Enarrationes in Psalmos*, ed. J. Fraipont, CCSL 40, p. 1459 lines 16–48 and p. 1461 lines 41–8; Cassiodorus, *Expositio Psalmorum*, ed. M. Adriaen, CCSL 98, p. 915 lines 75–86.

[23] For a list of surviving early Anglo-Saxon Gelasian sacramentaries, see Klaus Gamber, *Sakramentartypen. Versuch einer Gruppierung der Handschriften und Fragmente bis zur Jahrtausendsende*, Texte und Arbeiten 49–50 (Beuron, 1958), pp. 60–4; and Helmut Gneuss, 'Liturgical Books in Anglo-Saxon England and their Old English Terminology' in *Learning and Literature in Anglo-Saxon England: Studies Presented to Peter Clemoes on the Occasion of his Sixty-Fifth Birthday*, ed. Michael Lapidge and Helmut Gneuss (Cambridge, 1985), pp. 91–141 (at pp. 99–102).

[24] I quote this verse in the *Psalterium Romanum* version, as it is inscribed on the flowering rod held by Christ as Wisdom in Oxford, Bodleian MS Auct F. 4. 32, f. 1r: see *Saint Dunstan's Classbook from Glastonbury*, ed. R. W. Hunt (Amsterdam, 1961), p. vi; and E. Temple, *Anglo-Saxon Manuscripts 900–1066* (London, 1971), No. 11, p. 41, and Illus. 41.

have comforted me' ['virga tua, et baculus tuus, ipsa me consolata sunt'], Ps. 22: 4)[25] as well as being on occasion a symbol of Christ himself ('there shall come forth a rod out of the root of Jesse' ['egredietur virga de radice Jesse'], Isaiah 11: 1; 'a star shall rise out of Jacob, and a sceptre [rod] shall spring up from Israel' ['orietur stella ex Jacob, et consurget virga de Israel'], Numbers 24: 17).

St John seems to be represented as having raised the bird from a T-shaped perch, visible under the saint's arm. It may not be too fanciful to suggest that here, as in the pointing finger of John the Baptist and the crossed paws of the beasts who adore Christ, we have a visual pun. The Hebrew letter *thau* is the sign placed on the foreheads of those chosen from the midst of Jerusalem to become members of the new Israel (Ezechiel 9: 4). *Thau*, the final letter of the Hebrew alphabet, signified God, like the Greek letter *Omega*. Hebrew *thau* was identified with Greek *tau*: and Ezekiel 9: 4 finds its New Testament fulfilment in the sign of the one hundred and forty-four thousand (Apoc. 7: 3), who in St John's Apocalypse follow the lamb and who (together with the four evangelist-beasts) surround his throne 'having his name and the name of his Father written in their foreheads' (Apoc. 14: 1). The signing of the forehead in the Apocalypse apparently refers to early Christian baptismal usage: the first Christians were signed on the forehead with a *tau*, the name of Yahweh. The *tau* naturally became associated with the Cross (written both as + and as X), the sign of the Son of Man; signing with the cross was central to Christian rites of initiation.[26] The *tau* sign leads us back to baptism, the context already suggested by the bird, and to St John the Evangelist, author of the Apocalypse.

Is this lower panel related to the two figural panels above it? Canon 82 of the Quinisext Council, held at Constantinople in 691–2, had ordered that

---

[25] The 'rod' of Psalm 22 is particularly relevant, in view of the close association between this psalm and baptism: cf. its use by Ambrose, quoted below, pp. 25–6. In the Neapolitan liturgy, Psalm 22 was the first text solemnly 'handed on' to the catechumens. It seems likely that a Neapolitan list of festivals existed in Northumbria (perhaps at Monkwearmouth-Jarrow); and that such a list formed the archetype behind the references to the lectionary according to the use of Naples found in several insular gospel books (including the Lindisfarne gospels and the Durham gospels) which passed through Northumbrian scriptoria in the late seventh and early eighth centuries. See A. Dondeyne, 'La discipline des scrutins dans l'église latine avant Charlemagne', *Révue d'Histoire Ecclésiastique* 28 (1932) 5–33 and 751–87 (at pp. 19–21); and *The Durham Gospels: Durham Cathedral MS A. II. 7*, ed. Christopher Verey and others, Early English Manuscripts in Facsimile 20 (Copenhagen, 1980), pp. 26–8.

[26] See Jean Daniélou, *Primitive Christian Symbols* (London, 1962), pp. 136–45, and *The Bible and the Liturgy* (Notre Dame, 1966), pp. 54–69; Hugo Rahner, '*Antenna Crucis*, V: Das mystische Tau', *Zeitschrift für katholische Theologie* 75 (1953) 386–410. On the signing of the catechumens, see Ordo XI, pars 1–30: Andrieu, II. 417–25.

Christ should no longer be represented as a lamb.[27] It ordered that he should in future be represented only as a human figure. Because this council infringed papal prerogatives in various ways, Pope Sergius rejected its canons; and it may have been in the context of this iconographic controversy that Sergius introduced the 'Agnus Dei' chant into the Mass.[28] Awareness of such matters could well have made Anglo-Saxon clerics (who were in contact with Roman liturgical developments) interested in the ways in which symbolic creatures like the lamb and the eagle could express different aspects of Christ's nature and ministry. There is at Bewcastle a pleasing balance between, on the one hand, the top and bottom panels in which the two saints recognize Christ under the symbolic form of creatures, and, on the other, the central panel in which two creatures recognize Christ in human form.

St John's eagle, with its baptismal contexts, provides what might be called a prelude to (and to some degree a significant contrast with) the theme of the Eucharistic presence of Christ which seems to be reflected in the upper two panels. As we have seen, the text 'your youth will be renewed like the eagle's' (Ps. 102: 5) was used to link the eagle both with Christ and with the catechumen. The psalm refers to the legend that, when the eagle grows old, its hooked upper beak grows down over its lower beak so that the bird cannot open its mouth and begins to starve. It therefore rubs its beak on a rock so as to wear away the dangerous hook. Then it can feed, and its youth and plumage are renewed. This legend is told in their commentaries on Psalm 102: 5 by both Augustine and Cassiodorus (see above, p. 23 and note 22). For them, Christ himself is the rock against which the eagle rubs his beak to attain renewed life (cf. 1 Cor. 10: 4). Both Augustine and (more briefly) Cassiodorus bring out the Eucharistic possibilities of the legend of the eagle whose renewal depends on his ability to eat. But, in order to understand the progression between the lower panel of the Bewcastle Cross, on the one hand, and the two upper panels, on the other, the use of Psalm 102: 5 by St Ambrose is particularly illuminating. In each of his two explanations of the initiation ceremonies of the Easter vigil, Ambrose uses Psalm 102: 5 to explain why the catechumens, once they have been baptized and have received from the bishop the seal of the spirit (confirmation), proceed directly to receive communion:

> Signauit te deus pater, confirmauit te Christus dominus et *dedit pignus* spiritum *in cordibus tuis*. . . . His abluta plebs diues insignibus ad Christi contendit altaria dicens: *Et introibo ad altare dei, ad deum qui laetificat iuuentutem meam.* Depositis enim inueterati erroris exuuiis, renouata in aquilae iuuentutem, caeleste illud

---

[27] Charles Joseph Hefele, *Histoire des conciles*, trans. Henri Leclercq, 11 vols (Paris, 1907–52), III, Part 1, p. 573.

[28] Ó Carragáin, 'Liturgical Innovations', pp. 134–5.

25

festinat adire conuiuium. Venit igitur et uidens sacrosanctum altare conpositum exclamans ait: *Parasti in conspectu meo mensam.* Hanc loquentem inducit Dauid dicens: *Dominus pascit me et nihil mihi deerit. . . . Virga tua et baculus tuus ipsa me consolata sunt. . . .*[29]

[God the Father has marked you with his seal, Christ the Lord has confirmed you and sent his Spirit into your heart as a pledge. . . . Thus washed and rich in its adornments, the people proceeds eagerly to Christ's altars saying: 'And I shall go in unto the altar of God, to God who gives joy to my youth' (Ps. 42: 4). It has put aside the husk[30] of ancient error, its youth is renewed like the eagle's, and it hastens to approach that heavenly banquet. It comes then, and seeing the holy altar prepared for it, exclaims: 'You have prepared a table before me' (Ps. 22: 5). David has this people speak when he says: 'The lord feeds me, I shall not want. . . . Your rod and your staff have comforted me . . .' (Ps. 22: 1, 4).]

The way in which Ambrose brings out the dramatic implications of the renewal of the eagle's youth may provide us with an analogue for the way in which, on the Bewcastle Cross, the designer has kept the lower panel distinct from the two upper panels, while suggesting visual links between them: the new life of baptism was seen to lead naturally to a hunger for union with Christ in the Eucharist. The opening words of the runic inscription on the panel which separates the lower figural panel from the two upper ones fortunately survive. In view of the emphasis in the figural panels on rebirth to eternal life, and on Christ's divine nature, it is particularly appropriate that the opening words of the runic inscription refer to the monument as '+ [þ]is sigbecn' ['this token of victory', 'this victory-memorial'].[31]

All the panels seem designed to be multivalent; it is clear that the scene in which John the Baptist hails Christ as 'Agnus Dei' is associated not only with the breaking of the bread at Mass but also (through its scriptural context) with baptism. The documents which Northumbrian communities would have used when planning the Easter liturgy are likely to have reflected Roman use. References in these documents to the topography of Rome, and in particular to that of the Lateran, the Pope's cathedral church, had to be explained before a

---

[29] *Ambroise de Milan: Des Sacrements, Des Mystères, Explication du symbole*, ed. Bernard Botte, Sources chrétiennes 25 (Paris, 1980), pp. 178–80 (*De Mysteriis*, 42–3); cf. p. 104 (*De Sacramentis*, IV. 7).

[30] *exuuiis*: both 'clothing', and 'skin': perhaps a reference at once to the snake shedding its skin, and also to the catechumens putting aside their clothes before entering the font.

[31] Page, in Cramp, forthcoming. It is interesting that the fragmentary inscription recorded from the now-lost head of the cross apparently refers also to Christ's power: 'ricæs dryhtnæs' ['of a powerful Lord']. See Page, 'Bewcastle Cross', pp. 38 and 56.

1. Bewcastle Cross: west face.

2. Bewcastle Cross: St John the Evangelist.

3. Bewcastle Cross: east face.

4. Bewcastle Cross from the south-west.

Northumbrian community could have worked out its own version of the Roman liturgy. Explanations could have come from various quarters: from the accounts of those who had been to Rome, such as (to go no further) Bede's abbots Benedict Biscop, Ceolfrid and Hwætberht; occasionally from visiting authorities such as John the Archicantor of St Peter's, who taught the liturgy in Northumbria in 679–80;[32] from *libelli* or booklets which put into writing the Roman way of doing things (*ordo Romanus*) for particular seasons; and also from authoritative Roman documents such as the *Liber Pontificalis*, the official collection of papal biographies, known to and used by Bede.[33] In its account of Pope St Sylvester (AD 314–35) the *Liber* describes the golden statue of the Agnus Dei which stood in the font in the baptistery of St John Lateran. It stood at the foot of a porphyry column, and from it baptismal water poured into the font. On the right side of the lamb stood a statue of Christ, five feet in height, made from pure silver; on the left a matching silver statue of St John the Baptist, bearing a scroll with the inscription 'ECCE AGNUS DEI, ECCE QVI TOLLIT PECCATA MVNDI'.[34] An awareness of the existence of such statues at the Lateran baptistery at Rome may perhaps have encouraged patrons to provide representations of John the Baptist and the Agnus Dei at other sites associated with baptism. Even more interesting is the architectural setting provided by Pope St Hilarius (AD 461–8) for the Lateran baptistery. The *Liber* says that Hilarius erected three chapels, dedicated respectively to St John the Baptist, St John the Evangelist and the Holy Cross, all covered in silver and precious stones, as part of a unified building programme to adorn the baptistery:

> Hic fecit oratoria III in baptisterio basilicae Constantinianae, sancti Iohannis Baptistae et sancti Iohannis evangelistae et sanctae Crucis, omnia ex argento et lapidibus pretiosis.[35]

The chapels were evidently erected to provide a suitable setting for the Easter

---

[32] On John the Archicantor, see the references in *Venerabilis Bedae Opera Historica*, ed. Charles Plummer, 2 vols (Oxford, 1896), II. 484, s.v.; John's authorship of the baptismal *Ordo* XI, first proposed by Carlo Silva-Tarouca, 'Giovanni "Archicantor" di S. Pietro a Roma e l'"Ordo Romanus" da lui composto', *Atti della pontificia accademia di archeologia*, 3rd series, 1 (1925) 160–219, was rejected by Andrieu, *Ordines*, III. 6–15; but has been strongly defended by S. J. P. Van Dijk, who demonstrates that the *ordo* shows signs of having been compiled in St Peter's in the 670s: 'The Urban and Papal Rites in Seventh and Eighth-Century Rome', *Sacris Erudiri* 12 (1961) 411–87 (at pp. 455–65).

[33] On Bede's use of the *Liber*, see Plummer, I. li, note; II. 14, 82 and 84.

[34] Louis Duchesne, *Le Liber Pontificalis* (2 vols, 1886–92), reprinted with an additional volume, *Additions et corrections de Mgr L. Duchesne*, ed. C. Vogel, 3 vols (Paris, 1981), I. 174 (text), 192 (notes). *DACL*, II Part 1, col. 411, gives a hypothetical reconstruction of the statues.

[35] Duchesne, I. 242 (text), 245–6 (notes).

conferrings of baptism and confirmation. Entering the baptistery from the basilica, the baptismal procession of catechumens, sponsors and clerics would have encountered first the pair of chapels dedicated to the two Saints John: the chapel dedicated to St John the Baptist stands on the left of the font, that dedicated to St John the Evangelist on the right. The vaults of both chapels were decorated by Pope Hilarius with mosaics representing the Agnus Dei surrounded by symbols of the four gospels.[36] The third chapel, that of the Holy Cross, was the most important of the set, as it became the *consignatorium* of the Lateran basilica: the place in which confirmation was conferred by the Pope who signed the neophytes, fresh from their baptism, with the sign of the cross in chrism on their foreheads.[37] The neophytes finally returned to the basilica itself for the rest of the Easter vigil ceremonies, which included their receiving the Eucharist.

Thus the architectural setting for Christian initiation in the Roman liturgy encouraged the association of St John the Baptist with St John the Evangelist, and of both with the Holy Cross. The link between these three ideas becomes more striking when we realize that in the eighth century the post-baptismal catechesis of the neophytes at Rome included processions designed to fix in the imagination this sequence of chapels and the sequence of liturgical events with which they were associated. Easter week was a period of intense catechesis. Such ceremonies were not, of course, arranged simply, or even primarily, for the neophytes: at this period infant baptism had for long been the norm at Rome (but hardly at Bewcastle). In the persons of the neophytes and their sponsors, the whole congregation re-enacted in Easter week their original initiation into Christianity. A special sermon on this theme was preached at Mass each day. Vespers was a particularly solemn ceremony during this week. The neophytes gathered at St John Lateran, and the Pope himself presided over the ceremonies, which were designed as a re-enactment of the solemn initiation ceremonies of the vigil of Easter.[38] So that the stages of initiation could be 'revisited', the Vespers ceremony was divided into several 'stations'. The first three psalms, with the canticle (the Magnificat), were sung in the basilica itself. Then the neophytes, accompanied by the Pope and

---

[36] Philippe Lauer, *Le palais de Latran* (Paris, 1911), figs 19 and 20 and pp. 56–7. The mosaic in the chapel of St John the Evangelist still exists; the mosaic in that of St John the Baptist was destroyed in the eighteenth century, but is known from earlier drawings.

[37] Andrieu, Ordo XXXB, No. 52, note (III. 473), identifies the *consignatorium* of the Lateran as 'sans doute' the chapel of the Holy Cross. This chapel was separated from the baptistery itself by a little courtyard. See Lauer, *Latran*, pp. 57–61; *DACL*, II, Part 1, cols 382–469 under 'baptistère', especially cols 408–11 and the plan of the baptistery and chapels at col. 412 (*DACL* summarizes Lauer). The chapel of the Holy Cross was destroyed by order of Sixtus V (1585–90).

[38] The fullest account of the processions at Vespers on Easter week in the eighth century is in Andrieu, Ordo XXVII (III. 362–72); see also Ordo XXXB (III. 475–7).

clergy, proceeded to the baptistery. The neophytes proceeded into one of the two chapels dedicated to St John, the one known as 'St John *ad vestem*', before revisiting the scene of their confirmation, the chapel of the Holy Cross. There the final psalms were sung, and a collect said.[39]

The repetition of these ceremonies each evening in Easter Week (except on Friday, the octave of Good Friday, when Vespers was celebrated at the basilica of Holy Cross in Jerusalem)[40] must have linked the idea of Christian initiation very firmly with the topography and iconography of the Lateran baptistery and of the set of chapels which surrounded it. If a patron anxious to produce his own version of the *ordo Romanus* wished to associate his great cross with the idea of Christian initiation, he could hardly have done so more strikingly than by providing on the cross an iconographic analogue of the way in which, at the baptistery of the Lateran, the mother church of Christendom, St John the Baptist, St John the Evangelist and the Holy Cross were associated in a sequence at once architectural, iconographic and spiritual. The culminating chapel in the Lateran set, the chapel of the Holy Cross, would have its analogue at Bewcastle in the shape of the monument itself. The chapel could also have been recalled by the central figural panel at Bewcastle. The chapel of the Holy Cross was as we have seen the *consignatorium*, where the neophytes were signed with the sign of the cross in the oil of chrism. At Bewcastle the animals, with their crossed paws, hail Jesus as 'kristtus', 'the anointed one'. But the ceremony of consignation or confirmation symbolized the full union between the neophytes and Christ. In it they, like him, became 'anointed ones', sharing through his Spirit in his priesthood and kingship. This point is made very concisely by Isidore of Seville:

> Chrisma Graece, Latine unctio nominatur; ex cuius nomine et Christus dicitur, et homo post lavacrum sanctificatur. Nam sicut in baptismo peccatorum remissio datur, ita per unctionem sanctificatio spiritus adhibetur; et hoc de pristina disciplina, qua ungui in sacerdotium et in regnum solebant, ex quo Aaron a Moyse unctus est.[41]

[39] Andrieu, Ordo XXVII, no. 76 (III. 364–5 and notes). While proceeding from the baptistery to the chapel of the Holy Cross, the neophytes sang the antiphon 'Vidi aquam egredientem de templo, a latere dextro', which refers to the wound in Christ's right side. For a possible reminiscence of this antiphon, see É. Ó Carragáin, 'Vidi Aquam: the Liturgical Background to *The Dream of the Rood* 20a, "Swætan on þa swiðran healfe" ', *Notes and Queries* 228 (1983) 8–14.

[40] Andrieu, Ordo XXVII, no. 92, note (III. 371).

[41] *Isidori Hispalensis Episcopi Etymologiarum sive Originum Libri XX*, ed. W. M. Lindsay, 2 vols (Oxford, 1911), I, Bk. VI. xix. 50–1. On Christian initiation in this period, see Lionel L. Mitchell, *Baptismal Anointing*, Alcuin Club Collections 48 (London, 1966), pp. 80–171; and J. D. C. Fisher, *Christian Initiation: Baptism in the Medieval West*, Alcuin Club Collections 47 (London, 1965), pp. 78–87.

['Chrism' in Greek is called 'anointing' in Latin; from 'chrism' we get the name 'Christ', and by it man is sanctified after the [baptismal] laver. For just as remission of sins is given in baptism, so the hallowing of the spirit is added through anointing. This comes from the ancient custom of anointing into priesthood and into kingship, according to which Aaron was anointed by Moses.]

The iconographic fact that the animals on the centre panel are transformed and converted versions of the evil animals of Psalm 90: 13 thus takes on a more profound and specifically liturgical significance. The references in this central panel to the idea of conversion, to the unity between the animals (with their crossed paws) and Gessus Kristtus, and to the Eucharistic recognition of Christ on the Holy Cross 'in medio duorum animalium' all suggest that the panel is thematically as well as spatially central to the cross. It sums up all the themes of liturgical initiation reflected in the figural programme of the west side.

II THE EAST SIDE AND THE INSCRIPTIONS ON THE NARROW SIDES

One of the most striking visual characteristics of the Bewcastle monument is the structural balance between the figural programme on the west side and the single massive scroll which covers the east side (Plate 3). The scroll has eight volutes, and one creature feeds from a berry-branch in each of the lower seven of them; the topmost volute, uninhabited, rounds the pattern off with a knot of foliage. Its designer emphasized the unity of the panel by making the seven creatures face alternately left and right. The fourth and fifth of the creatures (reading from the bottom) are birds. The fourth (the central creature in the sequence of seven) is notably different from the three animals below it, which have fantastic tails merging into the scroll pattern itself. The body of the bird is realistically represented. Unlike all the other creatures in the scroll, it faces the spectator; but the bird's head is turned to its right, so that the right–left alternation between the creatures is preserved. Professor Cramp calls the bird 'thrush-like': but I am inclined to wonder whether it may have been placed where it is to remind the onlooker visually of the bird held by John the Evangelist in the lower panel of the west side. The designer has certainly placed at the centre of his scroll a motif which helped him to unify visually the two major faces of the monument.

The structural balance between the scroll and the Christological panels on the west face may be significant. If the upper two figural panels are unified by the idea that the body of Christ is to be recognized under symbolic forms, and in particular in the breaking of bread in the Eucharist, then the structure of the monument suggests that we should seek the significance of the scroll in Eucharistic images for the blood of Christ. The fact that all seven creatures are engaged in the act of feeding from the bunches of grape-like berries is interesting: the idea of 'feeding' was naturally central to the Eucharist. It seems on balance more likely that the scroll was symbolic than that it was merely decorative: in view of the virtuosity of the symbolism on the west side, the Bewcastle designer is unlikely to have planned the east side as simply a fine design, vacant of symbolic function. However, the great scroll is clearly not a naturalistic vine, nor are the berry-bunches naturalistic bunches of grapes. The seven creatures rear themselves among its branches as though it were a tree.[42] But the scroll lacks any naturalistic 'trunk': it clings vine-like to the 'trunk' of the monument itself. By his combination of grape-like berry bunches, tree-like foliage, and a clinging vine-like volute structure, the Bewcastle designer may have wished his scroll to combine the concepts of 'tree' and 'vine', and to suggest that the scroll was at once a symbol of the Cross, and something clinging to, hung from, the trunk of the Bewcastle Cross.

From the earliest Christian times, Christ's Cross was seen as a symbol of Christ's glorified body. This idea stemmed from the tradition that the Cross was the Sign of the Son of Man, which would appear in the East to announce Christ's return in glory to judge mankind.[43] In addition, the Cross was seen as the tree of life, the antitype of the tree of the knowledge of good and evil through which man had been expelled from paradise, and a symbol of the regeneration of the cosmos which was achieved through Christ's victory in death.[44] It is possible that the Bewcastle monument as a whole was conceived of as like a tree (it is certainly tall and tree-like). The emphasis on the Eucharistic recognition of Christ in the upper panels of the west side suggests that the monument as a whole might have been conceived as a symbol of Christ's body. The feeding creatures may indicate that the scroll also represented a regained paradisal state, in which men and animals could again be reconciled as at the beginning of man's history (cf. Isaiah 11: 6–9 and

---

[42] See W. G. Collingwood, *Northumbrian Crosses of the Pre-Norman Age* (London, 1927), Chapter 6 'The Tree of Life', pp. 39–55.

[43] Matthew 24: 27; Eric Peterson, *Frühkirche, Judentum und Gnosis: Studien und Untersuchungen* (Rome, 1959), pp. 15–35; Barbara Raw, '*The Dream of the Rood* and its Connections with Early Christian Art', *Medium Aevum* 39 (1970) 239–56 (at pp. 242–3).

[44] E. O. James, *The Tree of Life: an Archaeological Study* (Leiden, 1966), pp. 161–2; *The Dream of the Rood*, ed. M. J. Swanton (Manchester, 1970), pp. 42–52. I am grateful to my colleague Dr Jennifer O'Reilly for help with the symbolism of the tree of life, as well as with all aspects of crucifixion iconography.

65: 25), with the blessed Christian souls symbolized by feeding creatures. This theme is also reflected in the two converted beasts who recognize 'kristtus' in the central figural panel of the west face. Confirmation of such paradisal symbolism is perhaps to be found in the design of the narrow sides of the cross. Professor Cramp justly draws attention to the masterly variety in the decorative panels (which include interlace patterns and foliage scrolls) on these sides. None of these panels is inhabited by creatures, but the narrow sides are 'inhabited' in another way: between some of the panels runes have been inscribed. Weathering has rendered illegible the two runic inscriptions on the south side. At the top of the north side, the *nomen sacrum* '[ge]ssu/s' can be made out above the highest surviving panel (presumably it originally occurred just under the crosspiece). The name 'kynibur*g' is inscribed above the lowest panel on this side. The recurrence of the *nomen sacrum* may perhaps provide a hint of confirmation that the cross itself was seen as among other things a symbol of the glorified Jesus. 'kynibur*g', a feminine name, looks like a commemorative inscription: perhaps the name of a patroness or of an abbess. The embedding of this name (and the lost inscriptions on the south side may have provided other names) among decorative panels may possibly provide a hint of the symbolic meaning of the feeding creatures who, in a paradisal setting, inhabit the great scroll on the east side.

The 'kynibur*g' inscription, the lost inscriptions on the south face, and the names which seem once to have been inscribed on the panel on the west face, taken together, may indicate that for its original designers their 'sigbecn' was considered to be not only an *arbor vitae* (tree of life) but also a form of *liber vitae* (book of life), recording the most important benefactors and members of a community in such a way as to encourage prayers for their souls. Page (in Cramp, forthcoming) records that the penultimate line of the long inscription on the west face includes the runes '[.]gebid[.]', which as he points out may be a form of the verb *gebiddan*, 'to pray'. Such a list, ending with a request for prayers for the souls of those listed, would here have appeared in a most appropriate iconographic setting. It made sense to commemorate the dead between the eagle (which symbolized the promised renewal of youth after death) and the great image of Christ in Judgement, with his right hand raised in blessing and his left hand holding a scroll: presumably the sealed scroll, the *liber vitae agni* (Apoc. 13: 8; 21: 27), which only he can open. The custom of recording the benefactors and prominent members of a Christian congregation in a *liber vitae* grew out of the early Christian custom of recording such names on the reverse of ivory diptychs. Thus the combination of a commemorative inscription with appropriate iconography is of great antiquity. Diptychs were still used in the Roman Mass, at the commemorations of the living and the dead in the canon, up to the twelfth century. It is possible that such liturgical use of diptychs may have inspired the designer to combine figural panels (referring to eternal life, Judgement, and the Lamb) with a panel of runes in a single unified sequence balanced against the *arbor vitae* of the east side.[45] It seems reasonable to suggest that the feeding animals on the east side, and the names of Anglo-Saxon personages on the other sides, alike symbolize the hope of eternal life.

But the Cross, as well as being a paradisal and eschatological symbol, was also the gallows on which Christ hung, and on which his blood ran. It was possible, therefore, to see the Bewcastle monument as at once the tree of life, a symbol of the body of Christ, and also as a cross *on* which the body of Christ was raised and *on* which the blood of Christ had run. This ambivalence is fully developed in the Ruthwell Cross and poem, which dramatizes the way in which the Cross receives Christ, and the way in which it hands on Christ to his followers. But the same ambivalence seems implied by images at Bewcastle of Christ's body (images *on* the cross) and by the suggestions of grapes (which creatures feed on) and of a clinging vine in the great scroll on the east side. In his hymn 'Crux benedicta nitet' Venantius Fortunatus combines the ideas that the Cross is the tree of life, and that Christ is the vine who hanging on the Cross provided new wine for mankind:

> fertilitate potens, o dulce et nobile lignum,
>   quando tuis ramis tam noua poma geris. . . .
> appensa est uitis inter tua brachia, de qua
>   dulcia sanguineo uina rubore fluunt.

[You are powerful in your fruitfulness, O sweet and noble tree, seeing that you bear such new fruit in your branches. . . . hanging between your arms is a vine, from which sweet wines flow red as blood.][46]

If Venantius's poem does indeed provide an analogue for the symbolism of the scroll on the Bewcastle Cross, then an interest in the Eucharistic presence of Christ, body (recognized in the breaking of bread) and blood (received in the wine), unites the west and east faces of the monument.

---

[45] On the *liber vitae*, see further Philippians 4: 3, Apoc. 17: 8, 20: 12, 15 and parallels. The iconography and symbolism of scrolls are discussed by Hans-Jörg Spitz, *Die Metaphorik des geistigen Schriftsinns*, Münstersche Mittelalterschriften 12 (Munich, 1972), pp. 41–6, under 'Buchrolle'. See *DACL* III, Part 1, cols 1045–94 under 'Diptyques (Liturgie)', especially section iv, 'Le Liber Vitae', cols 1055–6; on the Roman use of diptychs, cols 1063–8 (esp. 1067), and cols 1074–81. For recent studies of the liturgical uses of diptychs, see A. G. Martimort, *The Church at Prayer, II: The Eucharist* (Shannon, 1973), pp. 127–9, 147–52 and 164–7.

[46] Lines 9–10 and 17–18; quoted from *Early Latin Hymns*, ed. A. S. Walpole (Cambridge, 1922), pp. 179 and 181. Walpole (p. 181) cites a parallel from Ambrose, *De Fide*, I, Chapter 20, par. 135, PL 16, col. 559A, where Christ is described as 'the new drink brought down from heaven to earth . . . who just like the grape on the vine, hung in the flesh from the wood of the Cross'.

III   THE SUNDIAL ON THE SOUTH SIDE

We can be sure that the present orientation of the Bewcastle Cross is original, because a sundial is preserved on the south side (Plate 4). Although several pre-Conquest sundials have been preserved, this is the only one to have survived on a cross. A sundial must have had practical uses, particularly for any community which recited the liturgical hours. But (especially in the case of liturgical objects) practical uses need not preclude symbolic meaning. The presence of a sundial complements the iconographic structure of the Bewcastle Cross in several ways. As we have seen, the figural panels on the west side are best explained in terms of the Roman liturgy of Holy Week and Easter. But Easter was calculated with reference to the sun's course: it fell on the first Sunday after the first full moon after the spring equinox. The equinox was theologically vital in the calculation of Easter. In his open letter (AD 707–10) to Nechtan, king of the Picts, Abbot Ceolfrid of Monkwearmouth-Jarrow explained why:

> We are commanded to keep the full moon of the Paschal month after the vernal equinox, the object being that the sun should first make the day longer than the night and then the moon can show to the world her full orb of light, because 'the Sun of righteousness with healing in his wings' [Malachi 4: 2], that is, the Lord Jesus, overcame all the darkness of death by the triumph of His Resurrection. So, ascending into heaven, he made His Church, which is often typified as the moon, full of the light of inward grace, by sending His Spirit down upon her. This plan of our salvation is what the prophet had in mind when he said, 'The sun was exalted and the moon stood in her order.'[47]

Ceolfrid writes that anyone who does not wait until after the equinox to celebrate Easter 'agrees with those who trust that they can be saved without the grace of Christ . . . and who presume to teach that they could have attained to perfect righteousness even though the true Light had never conquered the darkness of the world by dying and rising again': in other words, he is guilty of Pelagianism.[48] But in the same letter, Ceolfrid had already directed Nechtan and his people to look at a sundial if they wanted to confirm the fact that the equinox fell on 21 March: 'as we can also prove by inspecting a sundial' ['ut etiam ipsi horologica inspectione probamus'].[49] Ceolfrid's letter seems to be the earliest statement of the importance of the sundial for determining the equinox in a document emanating from

[47] *Bede's Ecclesiastical History of the English People*, ed. B. Colgrave and R. A. B. Mynors (Oxford, 1969), 5: 21, p. 545. 'The sun was exalted' is verse 11 of the old Latin version of the Canticle of Habbakuk sung at Lauds on Fridays.
[48] Ibid. On this reference to Pelagianism, see D. Ó Cróinín, ' "New Heresy for Old": Pelagianism in Ireland and the Papal Letter of 640', *Speculum* 60 (1985) 505–16 (at pp. 515–16).
[49] Ibid., pp. 542–3.

Monkwearmouth-Jarrow. In AD 703, when he composed *De Temporibus Liber*, Bede was still under the impression, like all western computists before him, that (Chapter 7) the Julian calendar corresponded with scientific fact when it placed the equinox on 25 March;[50] but in texts later than Ceolfrid's letter, Bede states in three separate places that the sundial confirms 21 March as the equinox.[51] Bede himself may possibly have drafted the letter to Nechtan for Ceolfrid, his abbot.[52] The inspection of sundials may have been merely a literary topos: C. W. Jones points out that, as the equinox had in fact moved forward to 17 March by Bede's time, Bede's advice cannot be based on acute observation of a sundial.[53] Therefore I do not wish to argue that at Bewcastle the sundial was put to practical use to calculate Easter or the equinox (Easter tables would have been less troublesome and more reliable). But the stress in Northumbrian literary texts on the *theological* importance of the fact that the sun (symbol of Christ) had to achieve ascendancy over winter darkness (in the equinox) before Easter could be celebrated, and their interest in sundials as instruments which track the sun's course, suggest that the Bewcastle designer might have incorporated the sundial into the design of his 'sigbecn' for symbolic reasons.

The sundial has been carefully incorporated into a panel of foliage, so that the dial is 'attached like a large leaf to the stem and sprouting from above [the sundial] is a large berry branch' (Cramp, forthcoming). The panel might be termed a 'time-tree', with the sundial as its fruit. Such an idea made liturgical sense. On the second Sunday in Advent (a day on which the Roman station was at Holy Cross in Jerusalem) the gospel (Luke 21: 25–33) told of 'signs in the sun and in the moon and in the stars' and of 'the Son of Man coming in a cloud, with great power and majesty'. In these verses, flowering foliage acts as a reminder that God's kingdom is at hand:

> See the fig tree and all the trees: when they now shoot forth their
> fruit, you know that summer is nigh. So you also, when you shall

[50] *Bedae Opera de Temporibus*, ed. C. W. Jones (Cambridge, Mass., 1943), pp. 297 and 127.

[51] *De Temporum Ratione*, Chapter 30, 'horologica consideratione docemur' (Jones, p. 237); and Chapter 38, 'horologii lineis in terra, quae necessaria quaerit, apprehendat' (Jones, p. 251); *Epistola ad Wichthedum* (AD 725–31), par. 12 'quod et inspectione horologica et aperta ratione probabitur' (Jones, p. 325). See also Plummer, II. 333.

[52] Plummer, II. 332. Colgrave and Mynors (p. 534 n. 1) suggest that Bede may have re-edited the letter for publication in his history, so this reference to the sundial may date from the 730s, not from two decades earlier.

[53] Jones, p. 127. On the difficulty, but possibility, of using a sundial for this purpose, see Kenneth Harrison, *The Framework of Anglo-Saxon History* (Cambridge, 1976), p. 43. Jones (loc. cit.) points out (following Adamnán, *De Locis Sanctis*, 13) that the equinox could also be determined by observing the shadow of a tall object: this suggests another way in which a tall cross might trace out patterns which reflected the liturgical symbolism of the sun's course.

see these things come to pass, know that the kingdom of God is at hand. Amen, I say to you, this generation shall not pass away till all things be fulfilled.[54]

The image of the Son of Man coming in power and majesty occurs next to the sundial at Bewcastle (see Plate 4, which shows the relation of the sundial to the design of the west side). The dial is placed at the level of Christ's shoulder, and the foliage on which the dial 'grows', sprouting at the level of Christ's waist, spreads aloft to slightly below the level of the Agnus Dei cradled on the arm of John the Baptist. An onlooker proceeding sunwise from the south side of the cross to the west, or looking at the cross from the south-west, might associate the sundial-tree with either or both of these figural panels. But the liturgical year linked the births of Christ and of John the Baptist by means of the sun's course. Christ was conceived (25 March: VIII Kal. Aprilis) and born (25 December: VIII Kal. Ianuarii) on 'the growing days' ['diebus crescentibus'], the spring equinox and winter solstice which marked the stages by which the sun overcame darkness. The Baptist was conceived six months before Christ (Luke 1: 36), and his vocation was to go before the face of the Lord to prepare his ways (Luke 1: 76); he was not himself the Light, but was to give testimony concerning the Light (John 1: 8–9). The Baptist's prophetic role was built into the liturgical year: his conception (24 September: VIII Kal. Octobris) and birth (24 June: VIII Kal. Iulii) were celebrated on the 'lessening days' ['diebus decrescentibus'], the autumnal equinox and summer solstice; for in John's gospel (3: 30) John the Baptist said of his relationship with Christ that 'he must increase; but I must decrease'.[55] It made symbolic sense to place a sundial as near as possible to paired representations of Christ and John the Baptist, whose advents marked into balanced quadrants the solar cycle incorporated into the liturgical year.

IV THE BEWCASTLE CROSS AND THE RUTHWELL CROSS

In her forthcoming study of the Bewcastle Cross, Professor Cramp comes down cautiously in favour of the Bewcastle Cross's having been erected before the Ruthwell Cross. At Ruthwell we find extended statements of several ideas that are briefly stated, or implied, at Bewcastle. Variants of the upper two

[54] On the eighth-century use of the lection, see Theodor Klauser, *Das römische Capitulare Evangeliorum*, 2nd edn (Münster, 1972), p. 43 (No. 239); p. 89 (No. 264), etc. On the station on this Sunday at Santa Croce, see Willis, 'The Roman Stational Liturgy', p. 83. For the idea that flowering foliage heralds the Last Judgement, see *The Seafarer*, ed. I. L. Gordon (London, 1960), pp. 39–40, lines 48–52.
[55] See Augustine on John 3: 30, Tractatus XIV, CCSL 36, p. 144, lines 23–5; Bede, *In Lucae Euangelium Expositio*, ed. D. Hurst, CCSL 120, p. 30, lines 439–54; Alcuin on John 3: 30 follows Augustine, and sums up the topos in the phrases 'diebus crescentibus . . . decrescentibus', PL 100, col. 787D; Alcuin is copied by Pseudo-Bede, PL 92, col. 676D.

panels at Bewcastle recur at Ruthwell. Their Eucharistic significance is confirmed by the context given them at Ruthwell, where the panel representing Christ over the beasts appears between an Agnus Dei panel (above) and a panel representing Saints Paul and Anthony breaking bread in the desert (below). At Ruthwell as at Bewcastle St John the Baptist cradles the Agnus Dei in his left arm, and points him out with his right hand: Augustine's 'huic autem digito ostendere' is relevant to both crosses.[56] Eucharistic ideas unite all the panels of this side at Ruthwell. It is striking that, in contrast with Bewcastle, there is on the Ruthwell Cross no inscription commemorating benefactors. The Ruthwell designer did not take up the Bewcastle idea of the *liber vitae*, but concentrated on exploring the idea that Christ was to be recognized in the Eucharist.

Presumably the sequence of Eucharistic panels originally faced west at Ruthwell, as the figural panels still do at Bewcastle. This would be liturgically appropriate. If Mass were ever celebrated at either cross these panels, facing west, would have been visible to a celebrant and congregation, who would have faced east so as to be correctly oriented for the Eucharistic sacrifice. That tall crosses were closely associated with altars in eighth-century Northumbria is made clear by Aethelwulf's *De Abbatibus* (written AD 803–21), which describes a marvellous cruciform church seen in a midnight dream:

> ast pauimenta domus medii sub culmine templi
> aurea mirifice portabant munera mense.
> crux ueneranda nitens precelso stipite surget
> uertice de mense nimium candente smaragdo.
> aurea cum gemmis flammescit lammina fuluis.

> [The floor of the building beneath the mid-point of the temple roof bore the weight of golden offerings on a wondrous table. A holy cross rose up shining upon a very long stem from the top of the table, and (upon it) emeralds shone full bright. Golden plating blazed there (set) with dark-hued gems.][57]

[56] See above, p. 18. Paul Meyvaert, 'An Apocalypse Panel on the Ruthwell Cross', *Medieval and Renaissance Studies*, ed. Frank Tirro (Durham, North Carolina, 1982), pp. 3–32, argued that at Ruthwell the Agnus Dei is held by God the Father, not by John the Baptist; but this was convincingly refuted by George Henderson, 'The John the Baptist Panel on the Ruthwell Cross', *Gesta* 24 (1985) 1–12, who also demonstrates the Eucharistic significance of the sequence of panels on the (originally) west face at Ruthwell (pp. 4–8).

[57] Text and translation from *Aethelwulf 'De Abbatibus'*, ed. Alastair Campbell (Oxford, 1967), lines 721–5 (*carmen* xxii), pp. 56–7; Campbell comments on the similarity between this vision and *The Dream of the Rood* (p. 56, n. 2). Otto Nussbaum, *Der Standort des Liturgen am christlichen Altar vor dem Jahre 1000: eine archäologische und liturgiegeschichtliche Untersuchung*, Theophaneia, No. 18, 2 vols (Bonn, 1965), I. 431–2, explains this and other passages within the developing relationship of cross to altar: great crosses, or crosses on high stands, were erected *behind* altars at this period; the custom of placing crosses *on* the east side of the altar table began c. AD 1000.

When a little later Aethelwulf describes another visionary altar, the standard of a tall cross again towers over it ('quae crucis excelse porrexit uertice signum').[58] The existence of panels at the foot of the west side of both the Ruthwell and Bewcastle Crosses suggests that their designers did not envisage a permanent structure standing in front of either monument: we should perhaps think of the use of a portable altar, on a table erected either to one side, or else one to two metres in front of the crosses so that none of the panels would have been obscured from the celebrant's eyes. In the latter case, congregations would see the crosses rising behind the altar-tables 'precelso stipite . . . uertice de mense'. If Mass were ever celebrated at the Bewcastle Cross, the panel of runic inscriptions on the west face of that monument could have been put to liturgical use. I wish to emphasize that the text on the panel clearly was not designed to be read out at Mass. It seems to have begun with some such words as 'this victory sign was set up by . . .', and to have ended with a formula such as 'pray for their souls'. The inscription was in English, not Latin, and in runes (with their associations of secrecy and mystery), not Roman letters. The key to the possible symbolic use of the panel may lie in a characteristic of the Roman Mass. In the Celtic and Gallican Mass the commemorations of the living and dead took place during the offertory (before the preface) and the diptychs containing the names of the living and dead were solemnly read aloud. But in the Roman Mass these commemorations had been since the sixth century incorporated into the canon, or central action, of the Mass; and consequently the names of the living and dead were not usually read aloud. Instead, the priest usually commemorated them implicitly, by pausing at the appropriate points of the canon for a moment of mental prayer while gazing at a diptych or at a *liber vitae*.[59] At a Mass near the Bewcastle Cross, the priest and congregation could make an implicit commemoration of all their benefactors (not just those actually listed on the cross) by simply glancing at the cross for a moment of silent prayer at the appropriate moments of the canon. The very inaccessibility of runic script could have contributed to its symbolic value: a Latin inscription, in Roman letters, would have focused attention too exclusively on a limited number of names. The runic panel may have been valued not simply because it preserved the names of certain well-known people, but also because it suggested the deeper mystery of the *liber vitae*, a mystery also suggested by the closed scroll in Christ's left hand in the panel just above. The Irish Stowe Missal refers to the full *liber vitae* which

---

[58] *De Abbatibus*, ed. cit., line 737, p. 59. Cf. the Bewcastle inscription 'þis sigbecn': 'becn' often glosses *signum* in the Lindisfarne and Rushworth glosses (Bosworth-Toller, *Supplement*, p. 64 under *beacen*).

[59] On the Celtic use, see F. E. Warren, *The Liturgy and Ritual of the Celtic Church* (Oxford, 1881), pp. 105–6. For the Roman and Ambrosian uses see *DACL*, III, Part 1, cols 1063–8 (especially col. 1067); and section xi, 'La place des diptyques à la Messe', cols 1074–81; also Martimort, pp. 149–50 and 165–6.

only Christ can read: in its prayers over the offerings it distinguishes between the loved ones whose names the priest recites, and those whose names he does not recite, but who are recited by Christ in the book of eternal life ('pro anima[b]us carorum nostrorum .n. et cararum nostrarum quorum nomina recitamus et quorumcumque non recitamus sed a te recitantur in libro vitae aeternae').[60] Similarly, the Durham *Liber Vitae* (London, BL MS Cotton Domitian VII, begun in the ninth century) was, it seems likely, always kept on the high altar so that celebrants could, by glancing at the manuscript each day for a moment of mental prayer at the appropriate parts of the conventual Mass, implicitly commemorate all the members and benefactors of the community.[61]

I have suggested that the John the Evangelist panel at Bewcastle is to be associated with the catechumenate and baptism. At Ruthwell a whole side of the cross (the side which presumably faced east originally) was devoted to images which recall the Lenten catechumenate. On it we have panels representing the Blind Man (lection for the Wednesday of the fourth week in Lent) and the conversion of Mary Magdalene. Above and below them appear panels representing the Visitation and the Annunciation, which are to be understood in the light of the idea that the catechumenate was a period of spiritual gestation, an imitation by the catechumen of Christ's own virginal birth (see above, p. 22). The importance of the spring equinox (symbolized by the Bewcastle sundial) is at Ruthwell indicated by the juxtaposition of Crucifixion and Annunciation panels at the foot of the originally east side. Both Crucifixion and Annunciation were understood to have taken place on 25 March (the spring equinox in the Julian calendar), thirty-three years apart.[62] The side appropriately culminated with a panel representing an eagle perched on a branch of berries (grapes?). This eagle provides a highly appropriate transition to the second half of the Ruthwell programme, the Eucharistic images of the west side. We have seen St Ambrose (as well as St Augustine and Cassiodorus) stress that the eagle of Psalm 102: 5 must be hungry when he can open his beak again, like the catechumen who after gaining new life in baptism hastens to the Eucharistic feast. The climax of the Eucharistic programme, on the crosshead of the west side at Ruthwell, was apparently a set of all four evangelist symbols, who probably surrounded an

---

[60] *The Stowe Missal*, ed. George F. Warner, 2 vols, Henry Bradshaw Society 31–2 (London, 1906–15), II. 9; also printed in Warren, pp. 232–3; Warren's note 41 (on pp. 257–8) lists Gallican references to the *liber vitae*.

[61] A. J. Piper, 'The Libraries of the Monks of Durham' in *Medieval Scribes, Manuscripts and Libraries: Essays Presented to N. R. Ker*, ed. M. B. Parkes and A. G. Watson (London, 1978), pp. 213–49, at p. 237. See *The Oldest English Texts*, ed. Henry Sweet, EETS OS 83 (1885), pp. 153–66; and *Liber Vitae Ecclesiae Dunelmensis: A Collotype Facsimile*, ed. A. Hamilton Thompson, Surtees Society 136 (1927).

[62] The Ruthwell crucifixion poem reflects the same idea, presenting the dilemma of the Cross, when Christ wishes to ascend upon it, in terms reminiscent of Mary's dilemma at the Annunciation: cf. Ó Carragáin, 'Liturgical Innovations', pp. 140–1.

image of Christ (perhaps as Agnus Dei, perhaps in human form).[63] Of the four evangelists, St John and his eagle were given the highest place at the top of the cross, 'eo quod nimis alta petierit'. In this position, John and his eagle are balanced against the eagle on the branch (on the opposite side). With his more extensive programme, the Ruthwell designer could represent two matched (and, to a certain degree, contrasted) eagles, and so articulate the multivalence of the eagle symbol (evangelist-symbol, catechumen, Christ): a multivalence already implicit in the unique and moving image at Bewcastle. Finally, inhabited scrolls, on the model of the great scroll on the east face of Bewcastle, cover the two narrow sides of the Ruthwell Cross. But around the scrolls the designer left broad margins; and on the margins a poem in English was inscribed in runes. The poem emphasizes the complete pouring out of Christ's blood, in such phrases as 'they mocked the pair of us together; I was drenched with blood pou[red from the man's side]':

> bismæradu ungket men ba ætgadre ic waes miþ blodi bistemid
> bi[goten of þæs guman sida]. . . .[64]

The imagery of the Ruthwell poem may help us to understand the symbolic meaning of the scrolls around which it was inscribed; if so, it also helps us to understand the great Bewcastle scroll.[65]

V   THE BEWCASTLE CROSS AND THE LITURGICAL YEAR

It is natural to suppose that the designer of a great public monument like the Bewcastle Cross would have intended his monument, which would be in place at all times of the year, to be appropriate to the liturgy of every season. Liturgical action itself would have determined which of the various potential symbolic dimensions of a text were relevant on a particular day. Texts which were used daily or weekly must have been particularly familiar, and so particularly important in interpreting the cross. The 'Agnus Dei' chant recalled a solemn moment in daily Mass, the moment of communion. The Mass is an especially interesting context for elements of a high cross, as it made present each day Christ's sacrifice on the Cross on Good Friday. John the Baptist, hailing Christ as the Agnus Dei, was prominent in the weeks after

---

[63] Rosemary Cramp, 'The Evangelist Symbols and their Parallels in Anglo-Saxon Sculpture' in R. T. Farrell (see note 3 above), pp. 118–30.

[64] I quote from D. Howlett, 'A Reconstruction of the Ruthwell Crucifixion Poem', *Studia Neophilologica* 48 (1976) 54–8.

[65] For a full interpretation of the Ruthwell poem, see Ó Carragáin, 'The Ruthwell Crucifixion Poem in its Iconographic and Liturgical Contexts', to appear in *Peritia* 5 (1987 for 1986).

Christmas, the season of Epiphany.[66] Psalm 90 was sung every night at Compline; and the canticle of Habbakuk was sung every Friday morning at Lauds. On the first Sunday of Lent, the texts of the Mass summed up the major themes of the following season: the sung texts were all drawn from Psalm 90, while the gospel (Matthew 4: 1–11) told of the temptations of Christ by Satan in the desert, in which the Messianic images of Psalm 90 (quoted by the devil, who is rebutted by Christ) are triumphantly fulfilled. The Bewcastle Cross must have been seen as especially relevant to the liturgy in the final weeks of Lent. On the fourth Sunday the Roman station was at Holy Cross in Jerusalem; the gospel (John 6: 1–14, the feeding of the five thousand) combined the Lenten theme of the desert with the Eucharistic theme of spiritual food.[67] The Roman stational practice affected the texts sung at Mass on the fourth Sunday in Lent: the introit began 'Laetare Jerusalem', and references to Jerusalem dominated the Mass for the day.[68] It was within the fourth week in Lent, as we have seen, that the catechumens were presented with the gospels and told of the eagle image. John the Evangelist was particularly important in the final weeks of Lent, when extracts from his gospel were read daily at Mass.[69] The Passion according to St John was, of course, the one read at the moment of Christ's death, at the ninth hour on Good Friday. On Good Friday the Roman station was again at Holy Cross in Jerusalem; and the neophytes and their sponsors went again in procession to that basilica for Vespers on the Friday after Easter, to commemorate the octave of Good Friday (see above, p. 29). On Good Friday, as we have seen, Psalm 90 and the Canticle of Habbakuk, familiar from daily or weekly use throughout the year, were at the moment of Christ's death brought into close and significant juxtaposition. We have seen that the imagery of the Bewcastle Cross was particularly involved with the initiation rites of the Easter vigil, and with the catechesis of the neophytes during Easter week; these initiation rites

---

[66] Bede, *Homeliarum Euangelii Libri II*, ed. D. Hurst, CCSL 122, Book I, Homilies 14–17; see the analytical table in the introduction, p. xi. Note that John the Baptist is also prominent immediately before Christmas, in the gospels of the third and fourth Sundays of Advent: Klauser, p. 43 (Nos 240, 241); p. 89 (Nos 265, 266), etc.

[67] Klauser, p. 21 (No. 74); p. 67 (No. 85), etc.

[68] The Northumbrian liturgy was almost certainly not 'stational' in the Roman sense of having an elaborate tradition of episcopal processions to particular sites on specific feasts; but Northumbrian clerics must have known of the Roman stations, and if so would have appreciated their symbolic importance: in particular, how the stations determined the texts sung at various feasts. The stational churches are usually recorded in the gospel *capitula* printed by Klauser; they are often noted in antiphonaries, as in *Antiphonale Missarum Sextuplex*, ed. R. Hesbert (Brussels, 1935), No. 60 (fourth Sunday in Lent), pp. 74–5, 'STATIO AD HIERUSALEM'; they are described in the surviving *ordines*, e.g. Andrieu, *Ordo XXIII* (III. 269–73) for Good Friday and Holy Saturday. G. G. Willis, 'Roman Stational Liturgy', discusses Santa Croce at pp. 40, 45, 56–7 and 83.

[69] Klauser, pp. 21–4, Nos 72–90, etc.

could be repeated (when need arose) at Pentecost. On 14 September, the Feast of the Exaltation of the Holy Cross (which had recently been given added honour by Pope Sergius I after his rediscovery in the sacristy of St Peter's of a lost relic of the True Cross) is likely to have emphasized once more the devotional relevance of a high cross.[70] Finally, on the second Sunday of Advent the Roman station was again held at Holy Cross (see above, p. 35), and references to Jerusalem again dominated the Mass, as on the fourth Sunday of Lent.

All the feasts mentioned above are major ones; they must have been celebrated by any reasonably well-run ecclesiastical establishment, however small. Bewcastle may possibly have been a station for preaching, the celebration of Mass, and the administration of the sacraments, staffed by one or more Mass-priests: there was an early tradition of the use of free-standing crosses to mark such mission-stations in Northumbria.[71] The appearance of a commemorative inscription in English on the cross may possibly indicate an *Eigenkirch* or foundation belonging to an aristocratic family.[72] The list I have given of possible liturgical contexts for the Bewcastle Cross is not exhaustive; but it is enough to show that the monument could from season to season, in unison with the ceremonies of the liturgy, take on new meanings and new emphases. The liturgy of Northumbria in the early eighth century provides contexts within which the multivalent but profoundly coherent symbolism of the Bewcastle Cross can begin to be understood.

---

[70] Ó Carragáin, 'Liturgical Innovations', p. 138.

[71] On the use of outlying 'little monasteries', *monasteriola*, for mission purposes, see John Godfrey, 'The Place of the Double Monastery in the Anglo–Saxon Minster System' in *Famulus Christi*, ed. Gerald Bonner (London, 1976), pp. 344–50. Godfrey emphasizes the use by St Cuthbert of free-standing crosses 'each surrounded by a fence or hedge and covered by a thatched roof' as stations for preaching, and thus presumably for celebrating Mass and administering the sacraments (p. 348).

[72] In view of the English runic commemorative inscriptions on the cross, and of the absence of Latin except for the *nomina sacra* (in striking contrast with the Ruthwell Cross), the sort of aristocratic monastery described by Patrick Wormald, 'Bede, "Beowulf" and the Conversion of the Anglo–Saxon Aristocracy', in Farrell, pp. 32–90 (at pp. 49–58), is possibly indicated. Bede's account of the proliferation of monasteries in the early eighth century (*HE* 5: 23; Colgrave and Mynors, pp. 560–1) may be relevant to Bewcastle, and in particular the monastery (with abbot Eanmund, its aristocratic founder) described by Aethelwulf in *De Abbatibus* (esp. *carmina* i–vii).

5. The godly and the ungodly in Psalm 1: the Harley Psalter.
British Library MS Harley 603 f. 1.

6. The fall of Lucifer: the Old English Genesis.
Bodleian MS Junius 11, p. 3.

7. Jacob's ladder: the Old English Heptateuch.
British Library MS Cotton Claudius B. IV, f. 43v.

8. God appears to Abraham: the Old English Heptateuch.
British Library MS Cotton Claudius B. IV, f. 29.

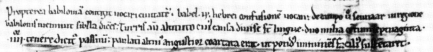

9. Building the tower of Babel: the Old English Heptateuch.
British Library MS Cotton Claudius B. IV, f. 19.

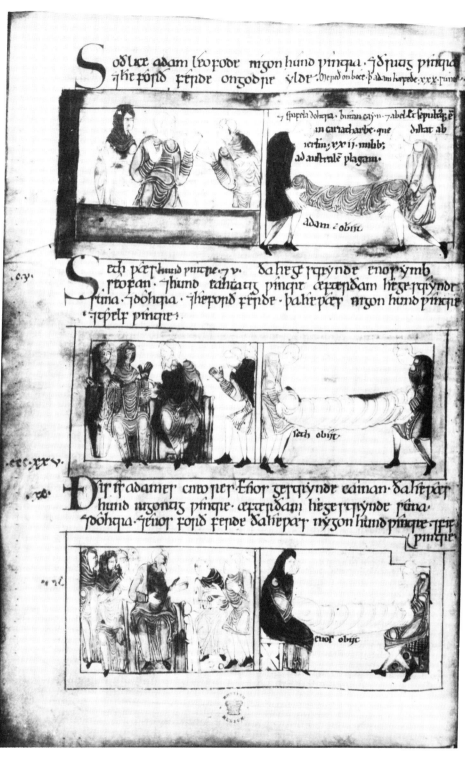

10. The lives and deaths of the early generations of mankind: the Old
English Heptateuch.
British Library MS Cotton Claudius B. IV, f. 10v.

Ē noch gecqÿnde machuʃalam ðahe paʃ fif ⁊ ʃixag
pinʒie. ⁊ ʃÿððan hēge cqÿnde runa ⁊ ðolihgia. ⁊ he paʃ
ðʃiðiʒon liʃe ðʃeo hund pintʃe. ⁊ fif ⁊ ʃixa pintʃe. ⁊ he ʃÿnde
mid ʒode. ⁊ hine nan man ʃÿððan neʒe ʃeah. ʃoʃðamðe
ðʃihten hine ʒenam mid ʃaple. ⁊ mid lice hama. 1.

tod lice maculʃalem gecqÿnde lamech ðahe paʃ e.
⁊ tpopan ⁊ hund tahtuag pintʃe. ⁊ axtepiðam hēge
cqÿnde runa ⁊ ðolihgia. ⁊ he xond ʃeiðe ðahe paʃ
n ŭ gon hund pintʃe. ⁊ nÿgon ⁊ ʃixag pintʃe.

11. Life and ascension of Enoch: the Old English Heptateuch.
British Library MS Cotton Claudius B. IV, f. 11v.

Ladders and Lines of Connection in Anglo-Saxon Religious Art and Literature

RACHEL CRABTREE

It was Dr Basil Cottle's undergraduate lectures on medieval art and architecture that first introduced me to the artefacts of the society whose literature I was studying, and I am grateful for the opportunity to thank him. It seems appropriate that the subject of this essay should be one that cuts across disciplinary boundaries to look at a particular concept in early medieval thinking: that is, the way in which Anglo-Saxon artists and writers use spatial devices to articulate verbally and pictorially certain abstract principles.[1]

The Harley Psalter (British Library MS Harley 603), an eleventh-century copy of the ninth-century Utrecht Psalter, has as a frontispiece a full-page illustration of Psalm 1, depicting the blessed man contrasted with the ungodly (see Plate 5). The illustration, faithfully copied from the Utrecht Psalter, is an effective example of the way two-dimensional space on the page can be used for didactic purposes. On the left-hand side is an enclosure where the blessed man sits in meditation on God's law, with an angel standing behind him; on the right-hand side a wicked man is seated holding a sword and surrounded by armed men, a devil at his side. These two features are separated by the width of the page, yet are connected by a line representing a path which runs between them and on which stand two men: one faces one way and one the other, each making a gesture in the opposite direction. E. T. De Wald in his introduction to the facsimile edition of the Utrecht Psalter (Princeton, 1933, p. 4) describes these two as 'discussing' the two seated figures; one could go further and suggest that they might represent the choice between the way of the ungodly and the way of the righteous—*via iustorum* and *iter impiorum*. The juxtaposition of the two figures and the fact that their hands and eyes are turned in opposite directions would be an indication by the artist of the choice that has to be made between good and evil, as represented by the two seated figures to the far left and right. The antithesis between the righteous man, blessed by God, and the ungodly man, doomed to perish, which is the theme

---

[1] The material contained in this essay is part of work to be submitted for a D.Phil. thesis at the University of York.

of the psalm, is thus dramatized on the page by means of the spatial organization, notably by the distance put between the two; righteousness and ungodliness have been polarized by the artist along a horizontal plane.

The vertical plane can similarly be used for the purpose of polarizing the forces of good and evil on a page. A marginal drawing in the Harley Psalter (f. 17v) shows a human figure leaping between a devil and an angel, the former below him trying to drag him down, the latter above him reaching down to pull him up to safety.[2] This is an example in miniature and in isolation of a principle of spatial organization found throughout the Psalter illustrations, that good should be seen to be above evil and therefore to be in command of the situation. The artists represent this spiritual hierarchy in terms of a standard pattern of spatial hierarchy: the Lord God, often framed in a mandorla, is to be found at the top of the picture, with the psalmist in a position either of detached observation or of besieged involvement, usually at a mid-point either vertically or horizontally, while enemies advance from the bottom corners or retreat into them. This basic hierarchical pattern is consistently used, with variations in arrangement.

These variations concern the exact nature of the relationship between the groups of figures in any one illustration, and particularly between the Lord God and the psalmist. In some illustrations, as in the marginal drawing mentioned above, there is a suggestion of violent action, requiring urgent intervention by the Lord or one of his angels. In others, the emphasis is on the symmetrical organization of the features on the page to create a static hierarchical structure. In both types, the artist creates for the reader an obvious visual connection between the Lord God and the psalmist: he may achieve this by a number of devices, such as placing the psalmist directly below the Lord, with the additional pointer perhaps of a hand stretched up or an arm stretched down, or leaving a clear space around the figure so that he stands out visually. The connection may be made apparent through eye contact between the two figures, usually along the vertical axis, and this is occasionally made visually explicit by the drawing of lines between the two. The hand of God (a common artistic convention to indicate blessing) on occasions has rays emanating from it, reaching down to the object of divine favour.[3]

By making these lines of connection—whether implicit or explicit—the artist is creating a visual representation of a concept inherent not only in the Psalms but in the Bible as a whole: that is, that the psalmist or the righteous man is blessed with God's favour, presence and protection, and that he is

---

[2] See E. Temple, *Anglo-Saxon Manuscripts 900–1066* (London, 1976), plate 204.

[3] Examples of divine intervention: Ps. 57 (f. 31), Ps. 114 (f. 59); of hierarchical structure: Ps. 118 (f. 60v); of an arm raised up: Ps. 105 (f. 52v); of space left: Ps. 47 (f. 27); of eye contact: Ps. 13 (f. 7); and of a hand in blessing: Ps. 27 (f. 15), Ps. 112 (f. 57v).

therefore in a particular relationship with God. The relationship is represented in terms of communication; the psalms themselves are expressions of prayer or praise addressed to God, which invite and expect a response, and the artist in illustrating the content of the psalms depicts the psalmist as in communication with God. The representation of this communication is achieved by the use of space, drawing particularly on the vertical axis because of the hierarchical nature of the subject matter. The spatial organization of the features on the page is used to signal spiritual relationships.

I want to look briefly at a few examples of the use of the vertical axis by artists and writers to make connections. In art, space on a page is used to place one thing in relationship to another, and certain principles can be seen to operate, such as the significance of hierarchical ordering.[4] In literature, spatial metaphors are used which equally serve to place one thing in a defined relationship to another. (Language, of course, is not confined to two dimensions; in literature, the distinction between inside and outside is a widely-used spatial relationship.) The concept of hierarchy is central to the Christian mythology. It is expressed openly in the psalms, mainly in terms of a static ordering of the universe; movement within the hierarchy underlies such central tenets of doctrine as the Resurrection and Ascension (in one direction) and the Incarnation, Descent into Hell and Fall of man (in the other). Anglo-Saxon poems such as the three *Christ* poems in the Exeter Book reflect this awareness of a cosmic hierarchy in their respective meditations on Christ's movements between Heaven and Earth, from the point of view of the latter. The hierarchy which informs the structure of *Genesis B* is the most interesting in this context, because it is a narrative poem, describing action in three separate locations—Heaven, Hell and Earth—and dealing with movements between them.[5]

The narrative progresses by means of the various ascending and descending movements. It begins with a hierarchical ordering within Heaven—God establishing ten orders of angels and creating one above the rest: 'hehstne to him on heofona rice' (254). Lucifer aspires to an even higher place—a 'strenglicran stol . . . heahran on heofonum' (273–4). The movement upwards in the hierarchy is found in Isaiah 14: 13–14, but the poet emphasizes it further by his choice of words to describe Lucifer's mental process at this point: 'ahof hine wið his hearran' (263). The spatial metaphor here is repeated also in 'ongan him winn up ahebban/ wið þone hehstan heofnes waldend' (259–60); and the reader's consciousness of the vertical plane is reinforced by the poet's placing of the action within the context of social hierarchy. The terms *hearra* and *geongra*

---

[4] The same principle is at work in the illustrations of royal donations, such as Cnut giving an altar cross or Athelstan a charter (BL MSS Stowe 944, f. 6, and Cotton Vespasian A. VIII, f. 2v), where the Lord is seated above in a mandorla.

[5] Quotations are from the text in *The Junius Manuscript*, ed. G. P. Krapp, Anglo-Saxon Poetic Records 1 (New York, 1931), pp. 9–28 (*Genesis*, lines 235–851).

are repeatedly used to characterize Lucifer's rebellion as that of the betrayal of a lord by a subordinate. The speech he gives expresses his denial of God as his *hearra* and his determination to set up an alternative hierarchical structure with his own subordinates. The relationship between lord and subordinate carries the implication of physical hierarchy; *hearra*, though not the same word as the comparative form of *heah* (*heahra* or *hearra*), is yet closely linked to it by the poet's constant association within the alliterative line of words with an ethical value with words of spatial value: *hearra, hyldo, halig, heah, heahra* and *heofon.*[6] *Geongra*, on the other hand, clearly does have its semantic origin in physical hierarchy; and, though the social hierarchy usually reinforces geographical position, it sometimes mocks it. In Hell, Satan, once higher than his colleagues, is now lower than his own subordinates, being chained to the bottom of Hell, yet he offers as a reward to a successful messenger equal status with himself: 'Sittan læte ic hine wið me sylfne' (438).

Satan's motive in sending up a messenger to deceive Adam and Eve is to prevent them from taking his place in Heaven, far above him; he wishes them to become instead his subordinates (407). They are spiritually at a mid-point in the hierarchy, just as Earth, justifiably here termed 'middle-earth', is set at a mid-point between Heaven and Hell. The poet confines his description of Earth to its two inhabitants and to the two trees which offer life and death and which display the qualities of Heaven and Hell respectively.

The messenger devil, on arrival *up* from Hell, as the poet stresses (446), makes continual reference to the long journey he has had in coming (supposedly) *down* from Heaven to Earth. He tempts Eve by offering her a sight of Heaven which, once she has eaten the fruit, she believes she possesses; she tells Adam:

> Ic mæg heonon geseon
> hwær he sylf siteð . . .
> geseo ic him his englas ymbe hweorfan. . . .
> . . . ic mæg swegles gamen
> gehyran on heofnum.   (666–76)

Once Adam too has eaten, they both realize that this line of communication with Heaven and God through sight and sound was a false one; the result of their disobedience is that they are cut off spiritually from God, and see and hear instead the unpleasant features of Hell:

> Gesyhst þu nu þa sweartan helle
> grædige and gifre. Nu þu hie grimman meaht
> heonane gehyran. Nis heofonrice
> gelic þam lige. . . .   (792–5)

---

[6] Even if it is merely a convenient accident that these key words all begin with *h*–, it cannot be chance that they are repeated so frequently in various combinations.

Once communication upwards towards Heaven and God has been cut off, the poet draws attention to the horizontal plane. Their world becomes a place where hunger and thirst close in on them (802) and they are oppressed by the weather from all points of the compass (806–9). As with the devils, whose surroundings in Hell seem narrow and restrictive after the freedom of Heaven, their experience is necessarily concentrated on the horizontal once the vertical—access to God—is denied. Adam and Eve can no longer look up to God in Heaven and bow their heads before him as obedient servants, and they now become perforce aware of their environment, taking shelter in a forest.

Throughout the poem the hierarchical dimension reinforces the moral interaction. The spatial metaphors of upward and downward motion are used to indicate spiritual transitions; the distance between Heaven and Hell, repeatedly stressed in the account of the Fall of the angels, is a measure of the spiritual change that has taken place:

> Acwæð hine fram his hyldo and hine on helle wearp,
> on þa deopan dala, þær he to deofle wearð. . . .
> . . . Feollon þa ufon of heofnum
> þurhlonge swa þreo niht and dagas,
> þa englas of heofnum on helle. . . .   (304–8)

Distance in spatial terms is an indication of distance in spiritual terms. During the temptation sequences the poet reminds the reader by the references to Heaven above and Hell beneath that Adam and Eve are making a choice between the two; hence Adam's choice of the latter occurs simultaneously with his acceptance of the fruit: 'He æt þam wife onfeng/ helle and hinnsið' (717–18).

The illustrations which accompany the poem in the manuscript show a similar concern for hierarchical organization in two-dimensional space, so that, as in the Psalter, the top of the page is occupied by Heaven and the bottom by Hell.[7] The illustration of the Fall of the angels (p. 3), though organized in four horizontal sections, reads vertically downwards (see Plate 6). Lucifer in the top section stands centre, slightly raised up on a footstool beside an empty throne space raised higher still. In the next section he is accepting palm branches from followers on each side; and in the section below the Lord God deals with the situation in a downward movement represented by his handful of spears. The final section contrasts with the upper three in its jumble of figures, some falling horizontally, some already contorted into devils. Satan himself is represented twice here, once falling, entangled in pieces from his broken throne, and once chained centre bottom to the teeth of the jaws of Hell. The artist's placing of Satan in the centre of the first, second and fourth sections assists the eye in following his descent—from

---

[7] See the facsimile edition of the MS (Bodleian MS Junius 11) published as *The Cædmon Manuscript of Anglo-Saxon Biblical Poetry*, ed. I. Gollancz (Oxford, 1927).

the top of the page to the bottom, from Heaven to Hell. This one composite illustration deals with the whole narrative sequence of the Rebellion and Fall, depicting details from the text and retaining the importance of its basic hierarchical structure.

Those scenes in which the artist is required to depict both Heaven and Hell, or both Heaven and Earth, or both Earth and Hell, show each as a distinct location, appropriately placed at the top or bottom of the page. For example, on p. 11, the Lord God stands above Adam and Eve to bless them, surrounded by the battlements of Heaven which stop at the point where the trees of Earth intersect them. The Lord is shown in colourful glory, in contrast to Adam and Eve in monochrome, but he is not completely remote from Earth and from his creation.

One scene, p. 28, shows an interesting example of connections on the horizontal axis, where the spatial relationship between the three figures—Eve, the devil and Adam—indicates their spiritual status at that moment. Eve has already accepted the fruit and is in fact eating it with her right hand; her left hand is linked to the devil's right hand over the apple they are both holding. Adam on the other side is not yet in tangible contact with the devil, though his hand is close to the apple in the devil's outstretched left hand. So, in this manuscript, the artist, like the poet, uses the principle that relationship in a spatial plane, predominantly vertical but also horizontal, can indicate spiritual relationship.

In the manuscript British Library Cotton Claudius B. IV, an Anglo-Saxon translation of the Heptateuch with accompanying illustrations, there are a number of scenes in which the artist makes a connection between the upper part and the lower part of the page in a specific way: that is, he uses the device of a ladder with its feet on the earth and its topmost rungs in Heaven. This obviously stems from the story in Genesis 28 of Jacob at Bethel and his dream of a ladder between Heaven and Earth. The passage is a significant one with regard to spatial relationships: the ladder, standing on the earth and reaching to the sky, connects the two; the angels ascending and descending suggest two-way communication. Jacob's immediate reaction is to say (in the Old English translation), 'Witodlice Drihten ys on þisse stowe, and ic hyt nyste',[8] a sentiment called forth by the very occurrence of the vision and by its nature. The purpose of the dream is to bring the covenant promise to Jacob that the Lord will be with him wherever he goes; it requires and provokes a response from Jacob—the acknowledgement of the Lord as his God, the vow to give a tithe, and the setting up of his stone pillow to mark the spot, which he calls Bethel: the House of God.

The illustration (f. 43v) shows Jacob asleep and the ladder of his dream

[8] *The Old English Version of the Heptateuch*, ed. S. J. Crawford, EETS OS 160 (1922), p. 111.

alongside him, with the Lord God at the top in the Heavens, which are depicted as a distinct location by a wide band of colour, as they are throughout the manuscript (see Plate 7). There is no extraneous detail to detract from the simple arrangement of the three basic features: Heaven, Earth, and the ladder spanning the space between them. Jacob's eyes are open and his face is turned upward to the Lord who is looking directly at him. The ladder in the text provides the artist with a device to pictorialize communication between God and man.

On f. 29 there is an illustration of the Lord appearing to Abraham (Genesis 17) to make a covenant with him (see Plate 8). It is not a dream this time, and Abraham falls on his face in front of the Lord, who has descended by means of a ladder, an object not mentioned in the text. The incident itself could have been illustrated solely by the two figures bottom centre, but the artist has chosen to represent both characters twice and to include a ladder and a host of angels. The inclusion of the ladder, attended by flying angels, allows the artist to portray the Lord in the act of descending (or possibly ascending), his head just touching the lowest line of the Heavens. It may be that this position, together with the kneeling figure of Abraham in the right-hand corner, portrays the Lord *appearing* to Abraham (v. 1), whereas the centre two figures portray the Lord *speaking* to Abraham (vv. 1–2, 3 ff.). The illustration as a whole demonstrates how a divine revelation can be depicted through the use of connecting lines.

A third use of the ladder device is in illustrating the building of the tower of Babel (Genesis 11) on f. 19 (see Plate 9). The Lord is positioned at the top of a ladder, slightly below the Heavens, yet above the topmost builder who himself is not far off his target. There is another ladder at the right of the picture, and the various stages of the building are depicted in ascending steps. The physical gestures and postures of the builders help to emphasize the sense of the vertical, since their arms are mostly stretched up or stretched down. The portrayal of their mutual assistance suggests that the penalty of non-communication will prove effective in stopping the work. Once again, no ladder is mentioned in the text, which states that the Lord came down to see the tower (Genesis 11: 5). The ladder is a useful means of depicting descent, followed by observation, and then judgement, since the Lord can be seen to be suspended at the vantage point of a superior position. The other ladder may perhaps be representative of man's attempt to raise himself up (through the pride and presumption originally displayed by Lucifer) and reach Heaven by human exertion and force; in that case, it is significant that the ladder reaches only halfway.

Fourthly, there is a series of pictures towards the beginning of the manuscript, concerning the lives and deaths of the earliest generations of mankind. The text—Genesis 5—is factual in the extreme, being a list of those generations, the number of years each man lived and who his sons were; and it might well be thought a difficult passage to illustrate. In fact, the artist has chosen a stylized representation of Life on the left half of the page and Death on the right, the two halves linked together for each generation by a border round both (see Plate 10). The reader's eye zigzags down the page from left to right, following the progression from life to death. 'Life' is characterized by a seated figure surrounded by wife and sons, and 'Death' by a swathed body, supported by two figures, lying across the middle of the right-hand section. The slight variations in this series of generations are due to the increase of relatives in the left-hand section, as the human race multiplies.

Otherwise, the series is consistent until it reaches its fifth member, Enoch, who was notable for having been translated to Heaven before death. The artist represents this effectively by interrupting the horizontal emphasis of the 'Death' sections with a vertical emphasis (see Plate 11). This is achieved through Enoch's upright stance, his raised arms, grasped by the Lord's hand reaching down, and also by a ladder drawn between Heaven and Earth, on which Enoch is standing.[9] There is an interesting verbal parallel to this in the Old English translation at this point. The word used for 'died' in the generations before Enoch is *forðferde*, a common term (which, incidentally, contains a metaphor of movement). The visual interruption of the sequence in the case of Enoch is accompanied by a felicitous verbal interruption, in that 'he forðferde' is replaced by 'he ferde mid Gode' (*Heptateuch*, p. 98).—A twelfth-century version of the same text (ibid.) puts it even more clearly: 'he ne forðferde na ac ferde mid Gode'.—There is a phrase at the end of the sentence added in translation from the Vulgate: '[Drihten genam hine] mid sawle ond mid lichaman'; the illustrations certainly point a contrast between the helpless mortality of the preceding figures and the upright movement of Enoch.

It seems that the artist in this manuscript is using the device of a ladder to pictorialize a particular concept—the fact of divine intervention on Earth; communication or access between Heaven and Earth is made concrete by its visual representation. The space on the page is organized so that certain features are linked together, not merely implicitly, as in the Psalter, but explicitly by the connecting quality of the vertical lines of the ladder. It follows that the point at which the vertical line of communication intersects with the horizontal plane of Earth becomes significant. This is explicit in the account of Jacob's dream, where he interprets the vision as investing that point in space with a particular importance. He recognizes it as sacred as a result of the Lord's presence, and he sets up a pillar to mark the spot, calling it *domus dei* and *porta caeli*. It is not surprising to find phrases from this incident being

[9] This is, incidentally, quite unlike the portrayal of the same incident in MS Junius 11, where Enoch is shown disappearing upwards beyond the upper edge of the page (Gollancz, p. 61).

used liturgically in the order of service for dedicating a church,[10] which is in effect the ceremony of creating a sacred space, in which the presence of God in his house allows men access to God in the Heavens. Consciousness of this is expressed in the pattern of movements made around the church inside and outside, by the exorcism of evil through marking crosses on the walls, by the choice of biblical passages selected for singing and reading, and by the episcopal prayers inviting God to dwell in his house.

The church equally in its inception and in its regular use is a sacred space in possession of special rights of access to God. The Old English word *gemana*, used of the sacrament of communion in the compound term *cyricgemana*, had the senses also of 'communication' and 'community', as its use in one of Wulfstan's homilies for Lent indicates.[11] Wulfstan gives instructions for dealing with men who because of 'healican synnan' are excluded from 'cyricgemanan' during the 'halgan tid' of Lent, and he cites as analogy Adam's excommunication from the company of angels ('of engla gemanan') after the Fall (lines 36–40). He is not referring to Adam's ultimate exclusion from Heaven and condemnation to Hell on account of his disobedience, but to his immediate loss of the companionship of angels, which he had enjoyed while still in Paradise. Wulfstan expands this in another homily, the 'Sermo de Cena Domini': 'God hine gelogode on fruman in paradyso on ealre myrhðe and on ealre mærðe, ðær he geseah Godes englas and wið spæc, and wið God sylfne he spæc' (p. 236). Having fallen, Adam lost those privileges until Christ's act of redemption brought him into the heavenly church to live for ever with God and his angels and saints.

Wulfstan makes explicit this analogy between Adam and contemporary Christians; men who have acknowledged guilt of a particular mortal sin are forbidden for a time to go to communion or even to enter the church: 'forbod huslganges and inganges into cyrican' ('Sermo in .XL.', lines 46–7). Men will be received back into God's favour and back into the church, he says, if they eagerly seek God's house day and night—'geornor and gelomor Godes hus sece dæges and nihtes and cneowige þær ute' (lines 52–3)—kneeling outside it and acknowledging that they are not worthy to go inside. Going to the sacrament of communion and entering the church are equally forbidden, and being received back into the church building by the bishop is an outward sign of being received back into God's favour, here likened to Adam's privilege in Paradise of being able to converse with God and his angels.

The concept of the inside as opposed to the outside is clearly marked here; communication with God is available inside, whereas outside such access is

[10] *Lanalet Pontifical*, ed. G. H. Doble, Henry Bradshaw Society (London, 1937); for example, pp. 2–38.
[11] *The Homilies of Wulfstan*, ed. D. Bethurum (Oxford, 1957), 'Sermo in .XL.', pp. 233–5.

denied. This is a principle which can be seen to operate in both literature and art; Cain is cut off from God by his act of murder, and the Junius 11 artist has drawn a vertical line down the page between the Lord and Cain to represent this (Gollancz, p. 51). Furthermore, access to God involves his protection, as demonstrated both by the Psalter illustrations discussed above and by Cain's first thought on being sentenced to exile, which is for his loss of protection (Genesis 4: 14). The church building was also an area of sanctuary, and it was in the interests of the Church to promote this idea of the sacred quality of the site (which endowed its immediate environs with a similar importance) in order to preserve the effectiveness of the sanctuary rights offered. These were frequently associated with a particular saint, usually the one to whom the church was dedicated; and if it was a local saint of some reputation, the sanctuary rights assumed greater local significance in proportion.

This may partly explain certain features towards the end of *Guthlac B*, a poem dealing with the death of that saint.[12] At the moment of Guthlac's death, the poet gives an account of various supernatural signs witnessed by the servant watching beside his master:

> Ða þær leoht ascan,
> beama beorhtast. Eal þæt beacen wæs
> ymb þæt halge hus, heofonlic leoma,
> from foldan up swylce fyren tor
> ryht aræred oð rodera hrof,
> gesewen under swegle, sunnan beorhtra,
> æþeltungla wlite.   (1308–14)

This is a direct communication between Heaven and Earth; the light is described as a fiery tower, ascending to Heaven and perceptible on Earth. There is a further communication—that of sound as well as sight:

> Engla þreatas
> sigeleoð sungon, sweg wæs on lyfte
> gehyred under heofonum, haligra dream.   (1314–16)

These are signs of spiritual power, also sensed in a sweet smell and felt in the trembling of the earth, and they signify the final victory of the saint over death. However, they are also used by the poet to make less absolute the inevitable separation between saint and servant. Guthlac promises on his death day not to leave his servant unprotected but to keep friendship with him: 'A ic sibbe wiþ þe/ healdan wille' (1262–3). At the point of death itself, there are

---

[12] Quotations are from 'Guthlac II' in *The Exeter Book*, ed. G. P. Krapp and E. V. K. Dobbie, Anglo-Saxon Poetic Records 3 (New York, 1936), pp. 72–88 (see pp. 85–6).

two separations: the soul from the body and the saint from his servant. The soul rises to Heaven, and the body is left on Earth with the servant:

> Ða wæs Guðlaces gæst gelæded
> eadig on upweg. Englas feredun
> to þam longan gefean, lic colode,
> belifd under lyfte.   (1305–8)

The separation involved is that of the distance between Heaven and Earth; body and soul are completely severed. But the separation between servant and saint is not complete, because the phenomena accompanying the event due to . . ., which connect Heaven and Earth, and therefore the saint with his servant, at that particular location, which happens to be the sanctuary of Guthlac's retreat. It becomes the sanctuary of the monastery of Crowland, founded by Guthlac's followers on that very site, thus ensuring that the promise of eternal friendship and the signs of spiritual power and protection are inherited by the monks, who of course are likely to have been involved in the writing of the poem.

This essay has endeavoured to show some of the ways space can be employed to indicate relationships of certain kinds. The use of the vertical axis in hierarchical structures and in connecting lines is found, as we have seen, in works widely separated in date within the Anglo-Saxon period; most of them are in fact indebted, directly or indirectly, to Carolingian and Classical sources, and the underlying continuity of thought derives from their overtly Christian content and their reliance on widely accepted authorities, both patristic and contemporary. A consideration of these spatial principles, however, may be valuable in helping us understand how certain concepts were articulated in the Anglo-Saxon period.

Editions of Texts

The Insular Connections of a Sermon for Holy Innocents

J. E. CROSS

The sermon for Holy Innocents is extant earliest (at present) in the Cambridge, Pembroke College MS 25 (saec. XI, Bury).[1] Its presentation and analysis here may both typify the nature of the collection of sermons within the manuscript and offer, I trust, a pleasing novelty to Basil Cottle, staunch Churchman, patriotic Kelt and avid antiquarian.

The Pembroke MS is the fullest representative of what Henri Barré regarded as a reading-collection for preachers to use on appropriate days of the liturgical year,[2] together with eight pieces on general Christian topics at the end.[3] But almost as large is a collateral descendant from the exemplar in Oxford, Balliol College MS 240 (saec. XIV);[4] and other manuscripts which contain, or indicate that they contained, sequences of items are: Chartres, Bibliothèque Municipale MS 25 (44) ff. 119–62 (saec. X/XI, Saint-Père, Chartres);[5] Cambridge, St John's College MS 42 ff. 13–62v (saec. XII,

---

[1] For a description of the MS, including place and date of origin, see M. R. James, *A Descriptive Catalogue of the Manuscripts in the Library of Pembroke College, Cambridge* (Cambridge, 1905), pp. 25–9.

[2] Henri Barré, *Les Homéliaires carolingiens de l'école d'Auxerre* (Vatican City, 1962), p. 24. Barré described and itemized the Pembroke MS, and in my general discussion on the collection (for which see below) I have followed his numbering of items.

[3] Barré thought that the general sermons at the end did not originally belong to the collection (ibid., p. 18), but there is evidence otherwise.

[4] For a description of the whole MS see R. A. B. Mynors, *Catalogue of the Manuscripts of Balliol College, Oxford* (Oxford, 1963), pp. 260–3. The collection, which occupies ff. 56r–136r, is preceded by a list of contents (f. 55r–55v).

[5] *Catalogue général des manuscrits des bibliothèques publiques de France: Départements XI: Chartres* (Paris, 1890), p. 12. At the time of the catalogue the collection occupied ff. 119–62 and included an item numbered XXXII, by caption corresponding to an item in Pembroke 25 f. 77r. The manuscript was burned in 1944 and is extant only as a box of fragments, now interleaved and numbered. Abbé Raymond Étaix considered the fragments and left a letter of 21 January 1957 at Chartres identifying many fragments

Worcester [?]);[6] London, British Library MS Royal 5 E. XIX ff. 21–37 (probably 1089–1125, Salisbury);[7] Canterbury, Cathedral MS Addit. 127/12 (saec. XI in.),[8] a fragment of two folios. All of these manuscripts are representatives of the original homiliary to a larger or smaller degree, but all at removes from the exemplar. Two more collections select and include items from the Pembroke-type collection: Paris, Bibliothèque Nationale MS lat. 3794 ff. 18–31 (saec. XII, Germany?)[9] and Grenoble, Bibliothèque Municipale MS 278 (470) (saec. XII, Chartreux).[10] From this copying in Latin, it appears that the collection had become popular in England and had influence on the Continent.

This popularity in England is also indicated in vernacular sermons of the Anglo-Saxon period. Eight anonymous Old English sermons (out of a limited corpus) use material from a text or texts of the Pembroke-type collection as a direct source: four from *The Vercelli Book*, III, XIX, XX, XXI;[11] and four identified under the names of their first editors, Assmann XI, XII, Belfour VI

from the non-homiletic items in the manuscript, and also six fragments from the sermon-collection. Through generous aid from the British Academy I have also been able to examine the fragments at Chartres, sometimes of two or three words or part-words. I have been able to confirm five of Étaix's identifications (parts of captions to individual items), have rejected a sixth (now generously agreed by Abbé Étaix), and have added ten more. The fifteen identified fragments indicate that the Chartres MS included folios within the range of Pembroke 25 ff. 81v–108v. These identifications, together with the record in the 1890 catalogue, indicate that Chartres 25 (44) was a text of at least a considerable section of the collection.

[6] For description and date and place of origin see M. R. James, *A Descriptive Catalogue of the Manuscripts of St. John's College, Cambridge* (Cambridge, 1913), pp. 57–64.

[7] N. R. Ker commented on this manuscript, among others, on two occasions: in 'Salisbury Cathedral Manuscripts and Patrick Young's Catalogue', *The Wiltshire (Archaeological) Magazine* 53 (1949) 154, 158, 168, 171, and 'The Beginnings of Salisbury Cathedral Library' in *Medieval Learning and Literature: Essays presented to Richard William Hunt*, ed. J. J. G. Alexander and M. T. Gibson (Oxford, 1976), pp. 23–49.

[8] Noted in N. R. Ker, *Medieval Manuscripts in British Libraries II: Abbotsford–Keele* (Oxford, 1977), pp. 316–17.

[9] R. Étaix, 'Le sermonnaire carolingien de Beaune', *Revue des Études Augustiniennes* 25 (1979) 106–21.

[10] *Catalogue général des manuscrits des bibliothèques publiques de France: Départements VII: Grenoble* (Paris, 1889), pp. 112–13.

[11] For an edition of Vercelli Homily III see *Die Vercelli-Homilien: I.–VIII. Homilie*, ed. Max Förster (Hamburg, 1932; rpt. Darmstadt, 1964), pp. 53–71. For an edition of Vercelli Homilies XIX, XX and XXI see Paul E. Szarmach, *Vercelli Homilies IX–XXIII*, Toronto Old English Series 5 (Toronto, 1981). Helen L. Spencer ('Vernacular and Latin Versions of a Sermon for Lent: "A Lost Penitential Homily" Found', *Mediaeval Studies* 44 (1982) 271–305) has already identified the source of Vercelli Homily III and printed the relevant item from the Pembroke collection. I shall present the sources of the other Vercelli Homilies (XIX, XX, XXI) in a forthcoming monograph on the Pembroke-type collection.

and Tristram III.[12] Directly or indirectly its influence extended in England after the Anglo-Saxon period. As Helen Spencer has illustrated (p. 274), a collection of sermons known as the *Collectio 'Filius Matris'*, attributed by early commentators to William de Montibus (c. 1140–1213), Chancellor of Lincoln Cathedral from 1191, contains one sermon which is based on one Pembroke item for Lent, but, as I add, also drew on one other.[13] The *Collectio* was copied well into the fifteenth century and a translation into the English vernacular was made at that time (see Spencer, p. 276).

I have just completed a preliminary analysis of the Latin collection, together with presentation of Latin items against Old English derivatives, as yet without firm title or place of publication, but I hope that others will read the collection in the clear script of the Pembroke manuscript, since it is unlikely that its potential influence on popular preaching has yet been fully realized.

Undoubtedly the composer worked in a well-stocked library and used material from its manuscripts to create his separate items, normally from a variety of sources. Not only did he draw on earlier homilies and sermons from named and anonymous authors, as might be expected, but he abstracted from moral florilegia such as Alcuin, *De Virtutibus et Vitiis* and Pseudo-Basil, *Admonitio ad Filium Spiritualem*; liturgical handbooks such as Amalarius, *De Ecclesiasticis Officiis* and Hrabanus Maurus, *De Clericorum Institutione*; an encyclopedia, Isidore, *Etymologiarum sive Originum Libri XX*; a history, Rufinus, *Historia Ecclesiastica*; an itinerary, Adomnán, *De Locis Sanctis*; a tract, Gildas, *De Excidio Britanniae*; a curious letter on the ills of the world from a rare author, Dynamius Grammaticus, *Ad discipulum*.[14]

The collection, as could be expected, contains moral precept presented in dogmatic terms, often with mnemonic devices such as numbered lists and titles (*vias domini*, *opera carnis*, *ornamenta celorum*, etc.) to aid the preachers, but, somewhat unusually, also a considerable amount of narrative. On the evangelist John, for the death of Peter, for the Nativity and the Assumption of

---

[12] The relevant editions are: *Angelsächsische Homilien und Heiligenleben*, ed. Bruno Assmann, Bibliothek der angelsächsischen Prosa 3 (Kassel, 1889; rpt. Darmstadt, 1964), pp. 138–50; *Twelfth-Century Homilies in MS. Bodley 343*, ed. A. O. Belfour, EETS OS 137 (1909; rpt. 1962), pp. 50–8; Hildegard L. C. Tristram, *Vier altenglische Predigten aus der heterodoxen Tradition* (Diss., Freiburg i. Bresgau, 1970), pp. 162–72. The sources will be demonstrated in my forthcoming monograph.

[13] A section entitled *Quare diem mortis ignoramus* from the sermon attributed to William de Montibus (Spencer, p. 284), which is not found in the main source from Pembroke 25 (cf. Spencer, p. 285), is abstracted from one of the Pembroke items on general topics (Pembroke 25 f. 167r).

[14] The works are named here merely to illustrate the variety of sources; details will be given in the forthcoming monograph. Two of the sources named, by Amalarius and Hrabanus Maurus, indicate a *terminus a quo* for the composition of the Latin sermon-collection, since *De Ecclesiasticis Officiis* was written towards AD 820 and *De Clericorum Institutione* was written under the abbacy at Fulda of Eigil, who died in AD 822.

Mary, and for Andrew, the composer abstracted from the appropriate apocryphal stories.[15] For the accounts of Martin and Michael the Archangel he went to hagiography.[16] But for a number of items he returned to Scripture: for the nativity and passion of John the Baptist; for the conversion and missionary journeys of Paul; for the story of the Maccabees, although with extension and misrepresentation; for the two items on Epiphany, which record the four manifestations of Christ—the coming of the Magi, the miracle of the five loaves and two fishes, the wedding at Cana and the baptism of Christ. Narrative, based on Scripture, is the mode for *In Parasceuen* and *In Caena Domini*, and 'facts' are inserted in other less-dominantly narrative items, as for Holy Innocents below.[17]

In the medieval period Scripture was rarely read or presented without commentary. The link between homily or explication of a Scriptural section (lection or pericope) and commentary on the whole, particularly of the Gospels, is often close. Earlier homilies influence sections of commentary; commentaries are useful reference-books for homilists. Our composer clearly used commentaries to offer significations and explications of Scriptural statement. For individual items he abstracted from the great authorities: Jerome on Matthew, Ambrose on Luke, Augustine on John, Bede on the Acts of the Apostles and Cassiodorus on the Psalms;[18] but (of more interest here) he also knew anonymous commentaries, some unpublished.

These have been placed within the sphere of Irish influence in a seminal essay by Bernhard Bischoff, who described distinctive attitudes and statements and recorded nearly forty such commentaries, a number on the Gospels and on Genesis, but even commentaries on the prophets and the Catholic

---

[15] All the Scriptural people named here have liturgical feasts under the names, which are clearly entitled in the Pembroke manuscript. The apocryphal stories are easily identified under the appropriate names from the lists in *Bibliotheca Hagiographica Latina*, ed. Socii Bollandii, 2 vols (Brussels, 1898–9, 1900–1).

[16] There are two items on both St Martin and St Michael. For the first on Martin our composer drew on two accounts of the saint, by Alcuin (PL 101) and by Sulpicius Severus in *Sulpicii Severi Libri qui supersunt*, ed. C. Halm in Corpus Scriptorum Ecclesiasticorum Latinorum 1 (Vienna, 1866). For the second, on the death of Martin, he used Alcuin, *Sermo de Transitu Sancti Martini* (PL 101). For the first item on Michael our writer copied Isidore *Etymologiarum*, VII. 5, *De angelis* (PL 82, cols 272–4). The second item on Michael is a composite piece including, however, a curious story of Michael's fighting a real dragon in Asia. For a detailed discussion of this item and publication of the Latin sermon see J. E. Cross, 'An unpublished story of Michael the Archangel and its connections', in *Magister Regis, studies in honor of R. E. Kaske*, ed. A. Groos, T. D. Hill *et al.* (New York, 1986), pp. 23–35.

[17] All the items are clearly entitled in the Pembroke manuscript, and the content will be discussed in my monograph.

[18] For details see the forthcoming monograph.

Epistles.[19] Apart from editorial work by Bischoff's pupil, the late R. E. McNally, and McNally's pupil, J. F. Kelly, which produced editions of some commentaries,[20] comparatively little has been done to present the material, until very recently. Now a vigorous general activity is continuing world-wide,[21] but, at present, many of Bischoff's named commentaries are still unpublished. Fortunately Thomas Hill and I came to the printed material by McNally and Kelly some time ago when we were tracing the ideas and phrases in the Old English question-and-answer lists known as *The Prose Solomon and Saturn* and *Adrian and Ritheus*.[22] We realized that connections existed between some of the questions and designated Hiberno-Latin material in print, and have continued, after producing the edition, to read microfilms of manuscripts. This reading has been successful in establishing further contacts and the microfilms have also been available for the present study of the Pembroke-type collection.

Our collection as a whole certainly used two collections of sermons,[23] some items of which contain features already noted as distinctive in Irish works. The collection cites intermittently a gathering of moral aphorisms known as the *Collectio Canonum Hibernensis*.[24] It clearly abstracted sections from four Hiberno-Latin commentaries[25] (one—probably two—in print),[26] and, within

---

[19] Bernhard Bischoff, 'Wendepunkte in der Geschichte der lateinische Exegese im Frühmittelalter', *Sacris Erudiri* 6 (1954) 189–281. Bischoff revised the paper in his collected essays, *Mittelalterliche Studien*, 2 vols (Stuttgart, 1966–7), I. 205–73, and this essay was translated in *Biblical Studies: the Medieval Irish contribution*, ed. M. McNamara, *Proceedings of the Irish Biblical Association* 1 (1976), 74–158.

[20] *Scriptores Hiberniae Minores Pars I*, ed. R. E. McNally; *Scriptores Hiberniae Minores Pars II*, ed. J. F. Kelly: CCSL 108 B and C.

[21] See M. McNamara, 'Early Irish Exegesis. Some facts and tendencies', *Proceedings of the Irish Biblical Association* 8 (1984) 57–96.

[22] *The Prose Solomon and Saturn and Adrian and Ritheus*, ed. James E. Cross and Thomas D. Hill, McMaster Texts and Studies 1 (Toronto, 1982).

[23] Our composer certainly used items from the collection known as *Catechesis Celtica* (partially edited by André Wilmart in 'Reg. lat. 49: Catéchèses celtiques', *Studi e testi* 59 (1933) 29–111), extant only in the MS Vatican Reginensis lat. 49, which I had seen, but have now been able to read at leisure in a typescript edition prepared by the late R. E. McNally. Our writer also used some sermons, extant only in Munich Bayerische Staatsbibliothek MS clm 6233, on which see below.

[24] For some details of this see Joan Turville-Petre, 'Translations of a Lost Penitential Homiliary', *Traditio* 19 (1963) 51–78. Mrs Turville-Petre notes this *Collectio* as a source for Vercelli Homily III; but the homily is a translation of a Pembroke item, as Spencer has shown. For fuller analysis see my monograph.

[25] Our composer used separate Commentaries on Matthew, extant in the Vienna MS 940 and in the Orléans MS 65 (62), as illustrated for Holy Innocents below. He also used a Commentary on Luke, printed by J. F. Kelly (see note 20 above) from the Vienna MS 997, for sections in the items on Circumcision and the Purification of Mary. The first item for *In Parasceuen* (Pembroke 25 f. 65v) describes creation and narrates

the sequence of the whole collection, presented themes and topoi which persist in writings under Irish influence.

Some of these influences on the whole collection are exemplified in the one item on the Holy Innocents, a sermon which, in my view, uses two such anonymous commentaries, both unfortunately unpublished at present, and a rare collection of sermons, some items of which, including a relevant sermon on the Holy Innocents, contain features persisting in works under Irish influence.

Both commentaries are on the Gospel of Matthew. The first is extant only in Vienna, Österreichischen Nationalbibliothek MS 940 ff. 13r–141v (saec. VIII/ IX, Salzburg),[27] and various errors indicate that it was merely a copy. The only complete text of the second is the copy in Orléans, Bibliothèque Municipale MS 65 (62) pp. 1–269 (saec. IX med.); but it is extant in section or fragment in four other manuscripts, two of which, unfortunately, have been destroyed but were recorded.[28] The Orléans commentary is now being edited by Jean Rittmueller, but I have seen only the complete manuscript. Both commentaries, being single copies, contain errors, and, obviously, neither may be the exact manuscript which the composer of the Pembroke-type collection used.

The third main source for this sermon on Holy Innocents is another sermon for the feast within a collection of thirteen in Munich, Bayerische Staatsbibliothek MS clm 6233 (saec. VIII,[2] South Bavaria, written by the named scribe Dominicus and his pupils, possibly from Tegernsee).[29] Besides the sermons, the manuscript contains a commentary on Matthew's Gospel, ff. 1r– 110v, which is included within Bischoff's list (I. 254–5), and, interestingly for those concerned with the Christian comradeship of Irish and English in the Continental mission-field, the manuscript has corrections in an Anglo-Saxon

the story of Adam and Eve as in Genesis chapters 1–3, but insertions of explanation are verbally as Paris, Bibliothèque Nationale MS lat. 10616, a commentary in question-and-answer form. This is linked by Bischoff with other material influenced by the Irish (see *Mittelalterliche Studien*, I. 237).

[26] Two sections from Pseudo-Bede, *Expositio in primum librum Mosis* (PL 91, cols 191 and 201) are verbally close to sections within the item *In Parasceuen* at Pembroke 25 ff. 65v. 8–16 and 66r. 4–5. Attitudes in much of the Pseudo-Bede material are reminiscent of those in designated Irish-influenced material.

[27] See Bischoff, *Mittelalterliche Studien*, I. 245–7, on the commentary.

[28] See Bischoff, *Mittelalterliche Studien*, I. 244–5, on the complete manuscript in Orléans 65 (62) and the fragments. J. F. Kelly, 'Frigulus: an Hiberno-Latin commentator on Matthew', *Revue Bénédictine* 91 (1981) 363–73, has reconsidered relationships, but it is worth noting here that one fragment, now destroyed, included Old Irish glosses and another fragment was 'probably written in Ireland' (p. 368). Kelly also argues that an eighth-century fragment now in Hereford Cathedral Library MS P II 10, written in Northumbrian uncials, has a close relationship with the Orléans commentary (p. 371).

[29] On the manuscript see E. A. Lowe, *Codices Latini Antiquiores* IX (Oxford, 1959), no. 1252.

hand. Dennis Brearley of Ottawa is editing the commentary; and he will also now edit the sermons with my collaboration—since the Pembroke-type collection draws on a number of the Munich MS sermons, extensively for eight sermons (including Holy Innocents) and slightly for two more.[30] The presence of a commentary, named as Hiberno-Latin, in a manuscript is no guarantee that the sequential sermons are under such influence, but I shall digress below on one distinctive feature within the Munich sermon on Holy Innocents which appears persistently in insular writings.

Our sermon, which is printed below, begins directly with a eulogy on the festival and a brief reminder of the main event and protagonists, in order to set the context for the flight to Egypt. Scripture (Matthew 2: 13–15) is then cited (lines 8–13), but the fulfilment of the prophecy *Ex Egypto uocaui filium meum* demands explication as in the Vienna 940 commentary f. 28v:

> Et fuge in Ægyptum; nunc impletur quod legitur; Ascendens (*corr. to*: ascendit) super nubem leuem et ingreditur Ægyptum et conterentur simulacra Ægypti ante faciem eius (cf. Isaias 19: 1). Nubem leuem dicit, id est, corpus sine peccato sanctae uirginis Mariae, in cuius umero Christus erat deportatus in Ægyptum. Et illud impletur: Erunt quinque ciuitates in terra Ægypti et una uocabitur ciuitas solis (cf. Isaias 19: 18); est uere ciuitas in qua uerus sol iustitiae (Malachias 4: 2) Iesus Christus habitat.

Similarities of detail with the corresponding passage in our sermon (lines 14–22) are the equation of the cloud of Isaias 19: 1 with the Virgin, of the 'city of the sun' with Christ, and the use of the non-Vulgate *conterentur* within the quotation of Isaias 19: 1, although a difference of phrase in Pembroke (*ante conspectum* for Vienna *ante faciem*, Vulgate *a facie*) suggests that the Pembroke composer did not read the Vienna copy of the commentary. But the details together with general similarity of idea and choice of Scriptural citation indicate a use of this commentary.

At this point and for the following passage (lines 22–35) our composer turns to the Orléans-type commentary, a section of which poses and answers questions on Matthew 2: 16, which records Herod's rage at being deceived by the Magi, and his order to massacre the Innocents. Orléans 65 (62) p. 38 reads:

> Sic et fuga Ioseph usque dum dicam quattuor annis . . . In Egyptum: in Hermopoli urbe ubi ut aiunt nocte aduentus eius omnia comminuta sunt idola . . . SPIRITALITER: Fuga Iesu in Egyptum significat Christum ad gentes iturum diabolumque;

---

[30] Sermons in the Munich MS are extensively used for our sermons on Innocents (as below); Circumcision; the second item for Theophany (Epiphany) (Pembroke 25 f. 24v); the first item for Ascension Day (Pembroke 25 f. 93v); Pentecost; Peter the Apostle; Paul; the Passion of John the Baptist; slightly for the Nativity of John the Baptist and for the first item for Theophany (Pembroke 25 f. 23r).

usque dicam: pater loquitur ad filium: Esto in gentibus donec omnes credant . . . Tunc Herodes . . . quoniam dilusus: potentes enim contempti iracundi fiunt. Iratus est ualde . . .: additur autem ualde quia a magis inlusus. Mittens: hic apparet quia lingua regis gladius est. Omnes pueros: more leonis qui de ore eius lapso agno totum deuorat gregem. In omnibus: in campis .xx. ut aiunt .c. pueri in unoquoque campo. A bimatu: regis iniqua malitia loco et tempore omnes antecedit quia non solum in Bethleem sed in omnibus finibus eius et non solum xii dierum/ p. 39/ uel unius anni sed duorum annorum pueros occidit . . . id est, a puero duorum annorum usque puerum unius noctis. Sed queritur cur sub hoc tempore filii occisi sunt. Nouit rex iniquus et subtilis quia regi et deo nascenti possibile est et utrum in breui tempore crescens oculis omnium quasi unius anni uel duorum puer appareret an crescenti uim in paruitatem corporis celaret; et ideo sub hac conditione temporis occidit siue quia magi annum natiuitatis domini aduenerunt et per annum alterum diu eos expectans ubi, dilusum se conperit, iratus, occidit pueros .ii. annorum.

The correspondence of idea and many phrases between our sermon and this commentary gives me some confidence to suggest that a similarly-close correspondence in such a long passage will not be found elsewhere, although the variation in name of the town (*Hieropolis/Hermopolis*) suggests that the composer of the Pembroke-type collection did not see the Orléans manuscript. Neither name, of course, equates the 'etymology' *ciuitas solis*, which should be *Heliopolis*, and such a lack of equation could confirm that our composer has conflated passages from two different sources, since the name does not appear in Vienna 940 and the meaning does not appear in Orléans 65 (62).

The background to some statements in this passage indicates that these originated in Irish spheres of influence. Among the attitudes distinguished by Bischoff was that 'unrestrained entrance was allowed to apocryphal narrative' (I. 222), although, clearly, it was not only the Irish who transmitted apocryphal story. In our passage the destruction of the idols in Egypt and the stay for *four* years in *Hermopolis* derives from the *Pseudo-Matthei Evangelium*.[31] But another statement is more distinctive: that as to the exact number of the Innocents, which persists in Irish texts or texts under Irish influence. In Orléans 65 (62) and in our sermon we see: *in campis .xx. ut aiunt .c. pueri in unoquoque campo*, that is, two thousand in all. Orthodox exegetes often linked the Innocents with the hundred and forty-four thousand who stood before the throne in the Apocalypse of John 14: 3, a verse included in the common epistolary reading for Innocents at this period (Apocalypse 14: 1–5). But medieval rationalism, which Bischoff notes as another feature of the writings influenced by the Irish (I. 222), demanded a smaller number. One com-

---

[31] See *Evangelia Apocrypha*, ed. C. Tischendorff (Lipsiae, 1853), pp. 85 (Hermopolis), 86 (idols destroyed), 88 (four years).

mentary, a derivative of that commentary on the whole of the Bible now named *Das Bibelwerk* or *The Reference Bible*,[32] makes the position impolitely clear.

Lyons, Bibliothèque Municipale 447 (376) (saec. IX),[33] a commentary presented in question-and-answer form, reads (f. 142v):

> Quanti infantes fuerunt occisi? RP.: Alii dicunt cxlīīī (i.e. 144,000) ut in Apocalipsi dicitur, quod falsum est, ut Primasius dicit;[34] cxlīīī hoc numero [e]lectos significare omnes finitus numerus pro infinito ponitur. Nullus estimet hunc numerum infantium esse; quis enim, imperitus et stultus, putat istum numerum de una tribu [n]ecasse (MS: mecasse) quando omnium tribuum nomina hic secuntur item de tribu Ruben xij milia et cetera, et una tribu Iuda tantum occidit Herodes infantes? Ideo uerius [ii] milia fuerunt infantes. . . .

Who so 'ignorant and foolish', indeed, to choose a hundred and forty-four thousand in the circumstances? The figure two thousand, or thereabouts, is a persistent Irish choice, as in Munich 6233 f. 122r (the sermon on Innocents noted above); in the marginal annotations to the Gospel-book of Armagh of AD 1138 (British Library MS Harley 1802 f. 11v); and in a sermon in the later Irish vernacular collection in the *Leabhar Breac*.[35]

Having presented the narrative background, our composer now eulogizes the Innocents and innocence in words drawn from Scripture. This section is clearly based on phrases found in the sermon from Munich 6233, a variant text of which is extant within a collection made for Hildebald, Archbishop of Cologne (AD 784–819),[36] but a collation of the two texts demonstrates that neither is the exemplar. Selections below are based on the Munich text with variants from the Hildebald collection, now Cologne Cathedral MS CLXXI. These are:

Munich f. 122v (cf. lines 44–52): Infantes autem ficuram (C: figuram) omnium sanctorum tenent. Ipsi (C: ipse) sunt primitiue (C: primitiuae) martyrum qui statim post aduentum Domini in carne coronam martyrii et uicturiam (C: uictoriam) meruerunt ante Petrum et Paulum et ante omnes martyres. Fortasse id est quod uideretur (C: ideoque uidetur) Dominus innocencia (C: innocentiam) paruulorum dilectari (C: dilectare *underpointed for deletion*; commendare *superscript*) cum dicit: Sinite infantes (C: paruulos)

[32] For the names see Bischoff, I. 222 and McNamara, p. 88.
[33] On the manuscript see Bischoff, I. 231.
[34] Primasius wrote a commentary on the Apocalypse, now printed in PL 68.
[35] For the references to the Gospel-book of Armagh and to the *Leabhar Breac* see M. R. James, *Latin Infancy Gospels* (Cambridge, 1927), p. 100.
[36] On the manuscript and its inscription to Hildebald see H. Barré, 'L'homiliaire carolingien de Mondsee', *Revue Bénédictine* 71 (1961) 79–80.

uenire ad me. Talium est enim regnum caelorum (cf. Mark 10: 14). Et iterum: Nisi conuersi fueritis et efficiamini sicut paruuli, non intrabitis in regnum celorum (Matthew 18: 13). . . .

Munich f. 122v (cf. lines 55–9): Hii sunt quos eligit Dominus quorum innocentia sicut paruulorum pura et munda est. Paruulus (C *adds*: enim) simplex et innocens ambulat (C *omits*: ambulat). Non dilectabitur (C: dilectatur) pulchre mulieres (C: mulieris) aspectu, non ambitiosus . . . nulli inuidit (C: inuidet), non cogitat malum. . . .

Munich f. 123v (cf. lines 60–5): Rachel autem (C *omits*: autem) ficura (C: figura) ecclesiae est que plorat . . . pro eo quod uideat filios suos . . . pro Christo cotidie sanguinem suum effundere (C: effudere) . . . hodie solempnitatem (C *adds*: passiones) et letitiam celebramus ut nos mereamur malicia esse paruuli sensibus autem perfecti (cf. 1 Corinthians 14: 20) et prudentes sicut serpentes (C *adds*: et) simplices sicut columbe (cf. Matthew 10: 16) . . . simplices in malo. . . .

Munich f. 124r (cf. lines 65–79): isti sunt . . . qui ante tempus martyrii martyres effecti sunt et ante baptismum baptizati sunt. Si dicat aliquis quomodo baptizati sunt, respondemus (C: respondebimus): Sicut baptizatus est Abraham, Isaac et Iacob et omnes sancti qui ante aduentu (C: aduentum) Domini nostri (C *omits*: nostri) Iesu Christi plaena fide/ 124v/ et bonis operibus placuerunt Deo, et sicut baptizatus est ille latro in cruce qui crederat in Iesum (C: qui Iesum crediderat) cui dicitur a Domino: Amen, dico tibi, hodie mecum eris in paradiso (Luke 24: 43), quibus omnibus fides pro baptismo erat. Ipsi sunt infantes qui lauerunt stolas suas et canditas (C: candidas) eas fecerunt in sanguine agni (cf. Apocalypse 7: 14) et secuntur agnum quocumque ierit (Apocalypse 14: 4) id est, Iesum Christum filium Dei per omnia regna caelorum (C: saeculorum) secuntur (C: sequentur) et canent (C: cantant) canticum nouum (cf. Apocalypse 14: 3), quod nemo cantare potest de his (C *adds*: qui se) cum mulieribus miscuerunt et non est locus illis prohibendus (C: prohibendi) est (C *omits*: est) in regno Dei.

Munich f. 124v (cf. phrases in lines 80–2): Ipsi sunt pueri (C: paruuli) quorum consortio (C: consortium) obtamus (C: optamus) et obsecramus in regno Dei et si meritis equari illis non possumus (C: illorum possib?) precibus et obsegrationibus (C: obsecrationibus) eorum Dominum inuocantes quoniam omnia possibilia sunt credenti ut in numero sanctorum suorum ab illo deputemur et /125r/ regni eius consortes esse mereamur. . . .

The overwhelming amount of verbal echo demonstrates the use of a text of the Munich sermon by our writer and the small differences (such as, for instance, his variant form of the last-cited section of the Munich text) may have been adaptations, but some may have arisen because our man read a text which is now lost.

In all, then, here is now a composite sermon, the originality of which lies only in the composing. Such sermons were common in the early medieval period, when composers revered and cited authority and thus guarded against heresy. But, in my speculative view, this sermon also testifies to the good sense of the 'insular' missionaries, in their desire to propagate simple morals of the faith in terms and with ideas acceptable to their listeners. The manuscripts of the sources are linked with the Continental missionfields (and, to some extent, with the insular homeland), but the ideas and attitudes include some which are typical of the insular peoples which supported the mission. When some unnamed writer wished to produce a helpful handbook for popular preachers he sometimes, as here in our sermon, found works such as these most relevant to his purpose. His collection, in turn, became popular back in the homeland with the very peoples from whom the ideas had originally come.

The Latin Text

Except for Balliol 240, which was read in manuscript, the texts below have been seen on clear microfilm and presented no problems. The spelling of the base text (Pembroke 25) is retained unless there could be misunderstanding and variant texts confirm a more recognizable spelling. Transpositions of words in variant manuscripts have not been recorded; abbreviations in the base text (Pembroke 25) have been expanded; punctuation, however, has been modernized for easier reading.

Manuscripts:

    i. Cambridge, Pembroke College MS 25 (P), saec. xi, Bury; ff. 19v–21r.

    ii. Cambridge, St John's College MS 42 (B 20) (J), saec. xii, Worcester (?); f. 18r–18v.

    iii. Oxford, Balliol College MS 240 (B), saec. xiv; f. 65r–65v.

f. 19v   XI. Omelia in Natale Innocentium

    Glorificare oportet et honorare hanc solemnitatem beatorum ac felicium infantium, fratres karissimi, quorum hodie triumphalem passionis gloriam caelebramus quos Herodes sacrilegus, postquam fefellerunt eum magi ab Oriente uenientes adorare dominum, pro Christo iussit
5 occidere. Meditabatur enim multum cupiens per dolositatem inter eos Iesum inuenire ad interficiendum, sed quoniam cura illi erat de amministra[tion]ibus domini sui apparuit angelus in somnis Ioseph dicens: Surge, et accipe puerum et matrem eius et fuge in Ægyptum, et esto ibi usque dum dicam tibi. Futurum est enim ut Herodes quęrat
10 puerum [ad] perdendum eum. Qui consurgens statim accepit puerum et matrem eius et secessit in Ægyptum et erat ibi usque ad obitum Herodis; ut adimpleretur quod dictum est a domino per prophetam dicentem: Ex Egypto uocaui filium meum (cf. Matthew 2: 13–15). Hanc quidem fugam longe ante Isaias prophetauerat dicens: Ecce dominus ascendet super
15 nubem leuem et ingredietur in Ægyptum et conterentur simulacra Ægypti ante conspectum eius (cf. Isaias 19: 1). Haec nubs leuis corpus

sanctae Marie uirginis est quod quia sine peccato semper fuit leue
reputatur super cuius igitur humerum Christus deportatus est in
Ægyptum; de qua dictum est: Erunt quinque ciuitates in terra Ægypti et
20   una ex illis uocabitur ciuitas /20r/ solis (cf. Isaias 19: 18). Uere ciuitas
solis est illa ciuitas in qua Iesus Christus inhabitauit, qui est uerus sol
iustitie (Malachias 4: 2). In illa igitur ciuitate, quae Hieropolis uocatur, in
nocte aduentus domini in eam comminuta sunt omnia et ad nihilum
redacta sunt idola. Haec autem fuga Iesu in Ægypto significat spiritaliter
25   Christum ad gentes iturum esse ut crederent in eum. In qua etiam per
quattuor expectauit annos iuxta preceptum patris loquentis ad eum: Esto
in gentibus donec omnes credant. Tunc autem Herodes cruentus cum
cognouisset quod inlusus esset a magis nolentibus Iesu [inuento ad se
reuerti] iratus est ualde. Et mittens ministros suos occidit omnes pueros,
30   qui erant in Bethleem et in omnibus finibus eius, a bimatu et infra,
secundum tempus quod exquisierat a magis. Hii autem pueri a Bethleem
et de omnibus finibus eius usque ad duo milia congregati in campis uiginti
constituti sunt et in unoquoque campo centum pro ea interfecti sunt; et
non solum duodecim dierum uel unius anni infantes sed a puero duorum
35   annorum usque ad puerum unius noctis occisi sunt.

    Quaerendum est autem quare sub hac temporis mensura rex crudelis
occidit pueros, id est, ut Christus inter innocentes filios occideretur.
Nonne rex iniquus nouerat quod regi et deo nascenti possibile erat utrum
cresceret in breui tempore et oculis omnium quasi unius anni uel duorum
40   puer appareret aut crescens in paruitate corporis se caelaret? Ideo autem
sub hac conditione temporis omnes occidit pueros siue quia magi post
annum a natiuitate domini ab Oriente aduenerant et per annum alterum
quia diu expectauit eos ualde iratus istos occidit infantulos. Refulgent
igitur isti in regno dei /20v/ figuram omnium sanctorum tenentes quia ipsi
45   sunt primitiui martyrum quoniam statim post aduentum domini in carne
coronam martyrii meruerunt et uictoriae ante Petrum et Paulum et ante
omnes martyres. Ideo dominus multum delectatur comitatu istorum et
innocentia; uirgines enim sunt et sequuntur eum quocumque ierit (cf.
Apocalypse 14: 4). De quorum persona in aeuangelio dicit: Sinite
50   paruulos uenire ad me, et nolite prohibere eos; talium est enim regnum
caelorum (cf. Mark 10: 14). Et iterum: Nisi conuersi fueritis, et efficiamini sicut paruuli non intrabitis in regnum celorum (Matthew 18: 3),
id est, si non tales sitis innocentes sicut infantes regnum caelorum non
possidebitis. Iuxta igitur paruulorum exemplum prouocat nos ad se
55   Christus; hos enim sibi elegit dominus quorum innocentiam puram et
mundam esse cognouerit sicut paruulorum. Paruulus enim simplicit[er]
ambulat et innocenter, non delectatur deliciis mundi nec mulierum
pulchritudine, non est ambitiosus, nulli inuidet, numquam cogitat
malum.

60   Horum igitur, fratres karissimi, qui hodie pro Christi nomine sanguinem
suum fuderunt solemnitatem et letitiam uoluntarię celebremus ut nos
mereamur malitia esse paruuli sensibus autem perfecti (cf. 1 Corinthians
14: 20) et prudentes sicut serpentes (cf. Matthew 10: 16), uigilantes
assidue circa gemmas in capite suo positas et simplices a malo sicut
65   columbae (cf. Matthew 10: 16). Isti sunt enim qui ante tempus martyrii
effecti sunt martyres et ante baptismum baptizati sunt. Si quis autem
dicat quomodo baptizati sunt respondebimus ei: Sicut baptizatus est
Abraham et Isaac et Iacob et omnes sancti qui ante aduentum domini
nostri Iesu Christi plena fide et bonis operibus placuerunt deo, et sicut
70   baptizatus est ille latro in cruce qui credidit in Iesum cui dicitur a domino
Amen, dico tibi; hodie mecum /21r/ eris in paradiso (Luke 24: 43),
quibus certissime omnibus uera fides pro baptismo erat.

    Isti sunt autem infantes qui lauerunt stolas suas et candidas eas
fecerunt in sanguine agni (cf. Apocalypse 7: 14) et sequuntur agnum
75   quocumque ierit (Apocalypse 14: 4), id est, Iesum Christum, filium dei
per omnia regna caelorum sequuntur et canticum nouum canunt (cf.
Apocalypse 14: 3), quod nemo cantare potest de his qui cum mulieribus
se miscuerunt, et nullus locus illis prohibetur in regno dei in quo non
possent intrare.
80   Obsecramus ergo, fratres karissimi, ut licet meritis coaequari illis non
possumus eorum intercessionibus in numero sanctorum consortes esse
mereamur in regnis caelestibus, largiente domino nostro Iesu Christo qui
cum patre et spiritu sancto uiuit et regnat in secula seculorum. AMEN.

1 felicium] fidelium B.   6 inuenire] uenire B.   7 amministrationibus] *from* BJ,
amministrantibus P; angelus] *add* domini B, *om*. J.   10 ad] *from* BJ, et P.
11 Herodis] *add* et J.   15 in] *om*. B.   16 nubs] nubes B.   18 cuius] huius B;
igitur] *om*. J.

22 Hieropolis] Ieropolis B.   23 in eam] ad eam J; comminuta] commutata BJ.
25 iturum] *add* uenturum B.   27 credant] credent J.   28–9 inuento ad se reuerti]
om. P.   29 et mittens] mittensque B.   38 nascenti] nascendi B.

43 infantulos] infantes J.   45 quoniam] *add* et B.   46 uictoriae] uictorie J;
uictoriam B; ante (2)] *om*. J.   47 comitatu] comitatum B; istorum] *from* BJ,
iustorum P.   48 innocentia] innocentiam B; eum] agnum J.
49 Sinite] *add* enim J.   51 et iterum] *om*. J.   56 simpliciter] *from* BJ,
simplicitate P.   57–8 non . . . pulchritudine] nec mulierum pulchritudine nec
deliciis mundi delectatur J.

76 canunt] cantant B.   77 mulieribus] *add* non B.

'A Bird in Bishopswood'
Some Newly-Discovered Lines of Alliterative Verse from the Late Fourteenth Century

RUTH KENNEDY

In 1980 the surviving muniments of St Paul's Cathedral were consigned to the care of the Guildhall Library, London, where they are now preserved. While sorting and labelling this material for new classification, the archivist, Mr Stephen Freeth, noticed some writing in English on a blank portion of a parchment roll: GL MS 25125/32—a rental and account of 1395/6.[1] This writing is alliterative verse, telling of a walking-out in May to the bishop's woods outside London and of an unfulfilling encounter with a bird there. Palaeographical analysis of this and of adjacent rent-rolls shows that whoever wrote the verse was closely connected with the financial workings of the late fourteenth-century Chapter, and it seems probable that the verse was written before the end of the century, almost certainly within or close to the precincts of the Cathedral.

This article is a summary of my MA dissertation: Ruth Kennedy, 'An Unpublished Alliterative Poem of the Late Fourteenth Century' (University of Bristol, 1985). I wish to thank especially the Dean and Chapter of St Paul's for permission to publish the verse and to work on their documents; Mr and Mrs S. Freeth, who graciously relinquished 'editorial rights'; Dr Caroline Barron, Dr M. B. Parkes, Professor J. A. Burrow and Dr Myra Stokes for their very generous help; the staff of Bristol University Library; and finally, Dr A. B. Cottle, for his invaluable teaching.

[1] A calendar of the muniments is found as H. Maxwell Lyte's 'Appendix i' of the *Ninth Report of the Royal Commission on Historical MSS* (London, 1883) 1–72 [*9th HMCi*]; the new classification now being made at the Guildhall Library is still in preparation, and reference must at times be made to *9th HMCi* (as 'SP -Box(es)-'). This series, formerly SP A-Boxes 43–8, is described thus in the provisional catalogue: 'Guildhall [GL] MSS 25125–25133: St. Paul's Cathedral. Dean and chapter estates:— account rolls of the collector of rents in London and its suburbs. 1315–1488. Incomplete. The contents of these rolls vary considerably for the period for which they survive. In particular, the text of the rental for London and its suburbs appears in full on these rolls for the first time in 1391, and regularly each year from c. 1400, but not before. Paper (nos. 27/60) and parchment, 99 rolls in 10 boxes.' For a study of comparable documents see Audrey M. Erskine, 'The Medieval Financial Records of the Cathedral Church of Exeter', *Journal of the Society of Archivists* 2 (1962) 254–66.

The total archive collection has survived two fires and pillage during the Commonwealth, but, whatever their previous history, the rolls are extremely well preserved. They present almost uniform exterior appearances: workman-like, cylindrical *rotuli*, sometimes slightly torn, and dirty with age and (apparently) handling. Inside they are clean and almost totally unblemished. Each document is made up of oblong membranes of sheep's parchment, sewn together chancery-fashion to form one fairly short roll. GL MS 25125/32 is formed from four such membranes, and is approximately 2100 mm in length and 290 mm across. It has vertical margins of about 41 mm on both sides of the face, cut by a sharpened point, but there is no evidence of horizontal pricking or ruling. There appears to be no pressmark on this or any other of the rolls examined, no signs of seals or fastenings, and virtually no decoration in headings, margins or capitals. Both rentals (i.e. indentures on the face) and accounts (entered in full on the dorse) are always carefully written out in the ecclesiastical engrossing hands of the Chapter scribes. The totals and corrections are often written in what are, almost certainly, the hands of the contemporaneous Collectors of Rents.

All surviving statutes show that the rent-collectors—whose names appear on their rolls—were directly accountable to the *camera* (at St Paul's the steward was called *camerarius*); at this period, individual officers such as clerks of works and accountants commonly retained their own documents for some time, often in their own lodgings—which can be the reason for a defective series of rolls such as, indeed, we have here.[2]

Below some varied rubrics at the mitred head of the document,[3] the protocol of the rental commences, inscribed in an attractive, plain and exceptionally clear engrossing hand: anglicana, with some of the secretary features that had been adopted by the St Paul's Chapter scribes during the previous few years. It describes itself, in Latin, as the account of John Tickhill, Collector of Rents of the Dean and Chapter of St Paul's, London, on each quarter day of the regnal years in 1395. The accounts are more likely to have been drawn up during 1396, perhaps being presented for auditing at Michaelmas.[4] The rental is left

---

[2] Kathleen Edwards, *The English Secular Cathedrals in the Middle Ages* (Manchester, 1967), p. 232; confirmed by Dr A. Piper of the Dept of MSS, University of Durham, in private correspondence. Some of the St Paul's Chapter documents can be seen to have been drawn up in private houses, e.g. GL MS 25121/1076: John Tickhill's notification of resignation of a chantry (1398).

[3] For example, a nineteenth-century pencilled numeral: '128'; and a note, possibly in the hand of Sir William Dugdale, which reads: 'Compotus John Tyckhill 19. Rich. 2'. For Dugdale's possession of the MSS see his *History of St. Paul's Cathedral*, 2nd edn, ed. H. Ellis (London, 1818), pp. xviii–xxiv.

[4] Cf. Erskine, p. 257; and *Registrum Statutorum . . . Cathedralis Sancti Pauli*, ed. W. Sparrow Simpson (London, 1873): 'Auditor . . . post festum S. Michaelis . . . diligenter . . . audiat computum omnium ministrorum' (p. 246); but the rolls do *not* appear to have been audited.

very incomplete (as was frequently the case, since rentals changed so little from year to year: a scribe could use a previous rental for entering the accounts); and directly below its three brief entries in Latin (and so about 500 mm from the head of the roll), without introduction, in a different hand, employing a finer quill and darker ink, are found the twenty-two lines of writing in English that comprise the poem. They are in continuous prose format, but marked so as to indicate a metrical structure. The writer has made use of the left-hand margin of the prepared parchment, but not the right-hand one. There is no MS indication that the poem is finished. The rest of this top membrane, and then the entire remainder of the face of the *compotus*, is blank.

On the darker dorse of the roll the accounts—which include receipts, debts, wages and expenses—have been entered in detail, covering the entire side, as is usual. The key items on a medieval account were the allowances (*allocationes*).[5] These are often found as the final entries on the dorse of the rolls, and the contemporary economic recession ensured that they appear with some frequency in this series. Allowances have provided very useful data for social historians, but a faint one (perhaps erased) among the accounts of GL MS 25125/32 provides unique palaeographical evidence of possible authorship, as it can be seen to be the same hand that has written the verse. Further, this hand can be seen—often in only minute details—in corrections, additions, interpolations and totals, on every one of the seven rolls pertaining to John Tickhill's term as *collector reddituum* from 1394–8, but on no others. Very different hands have annotated the adjacent rolls, with an abrupt change of hand with each change of rent-collector.[6]

---

[5] An allowance was basically the discrepancy between the amount due and the money actually received. The collector had, in each instance, to beg allowance (*petit allocationem*), with reasons given, for each amount missing, in order that rental and account might balance. (I am indebted to Dr Martha Carlin of The Social and Economic Study of Medieval London for translation and explanation in this matter, and for similar assistance with GL MS 25121/1952—see n. 28 below.)

[6] The consecutive collectors of rents whose names appear at the heads of the rolls (and are sometimes written informally within the mitre or on the outside of the cylinder), and whose hands seem to have annotated them, are: Phillip Keys (1388–9): small, neat anglicana; Richard Thurston (1390–1): large, spidery, cursive anglicana, much splayed; William Ruthyn (1392–3): gigantic graphs, anglicana with semi-textura features; John Tickhill (1394–7): small, concise anglicana with open stroke spacing; John Stormorth (1398–1402): large, very ungainly, semi-literate-looking script. The scribal hands appear similar throughout and exhibit regular anglicana scripts with some secretary features. The annotations on Keys's, Thurston's, Ruthyn's and Stormorth's rolls are minimal, consisting in the main of an occasional side-total. By contrast, Tickhill's rolls show, quite apart from their additions of verse and astronomy, a notable degree of greater involvement in the accounting, and supply even, for instance, the Christian names of tenants. There are no less than seven rolls rather than the four that would be expected for this term of office. It seems that three were duplicate or draft rolls, which helps to explain why the poet felt free to use them for his own purposes.

The most noticeable of the signs of life on John Tickhill's rolls appears on GL MS 25125/34: an incomplete or draft version of the 1396/7 accounts. Its face is devoid of superscription or rental,[7] but written on this face, with some large deletions, are sixty-six lines of scientific Latin prose.[8] These, like the verse, were apparently first noticed by Mr S. Freeth, and entered as 'Notes on Astronomy' in the provisional catalogue—where, additionally, they are identified as being in the same hand as the verse.[9]

This hand is a fairly neat and fluent cursive anglicana, with a total absence of secretary features.[10] It is not the hand of an Oxford or Cambridge graduate,[11] but is, however, confident and professional-looking—the hand of one obviously very used to writing, though in many ways different from the ecclesiastical scribal hands: a literate clerical hand which is rather similar is that ascribed to Chaucer in CUL MS Peterhouse 75.[12]

There are multiform indications on the MS that the work is a draft, and possibly a holograph: for example, deletions, signs of revision, and the wide

---

[7] There is a small inscription in the very point of the mitred head: 'Compotus . . .? J. Tychyll'; the hand cannot be identified.

[8] Part of the Alphonsine Tables (instructions on calculating the motions of the sun and of the planets). Discussion of these is reserved for a forthcoming article. For a working summary of the subject see the notes to line 1273 of *The Franklin's Tale* in *The Complete Works of Geoffrey Chaucer*, ed. F. N. Robinson, 2nd edn (London, 1957).

[9] This identification has been tentatively confirmed (from photographs) by Dr M. B. Parkes; and subsequent analysis of graph variants has provided further corroborative evidence.

[10] For an exposition of the contemporary scripts, see M. B. Parkes, *English Cursive Book Hands 1250–1500* (Oxford, 1969), pp. xiv–xviii. In the verse draft no apparent majuscules are employed except for the first *I*, but long *i* is used throughout for the personal pronoun and for the initial letter (appearing only in the word *in*, except when the latter is abbreviated). The only diacritic is in line 28 (*in a stody*). Short undotted *i* is used only twice initially: for *in likyng* (11) and *in my solas* (20), and three times medially: in *bisy* (4), *likyng* (11), and *wischyd* (39). Two forms of *s*, of *e*, and of *r* are employed, the 2-shaped *r* appearing after *o*, both medially and finally, except in three out of seventeen instances. Short *s* is used before a vowel and long *s* before a consonant: with the result that different alliterating groups are graphically differentiated. Long *s* is used only twice as a terminal letter: in *wys* (5) and *bryddys* (7). The letter *t* frequently carries an elongated headstroke which does not appear to indicate a curtailment.

[11] This is the view of Dr M. B. Parkes. Very few of the names of the cantarists and administrators found in the documents appear in A. B. Emden's *A Biographical Register of the University of Oxford to AD 1500* (Oxford, 1957–9), or *A Biographical Register of the University of Cambridge to AD 1500* (Cambridge, 1963).

[12] The *Equatorie*: a draft working copy in anglicana facilis, and possibly a holograph: reproduced in facsimile in *The Equatorie of the Planetis, 1392*, ed. D. J. Price (Cambridge, 1955). See e.g. f. 72. I am indebted to Dr M. B. Parkes for drawing my attention to this palaeographical analogy, and especially to the shared feature of the wide line spacing.

line-spacing (this last suggesting that the writer knew that he would be making corrections). Apart from three insignificant *currente calamo* errors, the deletion and amendment is found within the first seven lines of MS (see Plates 12 and 13). This suggests either that the author had composed the entire piece first and had commenced to revise it, getting about as far as line 14 (MS line 7), or that the formal nature of the opening *ver* topos caused him difficulties that resulted in much amendment, but which ceased to exist once he had passed into a personal, almost certainly autobiographical mode. One or both of these cases would imply that the writer was the author. Many of the corrections can be seen to be 'poetic' rather than scribal, effected as the line was actually being written: see especially *doun hys* deleted for *tyl vs*, and *alle* deleted for *doun*, line 3 (MS line 2); also *hede* deleted for *hert*, line 14 (MS line 7); and very different evidence that the writer was the author can be deduced from the content.

The punctuation in this draft presents problems. Because syntax and metre are so closely linked, it is just possible that the large markings that are found throughout delineate rhetorical pauses: i.e. that each apparent flourish is an elaborate current *punctus versus* or *punctus elevatus*, or a doubled *virgula suspensiva*. But owing to the informal nature of the writing one cannot be certain of this. There is also much variation in the strokes and formation of the marks. The point, or single *punctus*, is employed five times: at the ends of lines 11, 18, 28 and 40; and medially only once: in line 21, after *bough*. Three of these usages indicate a slight pause, where a comma would be employed today, and show a degree of consistency; but that four out of the five terminal points are *then* followed by the usual punctuating flourishes is convincing evidence that these flourishes are rather indicators of the *metrical* divisions. The most interesting feature of the punctuation is the occurrence of noticeably irregular markings in MS line 5, which could signify a bracketing or *punctus versus* placed *before* the metrical lines (thus setting apart lines 10 and 11).[13]

Several unrhymed alliterative works are written in prose format and punctuated so that a rhyming or rhythmical structure is made evident. The MS of *The Blacksmiths*,[14] found on a Norwich priory document, provides a useful analogy to the punctuation of this St Paul's draft. It, too, as shown in Elizabeth Salter's edition, manifests some apparent variations—the significance of which has not been explained—in the marks themselves. The greater proportion of rhythmical works punctuated thus in a prose format are those associated with Latin writings or prose sermons, as has been well illustrated in recent scholarship, the substance of which consistently emphasizes the

[13] For a survey of some problems in medieval punctuation see M. B. Parkes, 'Punctuation, or pause and effect' in *Medieval Eloquence*, ed. J. J. Murphy (Berkeley, Cal., 1978), pp. 127–42.
[14] Bodl. MS Arundel 292: edited in MS format by Elizabeth Salter in 'A Complaint Against Blacksmiths', *Literature and History* 5 (1979) 195–215.

contribution of clerical and monastic writers to the alliterative 'Revival';[15] and here we have yet further evidence of informal alliterative writing, almost certainly composed by a secular clerk, presented in this fashion.

Apart from those in the punctuation, flourishes are minimal; and contractions and abbreviations are familiar and clerkly, though not regular:[16] this is as might be expected in a working copy (see prefatory notes to the edited text on p. 82).

The author must almost certainly have been one of a group of clerks whose names are frequently found in conjunction among the Chapter muniments and in several London records. It seems that a group of about twelve mature men, who were all perpetual chaplains, and who included among them Chamberlain, Sacrist and Collector of Rents, had common material interests and stayed close to the daily workings of the Cathedral and its fabric and funds. This body of clerics appears to have been a responsible and conscientious group, and, as far as can be ascertained (from curiously conflicting evidence), seems to have consisted not of Minor Canons, who lived as a community, but rather of priests, some beneficed, holding a variety of administrative posts within the Chapter; and from the sources there emerges a picture quite different from the still prevalent one of dissolute and ill-regulated chantry chaplains.[17]

Among such responsible Chapter servants was John Tickhill, *collector reddituum* from 1394–8. In view of the MS evidence, it seems not unreasonable to believe that the verse was written by John Tickhill himself. It is just

---

[15] See e.g. A. McIntosh, 'Wulfstan's Prose', *Proceedings of the British Academy* 35 (1949) 109–80, the seminal ideas of which were developed by Elizabeth Salter in her important study, 'Alliterative Modes and Affiliations in the Fourteenth Century', *NM* 79 (1978) 25–35, and surveyed most recently by D. Lawton in 'Middle English Alliterative Poetry: An Introduction', and by I. Doyle in 'The Manuscripts', both in *Middle English Alliterative Poetry: Seven Essays*, ed. D. Lawton (Cambridge, 1982), pp. 1–19 and 88–100.

[16] Flourishes consist only of a lengthened transverse bar through final *t(h)*—as in *askyth* (16), *caght* (10), and *vnlyght* (35); in each of these cases, the word occurs at the right-hand edge of the parchment, and (in the last two instances especially) would be unlikely to occur with a final *-e*. Where a similar flourish is found elsewhere on *t* (e.g. *laxt' lust'*, MS line 6) it has similarly been read as otiose. þ9 and *thus* both occur, as do both full and contracted forms of *in*, *alle*, and *-er*. *And* is always a Tyronian *et*-Nota : ᚃ.

[17] This has arisen largely because of an equally prevalent confusion between perpetual chaplains and the more rootless Mass-priests. See e.g. K. L. Wood-Legh, *Perpetual Chantries in Britain* (Cambridge, 1965), esp. pp. 189–92. It must be emphasized that at St Paul's, as at some European cathedrals, the position of *capellani cantariarum* was of higher status than that of the very inferior vicars choral who were the ill-paid deputies of the rich and often-absent prebendary canons. This hierarchy was a reversal of the usual order in English secular cathedrals, and further indicates the respectable status of the chantry priests at St Paul's. It also well explains the attraction of the post, as described in Chaucer's *General Prologue* (507–10).

possible, though not probable, that it was inscribed by some other of the clerks or canons; but that anyone except a member of the Chapter could have had access to the rent rolls and annotated the accounts in the manner of John Tickhill's would have been highly irregular. The two most likely of the alternative candidates would be the Chamberlain or an unknown partner or *contrarotulator*, and it is only the possible existence of the latter that prevents us from coming to any definite conclusions about authorship.[18]

The absolute *terminus a quo* is 12 April 1395, but late in 1396 is more feasible. A pure anglicana script such as this could appear as late as 1450, but if the writer was as closely connected with the financial work on the dorse as appears almost certain, then it seems probable that the verse was set down before mid-1398 when John Tickhill became rector of St Gregory's and resigned both his chantry and his office.[19] The draft may well, therefore, have been penned in 1397 (perhaps even in the 'monþ of May'), on a document no longer required for its figures, after a particularly late Easter (22 April)—which accords well with the emphasis in line 12 on the apparent length of the 'Lentyn tyme'—and before the transitions of Spring 1398, when Tickhill was preparing to hand over his work to his successor.

Since John Tickhill is the most probable candidate for authorship, the available details of his career must be of interest.[20] He would almost certainly have been an ordained priest when he was recorded as one of seven chaplains at St Mildred, Bread Street (by the south-east end of St Paul's), in 1379 and 1381, which would make him, at the very minimum, thirty-five years old in 1396. He had licence to 'travel overseas' in 1390, and is next recorded as Collector of Rents and 'presbyter cantarie' at St Paul's in 1394, where he held at least two apparently desirable chantries. In 1394 he was one of a group of about twelve chaplains accused of intimidating ('averring threats' against) three other named chaplains. In 1398 he was collated to the rectorship of St Gregory's, a parish church which lay against the south side of the Cathedral; again this appears to have been an estimable benefice. Tickhill is recorded as

---

[18] See Kennedy, pp. 98–9. It is unlikely that the Chamberlain's hand would be in evidence on Tickhill's rolls and not on others. A later rent-collector would not enter *allocationes* or financial details; and if a contrarotulator had his own roll, he would be unlikely to write verse on a roll marked 'Compotus Joħis Tykhylle'.

[19] See *9thHMCi*: 'SP A-Box 11/1076' [GL MS 25121/1076], p. 12; also salary adjustments recorded in a margin of Stormorth's *compotus* of 1398 (GL MS 25125/38).

[20] For sources (largely Public Record Office documents, etc.), see Kennedy, pp. 115–16. An invaluable bibliography can be found in C. N. L. Brooke's 'The Earliest Times to 1488' in *A History of St. Paul's Cathedral and some of the Men Associated with it*, ed. W. R. Matthews and W. M. Atkins (London, 1957), pp. 1–99. For all episcopal registers cited, see D. M. Smith, *A Guide to Bishops' Registers in England and Wales* (London, 1981).

Rector of St Gregory's in 1414; and in 1423 a different person became rector, perhaps on Tickhill's death or retirement.

Tickhill is a small town in the West Riding of Yorkshire, virtually on the Great North Road, and almost equidistant from York and Lincoln. John of Gaunt held the castle there in the Honour of Tickhill, an ancient demesne.[21] Roche and Hampole were the nearest monastic foundations, but the York bishops' registers show that there were strong connections with Welbeck Abbey, a Premonstratensian foundation. The town also had a house of Austin Friars which may well have had a school. But it must be emphasized that the place-name is not a sure guide to provenance; there were Tickhills in London a generation earlier, butchers and mercers; and, in the lamentable absence of Northburgh's and Courtney's London registers, it is probably impossible to know whether a son of one of these guildsmen was ordained priest in London in the years 1354–61 or 1375–9. The name does not occur in Sudbury's or Braybrooke's registers, the ordinands of which come with remarkable regularity from the York, Lincoln or London dioceses. Naturally the York bishops' registers do not show whether any of the ordained John de Tickhills or John Page de Tickhills had migrated southwards, as Courtney's register *would* have shown; but the traces of non-London dialect in the composition are consistent with those of a South Yorkshireman who had been living and working in London for the greater part of the previous seventeen years.

The 'Byschopys Woode' is possibly the most likely of places within or near the city to which a clerk from the Cathedral might resort to sit 'in [his] solas' after a cheerless 'Lentyn tyme'. The place-name survives only in Bishops Way, Bethnal Green, where Victoria Park and the London Chest Hospital (located there for the healthiness of the situation) now replace the woods and manor that once lay around the Stepney Episcopal Palace. This edifice later became known as Bonner's Hall, after its most infamous occupant. It is possible to reconstruct the locale of the place as it would have appeared at the time: wooded parkland of free warren surrounding the chalk, brick and timber building.[22] The London citizens had strenuously objected to Bishop Richard Gravesend's efforts at enclosure for a deer park, saying that 'from the time when no memory is extant they had used to . . . hunt . . . within the Woods and without, Hares, Foxes, Conies, &c';[23] and Lydgate's *A Mumming at*

---

[21] See *John of Gaunt's Register, 1379–83*, ed. Eleanor C. Lodge and R. Somerville, 2 vols, Royal Historical Society Publications, Camden 3rd Series 56–7 (London, 1937), I. 139, entry 422: '. . . pris pur les moleyns del Tykhull, sys soldz et oyt deniers. Et auxint facez paier pur le cariage dun coffre ove vessellement dargent del esglise de Seint Poule de Londres . . .' (8 Sept. 1380).

[22] For a bibliography of maps, surveys, books and articles see Kennedy, p. 117.

[23] *Liber Horn*, f. 268; reproduced in Stow (see *Notes to the Text*, line 2), IV. 47.

Bishopswood provides further evidence of this exercise of assumed rights over the estate by the public. In order for the protagonist to walk there he would have had to leave the city through one of the north-eastern gates or Aldgate; to pass the wells, priories, madhouses and the like, and the growing suburban industry outside the walls; and to make his way to the quiet lanes and fields beyond.

Although it is possible that these unrhymed long lines were intended to introduce a longer work, the piece appears closer in mood to a lyrical vignette of a familiar bipartite narrative structure, where the walking-out precedes a meeting in the wood. There is a decided waning of impetus in the last line, but the word *somer* provides a verbal link back to line 1. This could be interpreted as evidence that the composition is complete, since there are other alliterative poems which end in such a way; in the latter, however, the concluding repetitions are rather more striking.[24]

Formally, the piece consists of natural verse paragraphs of unequal length. Rhythms are freely arranged around the four, or sometimes five, alliterative stresses. After the wooden encyclopaedic opening section, monotony is avoided, with rhythmic echoes coming rather from *alternating* lines; and, together with the balancing sounds from the half-lines, this gives, at times, an antiphonal effect (e.g. lines 23–8)—for some ear for rhythmic harmony is apparent in this amateurish draft.

Alliteration is dense, but neither clumsy nor forced, being for the most part based on a regular AA/AX pattern. Perhaps five hypermetric lines can be discerned, as well as other variations, such as the XA/AA of line 10. Only one line (21) is, by the rules of 'classic' alliterative metre, very defective; but this is not apparent to the ear, which is engaged by the pervasive alliterative concatenation, found on unstressed as well as stressed syllables. Although many of the alliterative phrases have echoes in other works, they here tend towards the discursive and naturalistic: for instance, the common collocation *bryd/bough* here functions not as an ornamental tag *to* the narrative, but as prosaic substance *of* the narrative.

Spelling is consistent and literate, despite the evidently informal nature of the fragment. The only spellings not recorded elsewhere are *laxt* (11), *naythyr* (26, 27) and *þorg* (38). There is a marked preference for the employment of *y*

---

[24] For examples of the walking out and meeting of a stranger in short poems, see e.g. 'Now Springs the Spray' (*English Lyrics of the XIIIth Century*, ed. Carleton Brown (London,1932), No. 62, p. 119), and 'The Meeting in the Wood' (*The Harley Lyrics*, ed. G. L. Brook (Manchester, 1948), No. 8, p. 39). And for examples of structural circularity cf. *Gawain, Pearl, Patience, Avow.Arth.*, where a similar *dúnadh* is found (on which see P. L. Henry, 'A Celtic-English Prosodic Feature', *Zeitschrift für celtische Philologie* 29 (1962–4) 91–100).

rather than *i* or *e* throughout.[25] The diction is disappointingly undistinguished, but vivified by some interesting words of diverse origin. Words of French derivation make up over one fifth of the total vocabulary, and are especially numerous in the central section which appears to illustrate the poet's more personal and fluent expression. It is difficult to assess whether the alliterative vocabulary has been artificially adopted or represents the poet's natural idiom.

The dialect is problematic. Professor A. McIntosh very kindly agreed to examine a facsimile and transcription. He gave it as his opinion that dialectal provenance could not be securely established on the basis of such a brief text, but added: 'It would not surprise me if the text were written in London, but the scribe and/or his exemplar manifests a few non-London features' (private communication). The basic dialect is SE Midland (pr. 3 sg. *-yth*; use of forms *her*, *sche* and *I*; and a predominance of rounded development of OE *ā*/ON *á*). There are virtually no traces of W, SW or S dialect apart from the anomalous S and W *ham*. There are, however, slight indications of N or NM features: the alliterative vocabulary (e.g. *bowyd*, *buskyd*); forms recorded elsewhere only in N and E texts (*grys*, *bentys*); the usage of *welk* and the phrase *to mak here*; the lack of inflexion (only one of fifteen infinitives has an *-n* suffix; adjectives and datives are nearly all uninflected); absence of *-en* plurals; the characteristically N *-yn* past participle in *comyn*; and unvoicing of medial and final *f* (*hafe* 24, *ȝyf* (v.) 8). Spellings also conform to the usual N practice. The 'non-London features' *are*, therefore, predominantly Northern. Furthermore, the preposition *tyl* is used in two different ways, which does suggest a genuine familiarity with it. Its use with the infinitive (as in line 6) is found only in N or NWM texts. The pronoun *ham* may not be so anomalous in a MS of EM provenance showing some N features, since an adjustment of an original *þam* or *þaim* might well result in the form *ham* rather than *hem*—an idiosyncrasy of a non-Londoner's accent.

The central description of the bird is reminiscent of the turtle-dove of the bestiary tradition whose role was to sit alone mourning for its mate. Here there is an observation and intensity of image that is like a focused, self-existing detail from tapestry or illumination—although it is plain that the piece relates closely to the genre of the *chanson d'aventure*, especially to that category in

---

[25] The use of *y* for *þ* (which one would expect in the orthography of a Northerner) does not occur; but the noticeable horizontal line at the beginning of line 10 (MS line 5) has been read as a deletion of a previously-written *y* which can just be detected beneath it. This suggests that the writer inadvertently wrote *y* for *þ* (the word *þus* follows). This would be feasible in the orthography of a literate Northerner who had lived and worked in London for at least seventeen years and had come to distinguish the two graphs. On this detail of regional orthography see A. McIntosh, 'Towards an Inventory of ME Scribes', *NM* 75 (1974) 608–9, and M. Benskin, 'The Letters <þ> and <y> in Later Middle English', *Journal of the Society of Archivists* 7 (1982) 13–30. I am grateful to Professor McIntosh for drawing my attention to this matter.

which there is an analogy suggested between a bird and the woman wooed by the clerk.[26] These elements, together with a mirroring in the bird of the protagonist's own solitary state, appear to inform content and style. The last two lines pose difficulties in interpretation, and, apart from the obvious one that the poet was decidedly flagging, the most plausible interpretation is that they suggest a parallel to the mood of the poet himself, expressed in lines 12–17: 'wery of þat wedyr' and once more able to enjoy 'somer'.

From the specific context of late fourteenth–century verse written in London we can perceive features shared with the verse of Langland, though fewer with those of his followers. An educated person living only steps away from the London *stationarii* would almost certainly have read *Piers Plowman*, and much more.[27] The collocations and verbal parallels testify to a *literary* sensibility, no matter how meagre the poet's own talent. It is notable that there are strong parallels from the works of the NE Midlands. Although the text suggests little of the courtly, professional or military influences discernible in contemporary London verse, various analogies can be made with aspects of all of the London rhyming poets—especially, perhaps, Hoccleve, as here we find echoes of that poet's recounting of psychological detail, something of the genre of complaint,[28] and a London setting. The landscape, as in Hoccleve, is secularized and demystified, and, just as Thomas Hoccleve wrote 'At Chestre ynne As I lay in my bed', here the *locus amoenus* has become Bishopswood—a place that (according to a rubric on a Lydgate MS) was used by the Sheriffs of London for a civic picnic. No longer are we taken into the wild *fryth* of the earlier lyrics; just as Hoccleve set forth 'To walk vnto the brigge and take a boot', this poet 'welk forth as oþer wyes dydene'—but to 'se' rather than joyously to hunt or play: an observer within his milieu, and speaking in wan, discursive and individual tones.

[26] For a full survey of the genre see Helen Sandison, *The 'Chanson d'Aventure' in Middle English* (Bryn Mawr, 1913).

[27] On the dissemination of the *PPl*. MSS see J. A. Burrow, 'The Audience of *Piers Plowman*' in his *Essays on Medieval Literature* (Oxford, 1984), pp. 102–16, and Ann Middleton, 'The Audience and Public of "Piers Plowman" ' in *Middle English Alliterative Poetry*, ed. Lawton, pp. 101–24. For the transmission of other alliterative works see e.g. Elizabeth Salter, *Fourteenth Century English Poetry: Contexts and Readings* (Oxford, 1983), esp. Ch. 3 and studies quoted therein. If *St. Erkenwald* had been circulated at St Paul's during Braybrooke's episcopate (for it was he who reinstated the celebration of that saint, and he was a bishop more than usually involved in the affairs of his chapter), then something of that author's balanced rhetoric and precision of meaning may have been assimilated.

[28] For a formal complaint by Tickhill see GL MS 25121/1952: an undated petition in French in the name of John Tickhill, addressed to the Crown and craving letters patent in order to secure lapsed quit-rents. It is very similar in tone to the later Bills of Complaint to the Chancellor that so occupied the working hours of Thomas Hoccleve.

Editorial Procedure

The manuscript is not difficult to read, and ultra-violet light has helped with its few uncertainties.

It is with some hesitation that the final ꝼ brevigraph has been expanded to -*ys* on each of the six occasions when it is used. Full forms in -*ys* (e.g. *bryddys, lymys*) occur fifteen times; and fully-written -*es* is found only once (*wyes*, 15). But in the fully-written plurals -*ys* never follows *t-* or *g-*; whereas the brevigraph is used *only* after *t-* and *g-* (four times and twice respectively: *bestꝼ, bentꝼ, hartꝼ, syghtꝼ*; and *songꝼ, wengꝼ*). So it might have been precisely when the writer intended -*es* that he employed the sign. Neither MS *folows* (19) nor *fethyrs* (21) shows a vowel in the plural ending. A similar variety of plural forms can be found elsewhere within a single text.

The sign ᵞ has been read throughout as a contraction for -*re* and not as *r* with a flourish. Seven words ending in -*r* do not have the sign (e.g. *flauour* (8, MS 4)). The -*re* expansion gives variant readings of only *somer(e)* and *her(e)*. In lines 11 and 41 *somer* is written with the ᵖ sign, as are *oþer* (27) and *euer* (33). It is possible that the -*e* was deliberately intended in the first line for an opening bravura. The word *somnor'* (3, MS 2) is expanded because the writer would normally use a 2-shaped *r* for a word ending in -*or* (cf. *for*, MS 2). In lines 30 and 31 *her'* has been expanded to *here* and *her* respectively for dative and accusative, despite the short form clearly written in 34—on the grounds that different parts of speech appear to have been differently terminated (cf. *all/alle*). In line 6 (MS 3) *busk'* has been expanded to *buske*, because the MS frequently shows an apparent confusion in the carry-over of graph *k*, e.g. *lakke* (24), *make* (30a), and *kepyn* (40). Both *askyth* (16) and *buskyd* (37) have biting between *k* and *y*. Where *k* appears to be final it is quite clear and written without the suspension, e.g. *spak* (38). *ll'* is always expanded in conformity with the full forms; in line 20 the word *alle* is a plural adjective, in 25 it is singular (see also n. 16). *vnpᵘayd* (16) is expanded in conformity with *fourmyd* (23).

ꝛ is expanded throughout; *þᵉ* is given its common value; *þˢ* and *wᵗ* are expanded to *þis* and *with* respectively; the letter *y* is actually employed far more often than *i* in the MS, but the *in*-abbreviation uses an *i*, and it is possible that the calligraphically simpler and more current *i* would be employed in the absence of surrounding minims (but see *ys*, MS 1 and 2). *þᵗ* is expanded to *þat* in accordance with the phonology. No distinction can be observed between long *i* and *j*, and the graph has been modernized throughout. Spelling has not been normalized, but word-division has been modernized. Capitals and punctuation are editorial, cognizance having been taken of the existing punctuation.

For further comments on letter-shapes, punctuation, and flourishes, see footnotes 10, 13, and 16 respectively.

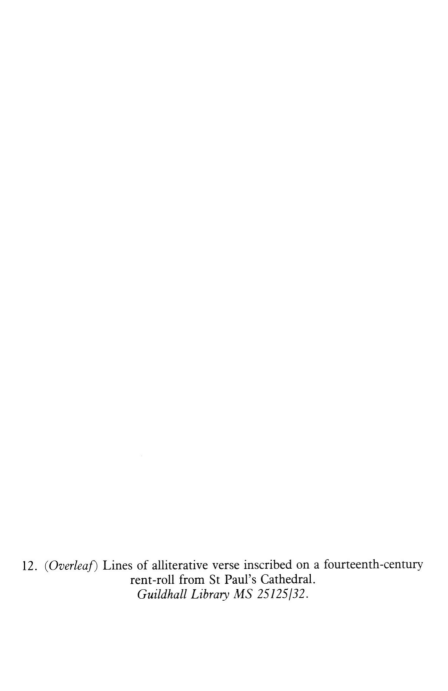

12. (*Overleaf*) Lines of alliterative verse inscribed on a fourteenth-century
rent-roll from St Paul's Cathedral.
Guildhall Library MS 25125/32.

MS Line		MS Line

		many
1	jn a sesone of somer' þᵗ souerayne ys of alle / þt was þᵉ myry monþ of may when (atte) myrthys spryng	1
	sonmor'	
2	þᵉ sonne ys (soᵘᵉrayne) ⁊ syr' – sendyth (dounys) tyl vs (atte) doun / ⁊ byddyth vs bisy for to be	2
3	our' bodys for to glade / man for to myrth hym in al maner wys / bestys for to busk' ham on bentys	3
4	tyl abyde / bryddys in buschys bysy ham wᵗ songys / flourys for to florych ⁊ flauour ʒyf a bout	4
5	grys for to grow grene ⁊ glade mennys hartys / (ᵞ)þus ech creatur' comfort hym caght' /	5
6	⁊ laxt' lust' for to lyf in likyng of somer. / ⁊ j had lenyd me long al a lentyn tyme	6
	hede	
7	jn vnlust of my lyf ⁊ lost al ^ᵐʸ joye / ⁊ þen j heuyd vp myn (hede) hert ⁊ myn (hert) aftyr /	7

Note ' signifies an additional calligraphic feature which may indicate a final *e*.

13. The opening lines (with transcription) of the alliterative verse on the rent-roll from St Paul's Cathedral.

The Edited Text

In a sesone of somere þat souerayne ys of alle,
Þat was þe myry monþ of May when many myrthys spryng,
Þe sonne ys somnore and syre and sendyth tyl vs doun,
And byddyth vs bisy for to be oure bodys for to glade;
Man for to myrth hym in al maner wys,   5
Bestys for to buske ham on bentys tyl abyde,
Bryddys in buschys bysy ham with songys,
Flourys for to florych and flauour ȝyf about,
Grys for to grow grene and glade mennys hartys;
Þus ech creature comfort hym caght,   10
And laxt lust for to lyf in likyng of somer.
And I had lenyd me long al a Lentyn tyme
In vnlust of my lyf and lost al my joye;
And þen I heuyd vp myn hert and myn hede aftyr
And welk forth to þe wodys as oþer wyes dydene,   15
Al vnpouruayd of play þat pryuete askyth.
And as I welk þus and wandryd, wery of myself,
I abode vndyr a busch at Byschopys Woode
For to se þe fayr fo[wly]s ech with his felaw play.
And as I sat in my solas and alle þes syghtys sawe,   20
A bryd bode on a bough, fast me besyde,
Þe fayrest fowyl of fethyrs þat I had say beforne;
Fyguryd in feturys fourmyd so clene
Þat sche nad lyme ne lyth þat lakke myȝt hafe;
Sade in al semblant, sayd bot a lytyl,   25
Naythyr chauntyd ne chatryd bot cheryd herself,
And naythyr fluschyd ne frayd as oþer fowlys dydyne,
Bot euer stode in a stody as sche astonyd were.
And as hyt semyd to my syght by semblant sche made
Þat sche myssyd a make myrth for to mak here.   30
Þen was I ferd of þis fowle þat I affray her schuld
Ȝyf I bowyd to þe bowgh þe bryd sat vpon,
And I was wo and euer waytyd when sche away wold flye,
For sche had wengys at her wylle and wantyd neuer a fethyr
And I vnlyght of my lymys and lyme had I none   35
Ne couth noght cheuysch me with charmys ne chauntyng of bryddys.
And thus I buskyd fro þis bryd and hyt abode stylle,
And þorg no spech þat I spak aspyed sche me noght;
And euer I wischyd in my wyl þat I her weld myȝt,
For to kepyn in my cage tyl wynter comyn were,   40
Þat sche were wery of þat wedyr and wold abyd somer.

19 fowlys] *McIntosh*, MS folows

Notes to the Text

(Abbreviated titles and line references for ME texts follow the usage of *MED*.)

1   Cf. *PP1.B* prol. 1: 'In a somer seson, whan softe was the sonne'; *Parl. 3 Ages* 2: 'And the sesone of somere when softe bene the wedres'.

2   Cf. *Destr.Troy* 12969: 'Hit was the moneth of May when mirthes begyn.' The 'maying' was not a mere literary convention in late medieval England; Stow gives details of the actual seasonal activities in London: 'In the Month of May, namely on May Day, in the Morning, every Man except Impediment would walk into the sweet Meadows and Green Woods, there to rejoice their Spirits with the Beauty and Savour of sweet Flowers, and with the Noise of Birds, praising God in their Kind . . . I find also that in the Month of May the citizens of London (of all Estates) lightly in every Parish, . . . had their several Mayings, and did fetch in Maypoles, with divers Warlike Shews, with good Archers, Morice Dancers, and other Devices for pastime all the Day long' (p. 252); *Sport with Birds and Dogs*: 'Many Citizens take delight in Birds, as Spar-hawks, Goss Hawks, and such like, and in Dogs to hunt in the wooddy Ground' (*Appendix*, p. 14). See J. Stow, *A Survey of the Cities of London and Westminster*, ed. J. Strype (London, 1720).

3   *sendyth*: 'sends a message' (down to us). See *OED Send* v.[1], 8: 'to send a message or messenger'.

tyl: use of this form as a preposition before a vowel conforms to N practice (cf. 6); *to* is used before a consonant.

6   *ham*: see above, p. 80.

bentys: plural of either *bent* 'coarse, long grass' (*MED, bent* n.(1), 1. (a); cf. *Patience* 392: 'Ne best bite on no brom, ne no bent nauþer'); or *bent* 'an open field' (*MED, bent* n.(1), 2. (a); cf. *Cleanness* 1679: 'Þou . . . on mor most abide . . . As best byte on þe bent of braken and erbes'). The plural form is recorded elsewhere only in the NEM *Florence* 1040: 'On felde they faght . . . Ovyr the bentys ranne the blode'; this might denote familiarity with common rather than poetic usage.

tyl: the usage here, as a preposition with the infinitive, is found only in N and NWM texts (see also 3).

8   *flauour*: MS *l* superimposed on previously-written *a* (i.e. *fa* was written first, in error).

9   *grys*: N and E dialect form of OE *gærs, græs*. Cf. *Parl. 3 Ages* 8: 'There the gryse was grene, growen with floures'; *Cursor* 8453: (Frf) 'grissis', (Göt) 'grisses'; *Quatref. Love* 66: 'grysse' (rhyming with 'blisse'). *MED*, s.v. *gras* n., records *i/y* forms in E. Anglia, Lincs. and Co. Durham; also (sense 5) in the Notts. place-name 'Grysthorp' [now Grassthorpe]. The metathesized form *girs(e)* occurs also in *Morte A., Awntyrs Arth.* and *BukeH*.

11 *laxt*: this must be a spelling or mis-spelling for *laȝt*. For *laȝt lust* = 'took pleasure in' cf. *Pearl* 1129: 'To loue þe Lombe his meyny in melle Iwysse I laȝt a gret delyt.'

somer: the repetition of this word from line 1 at the ends of lines 11 and 41 perhaps denotes an attempt at *dúnadh* (see n. 24).

12 *lenyd*: *n* and *u* are indistinguishable in the MS. *lenyd* has been preferred on the grounds of Langland's analogous phrase 'lened me to a Lenten' (*PPl.B* 18.5). Words common to the surrounding five lines of both contexts are: *I*, *tyme*, *long(e)*, *Lent(e/y)n*, *forth*, *aft(e/y)r*, *l(i/y)f*, *al*. The word *lenyd* comes either from (1) *lenen* (WS *hlinian*, N *hli(o)nian*) 'to lean on', as most probably in Langland: 'languished, laid low'—which would also make good sense here; but also 'to rely on', which would here give something like 'been self-sufficient'; or from (2) *lenen* (OE *hlænian*) 'to make lean'—thus 'fasted, abstained'. The ensuing phrases in line 13 lend weight to a reading based on (1).

16 *vnpouruayd* (of): 'unprovided, unfurnished, unsupplied' (with). *OED* states that the word was often stressed 'púrvey'; so the alliteration here is not at variance with the stress pattern. (For the expansion -*our*- see above, p. 82).

18 *Byschopys Woode*: land with rights of commons about three miles from the centre of the city (see above, pp. 78–9). Cf. Shirley's rubric to Lydgate's *A Mumming at Bishopswood* (Bodl. MS Ashmole 59 f. 62v): 'Bishop wood, Bishops hall, by Blethenhall greene'. Stow, using notes evidently taken from that MS, states: '. . . and of these Mayings [see note to line 2] we read in the reign of Henry VI that the Aldermen and Sheriffs of London being on May day at the Bishop of Londons Wood in the parish of Stebunheath [Stepney] and having there a worshipful dinner for themselves and other commers Lydgate the poet . . . sent to them . . . a ioiful commendation of that season' (IV. 252).

19 *fowlys*: MS *folows*. Although several readings are possible, *fowlys*, miswritten in anticipation of *felaw* later in the line, gives the most cogent reading. Professor McIntosh further points out, in correspondence, that *fol* deleted for *fowle* (22) furnishes supporting evidence that the writer has difficulty with the follow-on from graph *f* in the vicinity of graph *l*; see also note to line 8; and cf. *Cath.Angl.* (Monson) 137a: 'folowe (MS *fowlo*)'.

felaw: 'playfellow or companion'. Cf. *SLeg.Brendan* (Ld) 218: 'þe fowel . . . to his felawes wende'.

22 *fowle*: MS *fol* deleted before *fowle*.

27 *fluschyd*: 'moved rapidly or violently, rushed, darted or sprang': see *MED* *flusshen* v. (a). The etymology is uncertain, but the verb appears to be cognate with *flashen/ fleshen* (connected to *flashe* n. (partly imitative) from OF *flache* and MD *vlacke* 'a watery, swampy place') 'as if to splash water'—used also of the noise and movement of birds. Cf. *Mum & S. (1)* 2.166: 'But the blernyd boynard þat his bagg stall . . . Made þe fawcon to floter and flussh for anger'.

frayd: see *MED fraien* v. (1); *OED Fray* v.[1] The sense may be either 'made a noise or disturbance, quarrelled, fought' (*MED* 1. (a) or (b), *OED* 5) or 'was afraid' (*MED* 2. (b), *OED* †3), perhaps with the implication 'started for fear'.

28   *bot*: MS *b* superimposed on previously-written **t**.

30   *myrth for to mak here*: 'to bring her joy'.

34   *wengys*: a word of Norse origin which eventually replaced the ME *fether* 'wing', from OE *feþer* 'feather' and OE *fiðere/ fiþera* (pl. *fiþru*) 'wing'; e.g. Chaucer *Bo.* (Rob.) 4.pr.1.66: 'I shal fycchen fetheris in thi thought'. It first appears in ME in pl. forms (*wenge, wengen, wenges*) and is more commonly found with *y* as vowel in EM, WM and S dialects.

35   *lyme*: OE *līm*: 'anything sticky such as mud, glue or bird-lime'. (*PParv.*(Hrl 221): 'LYME, to take wythe byrdys. *Viscus.*') Bird-lime was a common and readily-available commodity. Although sour dough, oak gall, mistletoe or fish glue—or, more latterly, linseed—might be employed (see *Chauliac*, passim), in England bird-lime was mostly made from the bark and shoots of the holly tree (a detailed recipe is given by Gervase Markham in his *Hungers Prevention* (London, 1621), ff. 280–5). Although the substance was used in various ways (see J. M. Bechstein, *Cage and Chamber Birds*, ed. H. G. Adams (London, 1892), and Markham), it can be conjectured that to trap a bird that had alighted 'fast . . . besyde' a poet, the plan would be to touch it gently with a long limed rod to which it would stick fast and be his. Cf. Chaucer *CT.WB.* D 934; Lydg. *CB* 268; and Shakespeare (see the quotations in *OED s.v. Lime* sb.[1], 1.b).

36   *cheuysch*: 'supply' (OF *chevisser*).

charmys: charms were frowned on by the Church (see *Cursor* 28006–8; *Wycl.Apol.* 93–4; but cf. Chaucer *CT.Kn.* A 2712). There is widespread evidence of the charming of snakes (e.g. Trev. *Barth.* 269; *NHom.(3) Leg.Suppl.Hrl.* 257), but not of the charming of their prey by hunters or fowlers; and only *Wið Ymbe*, the eleventh-century Bee Charm (Corpus Christi College, Cambridge MS 41, f. 182), indicates something of the formulae that might have been practised: '. . . forweorp ofer great þonne hi swirman, and cweþ: Sitte ge, sigewif, sigað to eorþan. Naefre ge wilde to wuda fleogan' (edited in G. Storms, *Anglo-Saxon Magic* (The Hague, 1948), p. 132).

chaunting of bryddys: drawing birds to lime twigs or net could be effected either by one's skill in imitating their notes (see Markham, f. 128)—a superior skill, in the view of true fowlers; or by the use of a device named a 'bird call' (see Burton, *Anatomy* II. ii. 4: 'pipes, calls . . . Quail-pipes'). Bechstein mentions calls made of leather and leg bones (of cat, hare, goose or stork) which 'may be purchased for a trifle' (p. 477). Naturally one imitated the call of the opposite sex of the bird to be caught.

38   *þorg*: a spelling otherwise unrecorded. It seems likely that the writer employed a *g* for *ʒ*.

40   *kepyn*: MS *k* looks like *l*; but the writer appears to have had trouble with graph *k* whenever it is followed by another letter. The substitution of *l* for *k* is a common weakness in copying (see *Pearl* 369), and possibly also in handwriting. *kepyn* is the only -*yn* infinitive in the text—perhaps used because of the following vowel (but cf. *to lyf in*, 11).

    cage: on the keeping of birds in medieval England see the definitive article by B. Yapp, 'Birds in Captivity in the Middle Ages', *Archives of Natural History* 10 (1982) 479–500.

41   *somer*: see note to 11.

Middle English Literature

The Owl and the Nightingale *and the Bishops*

NICOLAS JACOBS

The argument against the customary attribution of *The Owl and the Nightingale* to Nicholas of Guildford on the grounds of the apparent plea for preferment made on his behalf implicitly in lines 187–214 and explicitly in lines 1751–78 is put most clearly by E. G. Stanley in his edition of the poem:

> The reason for doubting that Nicholas is the author is not that, if he were, he would be praising himself too much. . . . [but] in the poet's charge that Nicholas's superiors abuse their power and corruptly and nepotistically make over the emoluments from ecclesiastical offices to those unfit to discharge them. . . . he must have known that, if his superiors were to see O&N, his vague accusations would lead to resentful repression, not advancement.[1]

The charge against the ecclesiastical authorities of irresponsibility in refusing preferment to Nicholas, so that he languishes in the wilds of Dorset while parochial revenues are appropriated to provide sinecures for less worthy and able persons, is indeed one which might be expected to give offence to the very powers whose favour Nicholas needs.[2] Yet, placed as it is at the conclusion of the poem and constituting as it does, together with the high valuation placed on his talents, the one point of substance on which the two quarrelsome fowls are able to agree, it is inevitably thrown into prominence and is hard to interpret other than in promotional terms. But if, as a piece of self-promotion, the poem is destined to defeat its own object, there is no reason why it should be thought any more opportune by virtue of being someone else's work.

   Though Stanley does not directly address this objection, his hypothesis that 'the unknown poet sent his poem to Nicholas, his friend, a learned cleric,

[1] *The Owl and the Nightingale* (London, 1960; rev. 1962), p. 21; see also Kathryn Hume, *The Owl and the Nightingale: The Poem and its Critics* (Toronto, 1975), pp. 124–6.
[2] Dr Jeremy Catto reminds me that Stanley's argument is not absolutely conclusive, since the bishops were probably used to criticism of the kind here directed at them.

esteemed by all the world for his sound judgment'—as a consolation, we infer, for his failure to obtain advancement—suggests that he has taken note of it. But the suggestion is not convincing. A poem of the length and ingenuity of *O&N* is unlikely to have been intended as a merely private compliment; and the fact of its preservation in at least two copies demonstrates that it attained a wider circulation, whether or not it was originally intended to do so. In terms of the likely damage to the intended beneficiary's interest there is little to choose between deliberately making the poem public and allowing it to seep into circulation. Unless we are prepared to postulate an author who wished to flatter Nicholas to his face while at the same time contriving to discredit him in the eyes of higher authority, we should look for circumstances in which it might be possible to criticize in general terms the conduct of ecclesiastical authority without giving offence to its current representatives. The inauguration of the episcopate of a new bishop presents an obvious possibility, and it may prove useful to look in detail at the relevant instances.

The periods to be considered are limited rather severely by the reference in lines 1091–2 to 'þe king Henri—Iesus his soule do merci!' The arguments of H. B. Hinckley that this expression need not refer to a dead person have not been widely accepted by scholars;[3] further, the bare reference to the king's name without qualification appears to rule out composition in the reign of any king called Henry (see Stanley, pp. 131–2, for a detailed discussion). This confines the composition of the poem to the reigns of Stephen (1135–54), Richard I and John (1189–1216) or Edward I and his successors (after 1272). Even if a date as early as the reign of Stephen were credible on linguistic or metrical grounds, it would be excluded by the evidence that the poet knew Alexander Neckam's *De naturis rerum* (between 1187 and 1199) and, probably but less certainly, Marie de France's *Fables* and *Lais*, both of which were composed at some time in the last third of the twelfth century.[4] Stanley considered a date after 1272 to be too late (p. 132), but this depends on the conventional assumption of a date for the Cotton MS in the first half of the thirteenth century. N. R. Ker subsequently proposed a date in the second half of the century for both surviving MSS,[5] and this might permit the possibility of composition during an indeterminate period at the beginning of Edward I's

---

[3] 'The Date, Author and Sources of *The Owl and the Nightingale*', *PMLA* 44 (1929) 329–59; his arguments are conclusively exploded by F. Tupper in 'The Date and Historical Background of *The Owl and the Nightingale*', *PMLA* 49 (1934) 406–27.

[4] See *The Owl and the Nightingale*, ed. J. W. H. Atkins (Cambridge, 1922), pp. lxii–lxvii.

[5] *The Owl and the Nightingale*: Facsimile of the Jesus and Cotton Manuscripts, EETS OS 251 (1963 for 1962), p. ix; Frederick Madden had dated the MS 'probably at the close of Henry III's reign', *Laȝamon's Brut or Chronicle of Britain* (London, 1847), p. xxxv. Professor Stanley, accepting Ker's dating, would now place the poem in the second third of the thirteenth century (private communication).

reign. But the period 1189–1216, to which other evidence also points, remains the most promising possibility.

Portesham in Dorset, where Nicholas of Guildford is said to have resided, lies in the diocese of Salisbury; parts of Guildford itself were annexed to the church of Godalming, which was at the time in question appropriated to the prebend of Heytesbury in the same diocese.[6] It is thus natural to consider the position at Salisbury rather than elsewhere. There were two changes of bishop there in the reigns of Richard I and John. After the death of Bishop Jocelin in November 1184 there was an interregnum of five years during which the diocese was administered by Herbert Poore, archdeacon of Canterbury, Jordan, dean of Salisbury, and Richard fitz Ebrard (the last of whom I have so far been unable to identify). Herbert Poore was the natural son of Richard of Ilchester, bishop of Winchester 1174–88; in addition to his office at Canterbury he held at this time canonries at both Lincoln and Salisbury, and his abilities may be surmised from the fact that in 1186 both chapters chose him as bishop. The king, however, refused to accept his election at Lincoln, where St Hugh was subsequently elected; and when later in the same year Herbert was elected bishop of Salisbury with the king's approval, the election was disallowed on appeal to the pope on the grounds of Herbert's illegitimacy.[7] On 15 September 1189, shortly after Richard's coronation, Hubert Walter, dean of York, was elected bishop of Salisbury, and occupied the see until 1193, though absent from his diocese, and from England, on the king's service for almost the whole period. In the latter year, little more than a month after his return to England, he was elected archbishop of Canterbury.[8] Herbert Poore is on record as having appealed to the pope against this election, albeit only on the technical grounds that the king was in captivity at the time and that the bishops of England were not present at the election.[9] He himself was elected to the see of Salisbury in the following year, and occupied it until his death in 1217, when he was succeeded by his brother Richard.

[6] It was not, *pace* Gadow (see note 13 below), Atkins (p. xxxvi), and Stanley (p. 21), itself part of the diocese, or under its jurisdiction. Godalming was granted to the cathedral of Salisbury, together with some adjacent lands, by a charter of Henry I between 1109 and 1117: *Sarum Charters and Documents*, ed. W. Rich Jones and W. D. Macray, RS [97] 1891, p. 3. It was not a peculiar in the strict sense, in that presentations to the vicarage were subject to the consent of the diocesan (the bishop of Winchester) and institutions performed by him, and the church was subject to visitation by the archdeacon of Surrey. This is clear from the documents relating to Richard of Chiddingfold, perpetual vicar from 1185, which are transcribed in *Vetus Registrum Sarisberiense* (= *Registrum S. Osmundi*), ed. W. H. Rich Jones, RS [78] 1883, I. 298–303.

[7] 'Benedict of Peterborough', *Gesta Regis Henrici Secundi*, ed. W. Stubbs, RS [49] 1867, I. 346, 352.

[8] On his career, see C. R. Cheney, *Hubert Walter* (London, 1976).

[9] Roger of Howden, *Chronica*, ed. W. Stubbs, RS [51] 1870, III. 213.

Herbert Poore is celebrated, though the work was not carried out until after his death, as the prime mover in the abandonment of the site of Old Sarum and the refounding of Salisbury, together with the construction of the existing cathedral, on its present site. His zeal for the interests of his diocese is illustrated by his action at the council of Oxford in 1198, where he followed the example of Hugh bishop of Lincoln in refusing to supply, as a magnate of the kingdom, three hundred knights for a year for the king's service in France; thus incurring a severe financial penalty and provoking, if we are to believe Hugh's biographer, an explosion of rage on the part of the archbishop.[10]

The succession of Richard Poore to the bishopric in 1217 took place so early in the reign of the infant Henry III that the reference to 'þe king Henri' might conceivably be taken still to refer back to the earlier reign. But a reference to the shortcomings of the preceding bishop could hardly be expected to be well received when he was succeeded by his brother; in particular the allegation that bishops are altogether too inclined to bestow preferment within their families would seem inept in the circumstances. In seeking a period when such criticisms could be made without giving offence we are therefore restricted to the successions of Hubert and of Herbert to the bishopric.

It would be possible to construct, on the basis of some incidents already noted in the careers of the two men, a history of opposition between Hubert Walter and Herbert Poore which could be elaborated into a hypothesis that the complaints expressed in O&N might obtain a sympathetic hearing from Herbert. As an able and ambitious prelate with strong worldly concerns Hubert was certainly in a position to make enemies; the protracted dispute between him and the monks of Christ Church, Canterbury, over his attempts to found a college of secular canons at Lambeth demonstrates the intensity of antagonism which he could, perhaps inadvertently, arouse; and though his statements throughout the dispute appear to be characterized by patience and restraint, it should not be assumed that all the right was on his side: powerful men can afford to affect patience.[11] Hubert's willingness to enlist the secular power in his own interest lays him open to the charge of secularity of outlook: this certainly underlies the frequent disagreements between him and Hugh of Lincoln when he became archbishop (*Magna Vita*, IV. 6, 7; V. 3, 5, 7, 16); and, as he was hardly ever in the diocese of Salisbury during his tenure of the

[10] *Magna Vita S. Hugonis*, ed. Decima L. Douie and Dom Hugh Farmer OSB (London, 1961-2), v. 5.

[11] *Epistolae Cantuarienses*, ed. W. Stubbs as *Chronicles and Memorials of the Reign of Richard I*, II, RS [38] 1865, pp. 366–538. Hubert's proposal in establishing the college seems to have been to provide canonries for the scholars, lawyers and administrators of his circle; the monks evidently saw it potentially as a rival cathedral and as an infringement of their privileges, and at least claimed to be defending the jurisdiction of Rome against secular encroachment. For discussions, see Stubbs's introduction and Cheney, pp. 135–57.

see owing to his absence on crusade with the king, an ill-disposed observer could perhaps have regarded him as sacrificing the well-being of his flock to the interests of the state.

Whether all this is sufficient ground for supposing that the failure of Nicholas of Guildford to obtain preferment could have been attributed to Hubert's neglect of his duties and could have been put forward as a state of affairs that Herbert might be expected to rectify is, if we attribute to Nicholas any judgement at all, doubtful. Nor is nepotism evidently a charge which could reasonably have been brought against Hubert. Even if he had been so inclined, he had not been in a position to favour his family at Salisbury, and it is perhaps significant, given his talent for making enemies, that he appears never to have been seriously accused of it. His appropriation to his brother Theobald of the right to collect fees in respect of licences for tournaments, which Richard had entrusted to William earl of Salisbury (Roger of Howden, III. 268), is a trivial instance and has nothing to do with ecclesiastical preferment. That he owed the rapidity of his promotion, at least in part, to his being the nephew of Ranulf Glanvill, chief justiciar 1181–9, can hardly be doubted; but in the acrimonious controversies in which he was later to be involved there is no hint of improper favours to his family. To accuse him of intending to fill his proposed college at Lambeth with his own kinsmen would have been an irresistible debating point for the monks of Canterbury had there been the least foundation for the charge; and even Gerald of Wales, whose quarrel with Hubert was to a large extent over the intrusion of unworthy nominees at St David's and Bangor, refrains, while charging him with heresy, simony, unchastity and bad grammar (not to mention such trivia as arson and murder), from accusing him of nepotism.[12] It is easiest to believe that, whatever defects Hubert may have had as a pastor, he was at least scrupulous, and was known to be so, in such matters. Further, the circumstances in which Herbert's election as bishop of Salisbury had been nullified some eight years earlier probably constitute a conclusive argument against reading the relevant passage of *O&N* as a plea directed to him. The late bishop of Winchester's bastard, however well he may have overcome the reproach of his birth, could hardly be expected to look favourably on the assertion that bishops unfairly promoted their kinsmen.

If we may accept rather that the poet's strictures are in large part a commonplace of complaint (see Atkins, p. 150, for evidence that such abuses were in fact widespread), the unfair neglect of Nicholas of Guildford may be

---

[12] Giraldus Cambrensis, *De Invectionibus*, ed. W. S. Davies, *Y Cymmrodor* 30 (1920), I. 5, 10. Gerald himself was guilty of a particularly shameless instance in 1203, and that apparently with Hubert's connivance; see Brynley F. Roberts, *Gerald of Wales* (Cardiff, 1982), pp. 50–1. But nothing we know of his character suggests that he would have refrained earlier on from accusing Hubert of the abuse had there been any basis for doing so.

as well attributed to the absence of any bishop whatsoever as to the irresponsibility of any particular one; and it would be perfectly reasonable to see Hubert Walter himself as the bishop who would rectify the situation: whether at the time of his succession after the lengthy interregnum in 1189 or at the time of his return to England in 1193 (when there was reason to hope that he would at last be able to resume his long-interrupted diocesan duties). In the event, of course, even if the administration of the diocese was in need of reform, Hubert had no time to reform it at either juncture; and if the Nicholas of the poem is the *Nicholaus capellanus archidiaconi* of 1209 (*Sarum Charters and Documents*, p. 73) or the *Nicholaus submonitor capituli de Gudeford* of 1220,[13] he must have been rescued from the tedium of rural existence in the time of Herbert Poore, whatever offence the poem might have given to the latter; but then there is no evidence that any contemporary bishop ever read the poem.

As between 1189 and 1193, the internal evidence favours the later date. The reference in line 1732 to the king's being neither dead nor incapacitated was taken by F. Tupper, in his still valuable study of the historical allusions in the poem (pp. 416–17), to refer to Richard's frail health during the Crusade, 1190–3, and in particular to John's false claim before the justices of England in January of the latter year that Richard was dead: a claim which, like the Wren, they did not believe (Roger of Howden, III. 204–5). Whether or not the allusion is as specific as this, a reference to Richard's captivity seems inevitable, and would fit well with Hubert's return to England on 20 April 1193 and the consequent reassertion of royal authority. The reference in line 1731 to the king's peace[14] may also suggest a compliment to Hubert as the king's trusted representative and defender of his right against the supporters of John, even though he was not appointed justiciar until January 1194, nor was his proclamation for the preservation of the King's peace issued until 1195.

As a man already distinguished in ecclesiastical administration Hubert might be expected to take a vigorous interest in church appointments; as one whom both family background and personal experience had made familiar with the operations of the law he might be disposed to enjoy the elegant

---

[13] *Vetus Registrum Sarisberiense*, I. 297. Since none of the churches in Guildford was collegiate the significance of the expression is rather obscure, unless the chapter is that of Salisbury and Nicholas of Guildford is the man's usual name. The possibility of these identifications was first raised by W. Gadow ('Das me. Streitgedicht Eule u. Nachtigall', *Palaestra* 65 (1909) 12–13), who characterizes the *submonitor* as one 'der die Mitglieder eines Kapitels zur Versammlung zu rufen hatte.' W. H. Rich Jones thought he was 'probably a similar officer to the one that in Chaucer is called the "Sompnour"': in which case poor Nicholas, if it was he, had indeed come down in the world.

[14] A reference to the king is clearly intended here, though the word *kinge* was lost from the archetype and, curiously, not restored in either surviving manuscript.

parody of legal procedures and the shrewd exposition of forensic shifts and prevarications presented in *O&N*. As an ambitious churchman strongly aware of the claims of the secular world he might well appreciate a poem in which that world, if not allowed the final triumph, is at least given its due. Nicholas of Guildford, if he was the author, could reasonably have hoped that the return of such a bishop to his diocese would occasion a change in his own fortunes, and that the circulation of *O&N* would be one way of bringing his talents to the bishop's notice in not too heavy-handed a manner. All this is speculation, but it is not implausible. What remains curious is that he should have chosen to keep those talents concealed in the decent obscurity of an unlearned language.

So far I have assumed that the poet's praise of Nicholas, his complaints at his continuing neglect, and his promotion of his cause are to be taken, at least to some degree, seriously. But it is equally open to us to take them ironically. If Nicholas was not a man of talent languishing in undeserved obscurity but a well-known figure of fun whose notorious ineptitude made the remotest corner of the diocese the safest place to put him, everything that is adduced in his favour (from his reformation after a misspent youth and his present judicious sobriety to his discernment in dialectic and music) could be taken as a joke; and the claim that his obscurity is the result of the negligence or nepotism of bishops would be so far off target that no bishop could possibly take umbrage at it. The evident absurdity of the two avian disputants and the difficulty of finding a coherent subject in their debate have led some commentators (notably Kathryn Hume, pp. 101–32) to interpret the poem as a burlesque, and the submission of the dispute to the arbitration of a well-known nonentity would fit well with such a view. To have composed the burlesque not only in English but in English verse modelled, with a combined meticulousness and lightness of touch for which there is no precedent and no parallel for another hundred and fifty years, on the French octosyllables of polite literature, could then be seen as a *jeu d'esprit* comparable in technical terms to composing such a poem in a highly-wrought literary language—with the added refinement or anti-refinement that the chosen language was not, say, Provençal or neo-classical Latin, but the despised vernacular of the lower classes in England.

Such a hypothesis would have serious consequences. It is of little account that Nicholas of Guildford could hardly be considered any longer as a likely candidate for authorship: we are too obsessed already with putting names to anonymous works, and as a compensation we should be able to accept Tupper's arguments in favour of a date around 1196 without having to worry about which bishop might or might not be offended. But the status of the poem as an unexpected but prophetic manifestation of the English genius in an obscure period, or as a miracle of freshness, wit and urbanity in which for the first time we see the twelfth-century renaissance reflected in an English-language culture—and few who have taught the poem can have avoided making judgements of this kind at some stage of their career—would be considerably undermined if much of its point could be demonstrated to lie in the incongruity between the urbanity of the matter and the rusticity of its medium. That, to those of us who have come to love the poem, would be a pity.

The Avowing of King Arthur

J. A. BURROW

It has been the fate of *The Avowing of King Arthur* to be overshadowed by another Northern Middle English romance of a similar, indeed a confusable, name: *The Awntyrs of Arthur*. Whereas the *Awntyrs* survives in four manuscript copies and has been edited no less than twelve times, the *Avowing* is found only in the Ireland Blackburne Manuscript (preceded even there, ominously, by the *Awntyrs*) and has only lately become available in a scholarly edition.[1] Nor have critics or literary historians paid the poem much attention: there have been no studies of it to compare with recent discussions of the *Awntyrs* by Hanna and Spearing.[2] In his edition of the *Awntyrs*, Hanna has occasion to refer to the *Avowing* because it shares with his text a setting at Tarn Wadling; but he is evidently not impressed: 'Although [the *Avowing*] is intended to be a comic production, its jokes suffer from the poet's crude execution. The poet establishes certain expectations, only to destroy them in rather broad ways; for example, the title refers to a series of vows, only two of which are successfully completed. In the last half of the poem Baldwin reveals (and is applauded for) some most unchivalrous sentiments about women' (p. 34).[3]

---

[1] *The Avowing of King Arthur*, ed. Roger Dahood, Garland Medieval Texts 10 (New York, 1984), entirely superseding the edition by Christopher Brookhouse, '*Sir Amadace*' and '*The Avowing of Arthur*', Anglistica 15 (Copenhagen, 1968). The poem has otherwise been available only in *Middle English Metrical Romances*, ed. W. H. French and C. B. Hale (New York, 1930). The two most recent editions of the *Awntyrs* are by Robert J. Gates (Philadelphia, Pa, 1969) and Ralph Hanna III (Manchester, 1974).

[2] Derek Pearsall's single mention of the *Avowing* on p. 144 of his *Old and Middle English Poetry* (London, 1977) may be compared with his discussion of the *Awntyrs* on pp. 185–7. The only substantial study of the *Avowing* was published eighty years ago: E. A. Greenlaw, 'The Vows of Baldwin: A Study in Mediæval Fiction', *PMLA* 21 (1906) 575–636. On the *Awntyrs*, see Ralph Hanna III, '*The Awntyrs off Arthure*: An Interpretation', *MLQ* 31 (1970) 275–97, and three discussions by A. C. Spearing: '*The Awntyrs off Arthure*', in *The Alliterative Tradition in the Fourteenth Century*, ed. Bernard S. Levy and Paul E. Szarmach (Kent, Ohio, 1981), pp. 183–202; 'Central and Displaced Sovereignty in Three Medieval Poems', *RES* NS 33 (1982) 248–52; and his *Medieval to Renaissance in English Poetry* (Cambridge, 1985), pp. 121–42.

[3] Similarly, Dahood's critical remarks in his edition of the *Avowing* (pp. 36–8) are unduly apologetic.

When Hanna speaks of 'crude execution', he presumably has in mind the poet's rather rough handling (to judge from the surviving copy) of his sixteen-line tail-rhyme stanza—a metrical form which the *Avowing* shares with two other Northern romances of the time, *Sir Perceval of Galles* and *Sir Degrevant*. The effect is indeed sometimes negligent, not least by comparison with the much more elaborate thirteen-line stanzas of the *Awntyrs*, where rhyme combines with alliteration and stanza-linking to produce an impression of sustained and strenuous artifice. The *Awntyrs* must certainly have been a more difficult poem to write. Yet the author of the *Avowing* is also capable, as we shall see, of strong and memorable writing; and the organization of his poem, which resembles that of the *Awntyrs*, quite surpasses it in subtlety of conception. Indeed, for its conception if not for its execution, the *Avowing* deserves to rank with the best of the English medieval romances.

Spearing has given a good account of the structure of the *Awntyrs*, comparing it to a diptych. The poem is composed, he argues, of two parts of roughly equal length which are juxtaposed in such a way as to generate or create meaning by their conjunction: 'In both parts of the poem, the Arthurian civilization is faced with the challenge of an apparently hostile outsider: supernatural in the first, in the form of Guinevere's mother risen from her grave; human in the second, in the form of Galeron, come to demand his lands'.[4] The ghost's prophecy of doom, in the supernatural first part, casts a shadow across the second panel of the diptych, upon which the activities of Arthurian knighthood are displayed in all their customary splendour, threatened but not invalidated by what is to come. Spearing cites *Golagros and Gawane* as another 'diptych' romance, but not the *Avowing*. Yet the *Avowing* offers a more striking parallel. It falls—if allowance is made for one stanza which has clearly lost a quatrain in transmission—into two exactly equal halves, of 576 lines each.[5] The first half, set in the adventurous forest of Inglewood and its environs, corresponds to the second part of the *Awntyrs* in that it concerns a series of Arthurian encounters of the conventional sort. In fulfilment of their respective vows, Arthur kills a fearsome boar, Kay meets and is unhorsed by a stranger knight, Sir Menealfe of the Mountain, and Gawain succeeds in defeating Sir Menealfe and rescuing the damsel whom he

---

[4] *The Alliterative Tradition*, pp. 185–6. On 'diptych' structure in medieval narrative generally, see William W. Ryding, *Structure in Medieval Narrative* (The Hague, 1971), pp. 25–7, 40–3, 112–39. Ryding finds this kind of structure to be characteristic of such twelfth-century romances as those of Chrétien de Troyes, being superseded in the thirteenth century by *entrelacement*.

[5] The defective stanza is no. xviii. Dahood thinks that its short form 'may be authorial' (p. 31), but gives no reason why. A scribe could easily lose a quatrain by eye-skip in such tail-rhyme stanzas. The Lincoln MS of *Sir Degrevant* has clearly lost quatrains in this way after lines 220, 296, and 1188: see *The Romance of Sir Degrevant*, ed. L. F. Casson, EETS OS 221 (1949), pp. xvi, xxviii.

has abducted. Like the second part of the *Awntyrs*, this first half of the *Avowing* ends with the return of Arthur and his knights to Carlisle and the reception of Gawain's defeated adversary into the fellowship of the Round Table:

> And sekirly, wythouten fabull,
> Þus dwellus he atte þe Rowun Tabull
> As prest knyʒte and preveabull
>   Wyth schild and wyth spere.   (569–72)[6]

However, the reception of Sir Menealfe into the Round Table, unlike that of Sir Galeron in the *Awntyrs*, does not mark the end of the story. A fourth knight, Sir Baldwin, had accompanied Arthur, Kay, and Gawain into Inglewood. Since his vows were of a somewhat peculiar kind and so did not require his continued presence in the forest, he had gone straight home to bed in his lodgings; but once the business of his three companions had been completed, Kay reminds the king—not without a touch of his characteristic stirring malice—that Baldwin has still to be tested, thus neatly introducing the second half of the poem. This half matches the first not only because it occupies precisely the same number of stanzas, thirty-six, but also because it too concerns three vows. For Baldwin, unlike his companions, had made not one but three vows: never to fear death, never to refuse any man his meat, and never to be jealous of his wife. The rest of the poem, most of which takes place at Baldwin's castle home, describes how he fulfils each of these resolutions in turn, winning at last the highest praise from his comrades:

> And þou hase holdin all þat þou hiʒte
>   As a kniʒte schulde.   (1143–4)

The comment by Ralph Hanna just quoted quite wrongly suggests that the plot of the *Avowing* is not well developed from its initial postulates ('the poet establishes certain expectations, only to destroy them in rather broad ways'). No reader of Arthurian stories would expect Kay to match his words with deeds; but the vows of his three companions are all fulfilled in varied and interesting ways, culminating in the triumph of Sir Baldwin. Unlike the *Awntyrs*, in fact, the *Avowing* is held together by a strong and well-articulated plot: the two panels of the diptych are firmly hinged. The fact that the second half of the *Avowing* has already been set up by Baldwin's vows in the first distinguishes this narrative from the looser kind of diptych structure to be found in the *Awntyrs* and in most of the instances discussed by Ryding. Yet it

---

[6] This conclusion is marked by echoes of the opening description of the Round Table: 'Þis is no fantum ne no fabull./ ʒe wote wele of þe Rowun Tabull,/ Of prest men and priveabull/ Was holdun in prise' (17–20). The whole poem is rounded off by a similar echo of its first line in its last: 'He þat made us on þe mulde', 'That made us on þe mulde'.

is true that the second half of the poem, like the first part of the *Awntyrs*, does offer something of a contrast and a surprise, set off against the more conventional Arthurian subjects of its facing panel. Indeed the chief interest of the *Avowing*, as of the *Awntyrs*, lies in the teasing relationship between its two parts: 'Look here upon this picture, and on this. . . .'

To call the first half of the *Avowing* conventional does less than justice to the vivid night-scenes which the poet paints on his left panel. The sun is already setting on the forest of Inglewood, with its mysterious tarn and its 'adventurous oak', when the four knights make their vows in the presence of the great boar.[7] The first of the three adventures which follow, Arthur's fight with the boar, is a wild and perilous affair: the boar is broader than a bull, higher than a horse, and as black as a bear, with tusks three feet long, and his den is full of the bones of dead hounds and men. Yet despite these childish extravagances, the shaping power of chivalry is such that even this encounter takes the orderly form of a knightly joust. Arthur first rides a course against the monster and shatters his spear against his adversary's 'shield'—here an aptly used technical term for the thick hide of a boar:

> Þenne þe kinge spanes his spere
> Opon þat bore for to bere;
> Þer may no dyntus him dere,
>   So sekir was his schilde.
> Þe grete schafte þat was longe
> All to spildurs hit spronge;
> Þe gode stede þat was stronge
>   Was fallun in þe filde.   (193–200)

Like any jousting knight who has lost his spear and his horse, Arthur now tackles his adversary with a sword on foot; and this second phase of the encounter ends with the death of the boar, impaled through the throat up to the hilt of the king's sword. After 'brittening' the carcase according to the laws of venery, Arthur falls asleep, exhausted.

There follow the adventures of Kay and Gawain, both of whom have vowed in true chivalric fashion to 'wake' the night through and encounter whatever chance may bring—Kay at the adventurous oak, Gawain at Tarn Wadling. Hanna rightly observes that the ensuing events are less thrilling and outlandish than their nocturnal settings promise (ed. cit., p. 34); but what the poem requires at this point, as I understand it, is precisely some rather plain and workaday Arthurian action—something drawn out of stock. Accordingly, the poet turns to the traditional twin themes of prowess and courtesy, and exemplifies these essential knightly qualities in a time-honoured way, by

---

[7] Greenlaw (p. 577, n. 1) notes other examples of the custom of vowing upon an animal.

contrasting Gawain's conduct with Kay's. When Kay encounters Sir Menealfe leading his abducted damsel through the forest, he makes all the right noises, swearing to take vengeance on the recreant knight and to release his captive; but he ends up flat on his back in the grass. This experience sobers him temporarily. Addressing Menealfe now as 'Sir' and using the polite plural form 'ye', he pleads that Gawain should have the opportunity to ransom him by jousting with his captor. There follow at Tarn Wadling two courses of joust, in which Gawain wins first Kay and then the damsel from the stranger knight. When Kay first arrived with Menealfe at the tarn, he was still subdued, answering Gawain's soldierly 'Who is there?' with an uncharacteristic humility:

> He sayd, 'I, Kay, þat þou knawes,
> Þat owte of tyme bostus and blawus.
> Butte þou me lese wyth þi lawes,
>   I lif nevyr more.'   (353–6)

But once Gawain has defeated Menealfe at the first encounter, Kay reverts to his boasting and blowing, crowing most uncourteously over an adversary defeated by another's prowess. When the stranger is knocked off his horse at the second encounter, Kay's renewed jeering draws from Sir Gawain a memorable reproach:

> Quod Kay, 'Þi leve hase þou loste,
> For all þi brag or þi boste.
> If þou have oȝte on hur coste,
>   I telle hit fortente.'
> Thenne speke Gavan to Kay,
> 'A mons happe is notte ay.
> Is none so sekur of asay,
>   Butte he may harmes hente.'   (429–36)

Here, just as in the episode of Chrétien's *Perceval* where the same two knights make their very different approaches to Perceval in his love-trance, Gawain's famed courtesy is shown off, by contrast with the egregious Kay, as a noble manifestation of fine feeling and humanity.[8] His proverbial utterance, 'A mons happe is notte ay', while handsomely attributing whatever success he may have enjoyed to 'hap' or good fortune, suggests also something deeper than a mere courteous disclaimer. Courtesy here springs from a grave sense of those uncertainties of life to which all men are equally subject as fellow-

---

[8] *Le Roman de Perceval*, ed. W. Roach, 2nd edn (Geneva, 1959), lines 4164–509. Compare particularly the 'gab' addressed by Kay to Saigremors, who has just been unhorsed by Perceval, and Arthur's reproof: 'ce n'est pas buen/ Qu'isi vos gabez des preudomes' (4280–1).

sufferers.[9] It is an impressive moment, which should discourage one from looking for any easy critique of Arthurian chivalry in the second half of the poem. Such chivalry, as Sir Gawain here represents it, is no light matter.

Dawn breaks and rouses King Arthur from his sleep in another part of the forest. Summoned by his bugle-call, Gawain and Kay, together with Menealfe and the damsel, join him for their return to Carlisle:

> And hiet hamward gode spede.
> Bothe þe birde and þe brede
>   To Carlele þay bringe.   (490–2)

The spoils of the night, here so unceremoniously coupled in a single chiming line (the maiden and the meat!), are carried back to court; and the stranger knight, commanded by Gawain to submit to Guinevere's will, is commended by her to the king as a worthy addition to the Round Table. Thus the first half of the poem ends as it began, in fine traditional Arthurian style.

Nothing is known about the immediate sources of *The Avowing of Arthur*, but it is clear that the materials of its two parts have quite different origins. Whereas the first part is drawn out of Arthurian stock, the second has its affiliations not with courtly romance but with popular fiction. The story of Baldwin's three vows belongs, as Greenlaw showed in his excellent essay, to a very common type of tale, 'The Three Counsels', here adapted to its chivalric context by converting counsels into vows (p. 600). The story in its favourite form, summarized by Greenlaw (who gives numerous examples), runs as follows: 'Three counsels as to one's conduct are obtained by a person either as a wage for work performed or as a purchase; afterwards the life of the fortunate possessor of these maxims is saved by his observance of them in time of peril; or, in case he forgets them, he suffers the loss of property or of life' (p. 581). Greenlaw further observes that the maxims commonly enshrined in these stories are of a popular kind: 'We are in an atmosphere quite different from that of courtly romance. These are stories born of the people. There are cautions against hasty temper, cautions against the dangers of travel, cynical remarks about women, emphasis on the homely virtues' (p. 595).

This double ancestry of the *Avowing* might lead one to look for some direct opposition or violent clash between its two parts, the courtly and the 'popular'—to the detriment of the unity of the piece. Yet the poet's *conjointure* does not fall apart in this way. Contrasts between its two parts there certainly are, but these are of a subtle and muted kind. A comparison of Baldwin's vows with those of his three companions will illustrate this.

---

[9] 'A man's hap is not ay' is cited as a proverb by B. J. Whiting. He gives no further examples, but compares other proverbs, 'Fortune is changeable' and 'Hap is unstable and unsteadfast': *Proverbs, Sentences, and Proverbial Phrases from English Writings Mainly Before 1500* (Cambridge, Mass, 1968), M164.

Greenlaw rightly insists that Baldwin's 'vows' take an unusual form: they 'relate not to deeds which he swears to perform but to a philosophy of life which he has already long held' (p. 578). They are not resolutions newly made in Inglewood, for each of them had its origin, as Baldwin later explains, in his experiences campaigning in Spain when Arthur's father was king. So Baldwin only pretends, as it were, to join in with the 'avowing' of Arthur and his companions. At best, his vows do no more than confirm and reiterate settled principles of conduct. Furthermore, they do not fulfil the purpose customary in the vows and resolutions af Arthurian romance, which is to prompt adventure. Although the vow of Arthur himself serves a practical purpose—to deal, albeit single-handedly, with a menace to his dogs and men—the vows of Kay and Gawain to wake the night through at the adventurous oak and the tarn are entirely true to chivalric type. Knights live by adventure; and when it does not come their way, they go out and trawl for it, as Erec does in Chrétien's romance when he resolves that Enide shall ride ahead of him alone in her richest attire. Baldwin's vows are not of this adventure-provoking sort. They may be called defensive vows, in that they are concerned with responses—the right handsome responses to attackers, visitors, and sexual rivals. It is therefore appropriate that after making his vows Baldwin should simply go back to bed: his one night out of bed is spent, in the second half of the poem, peaceably hunting in his home marshes. He does not look for trouble.

To explore further Baldwin's distinctive version of chivalry I will now consider each of his vows, as he first fulfils and then explains them. As he rides from his lodgings to dine with the king, Baldwin is confronted by Kay and five other knights, disguised and armed; but he refuses to be driven off his 'right way', unhorses Kay and four of his companions, and rides on to Carlisle.[10] Since Arthur has warned Kay to 'save wele my knyȝte', Baldwin stands in no real danger; but, as he cannot know that, he is acknowledged to have fulfilled his first vow: 'nevyr to . . . drede my dethe for no threte'. The episode is commonplace enough, but it serves to establish that unperturbable eq̇ ̇: ̇mity which characterizes Baldwin throughout. He follows the path to Carlisle that he has chosen to take, even telling the king, when he arrives, that nothing worthy of note occurred on the way: 'I herde ne se butte gode'. Later, when all three tests are done, Arthur asks him to explain this remarkable fearlessness. In reply, Baldwin recalls the true, first occasion of his vow never to fear death (1013–45). Besieged by Saracens in a castle in Spain, Baldwin and his knights returned from a successful sally to find one of their

---

[10] Greenlaw notes 'Keep the proper road, don't leave the highway for the byway' as one of the 'counsels which illustrate the virtue of caution' in his Three Counsels tales (p. 596); but Baldwin's reason for not allowing himself to be diverted has nothing to do with caution.

companions, who had cravenly hidden in a barrel, blown to pieces by a stray cannon-ball. Like those stories current in the Second World War about children who were evacuated from London in the Blitz only to be killed by a stray jettisoned bomb in some remote country spot, this story occasions a little homespun philosophical reflection:

> Þen owre feloys con say,
> 'Schall no mon dee or his day,
> Butte he cast himselfe away,
>   Throȝh wontyng of witte.'
> And þere myne avow made I—
> So dyd all þat cumpany—
> For dede nevyr to be drery.
>   Welcum is hit:
> Hit is a kyndely thing.   (1037–45)

Here, as in *Sir Gawain and the Green Knight*, to act out of fear of death is, paradoxically, to court death before one's 'day'. Courage is therefore not only the right but also the sensible thing (hence the reference to 'witte'). No one wants to die prematurely; but death, coming at its appointed time, is to be welcomed not feared: 'Hit is a kyndely thing'. This is the best kind of broad proverbial philosophy, rather like Gawain's earlier thoughts on 'happe'. Baldwin's story does suggest a basely prudential, and therefore unchivalrous, motive for courageous conduct (cowards get killed); but this argument is subsumed in the grand concluding reflections on death—reflections which serve not to undermine but to underpin the knightly ideal of un-self-regarding valour.

Baldwin's second vow, to 'werne no mon my mete', is developed in a somewhat similar way. While he is still with the king at Carlisle, Arthur secretly sends a minstrel to his castle seat, where he finds Baldwin's lady keeping open house. There is no porter on the gate, a large company of guests is being entertained, and the minstrel himself is courteously and hospitably received, along with messengers, pilgrims, palmers, and poor men. Like Chaucer's Franklin, Baldwin is evidently a great householder and, even in his absence, the St Julian of his country. This proof of Baldwin's lavish hospitality, like the earlier proof of his fearlessness, marks him as a great gentleman; for niggardliness, like cowardice, was always held to be a churlishly mean and self-regarding vice in a knight. Yet Baldwin's explanatory story suggests that the road of excess can be trodden not only with honour but also with advantage; for he tells how he persuaded his Saracen enemies in Spain to raise their siege by treating their emissary to a display of lavish feasting with what were in fact the last day's supplies left in the castle.[11] Like

---

[11] Dahood gives references to the numerous analogues of this story (pp. 33–4).

Baldwin's other siege story, this may be thought to make too direct an appeal to vulgar self-interest, much in the manner of the popular Three Counsels tales studied by Greenlaw; but I think that Greenlaw is wrong to speak of a 'strong tinge of cynicism' in Baldwin (p. 577). Medieval moralists were not generally very sensitive to the distinction between self-interest and other more noble motives, provided the resulting actions were good. Baldwin's story of his Spanish stratagem, so far from casting a shadow of cynicism across his accustomed hospitality, serves rather to enhance his standing as a man of experience and good 'counsel' (1064). In any case, his generous habits have another, purer source, in that philosophy of life to which he again gives proverbial utterance. When Arthur first arrives at Baldwin's castle and congratulates his host on the lavish supper, Baldwin smiles and replies:

> 'Sir, God hase a gud pluȝe;
> He may send us all enughe.
> Qwy schuld we spare?'   (778–80)

Later, when telling his siege story, he expresses the same thought: 'God helpus ay his man'.[12] Something like that religious spirit of *fiat voluntas tua* which in *Piers Plowman* supports the doctrine of patient poverty is here enlisted in support of liberal wealth. Baldwin is no preacher, but his mature philosophy of life is here touched momentarily with religious feeling. God will provide.

As Greenlaw observes, the testing of Baldwin's third resolution, 'nevyr to be ielus of my wife', forms a climax to the series: 'the second test is more severe than the first, while the last is even more difficult than the second' (p. 601). The relative severity of the first two tests is disputable, but it is indeed hard to imagine a more severe test of husbandly equanimity than to return from hunting and find your wife in bed with one of your guests. Of course Baldwin no more stands to be cuckolded by the knight than to be killed by Kay or eaten out of house and home by the minstrel: he is strong, wealthy, and happily married, and in any case the tests are all strictly controlled by Arthur, who personally stage-manages the final bedroom scene. Yet the jealousy test is, while it lasts, so severe that it invites comparison with those tests of patience to which Walter subjects Griselda in the *Clerk's Tale*;[13] and it elicits from Baldwin what is clearly meant to be understood as a supreme manifestation of noble equanimity. In his first responses to the scene which Arthur discloses, he gives three reasons for not being angry. The young

---

[12] Proverbial: Whiting G211. Whiting also records 'God has a good plow' (G207), but only in the *Avowing*.

[13] Greenlaw makes this comparison (pp. 603–4). He assigns the jealousy-test story to the type 'The Woman Falsely Accused' (pp. 607–36), citing Shakespeare's *Cymbeline* among many other examples.

knight could only have been admitted to his wife's bed 'atte hur awen wille', so:

> gif I take hitte þenne to ille,
> Muche maugreve have Y.   (899–900)

One may take this to refer only to the knight (one can't blame *him*); but Baldwin evidently had his wife in mind too (she is a free woman?), for he goes straight on to give a further reason for not being angry with her:

> For mony wyntur togedur we have bene,
> And ȝette ho dyd me nevyr no tene.   (901–2)

And in any case, he concludes, if she has indeed sinned, that is for God to expose and punish at the Last Judgement:

> And ich syn schall be sene,
> And sette full sorely.   (903–4)

It is a powerful speech, expressing acceptance of the fact of his wife's adultery as a manifestation of her independent will, yet touched by doubt that such a thing could be after their many happy years together, and leaving the whole matter at last to the judgement of God. When Hanna speaks of Baldwin's 'most unchivalrous sentiments about women', he must have had in mind not this speech but the story which Baldwin goes on to tell (913–88). This further episode from Baldwin's Spanish campaigns displays women (or at least serving-women) in a very unflattering light, as murderously jealous in their relations with each other and sexually insatiable in their relations with men. It is no surprise to find an analogue to this story among the French fabliaux.[14] One might imagine, if the whole context did not forbid such a supposition, that Baldwin is here giving vent to his true feelings on a trying occasion. I think rather that, for once, the poet made a bad choice of story. The stanza in which Baldwin himself draws the required moral against jealousy (973–88) is uncharacteristically weak and muddled. His point seems to be that women are free to be good or bad as they please, so men must take them as they find them. But the story illustrates that truth only in a very peculiar way (the 'good' woman ends up, after killing her two rivals, satisfying a whole garrison of more than five hundred men in bed and at board); and Baldwin's final reflection, 'Ich ertheli thinke hase ende', hardly follows from

---

[14] 'D'une seule fame qui a son con servoit .c. chevaliers de tous poins', no. XXVI in *Recueil Général et Complet des Fabliaux*, ed. A. de Montaiglon and G. Raynaud (Paris, 1872–90). G. L. Kittredge, *MLN* 8 (1893) 251–2, cited a further parallel from the *Parisiana Poetria* of John of Garland: see the recent edition with translation by Traugott Lawler (New Haven, Conn., 1974), Chapter 7, lines 28–153. When judging the incongruity of the story in a romance such as the *Avowing*, it should be noted that John of Garland tells it (albeit with a different outcome) as a *tragedia* in high-style Latin hexameters.

what has gone before, though it does indeed express a sentiment highly characteristic of his mind (it is again proverbial: Whiting T87).

But King Arthur himself is not at all shocked by the soldier's tale ('þou says wele'); and it is clear that the poet does not otherwise represent Baldwin as cynical or unchivalrous. On the contrary, Baldwin's vows declare his dedication to the highest ideals of the noble life, in opposition to the churlish vices of cowardice, niggardliness, and jealousy. Even Kay had recognized that Baldwin vowed not less but more than his companions ('wele more thenne we thre', 580); and so it proved to be. Yet the second panel of the poet's diptych does not simply repeat the first. As the poem progresses, we come to see Sir Baldwin not as an adventurous knight but as the married lord of a great household, like Sir Bertilak de Hautdesert; and I have suggested elsewhere that the stories which he tells Arthur of his experiences in Spain 'in ʒour fadur tyme' (913) further identify him as an older, more mature knight.[15] It is not that he has given up the life of chivalry; but his sense of its values has been deepened and to some degree darkened by experience. Experience has taught him that one must be ready, when called upon, to risk one's life and one's property and one's love; for to hang on to them anxiously and possessively is the surest way to lose them—as one nevertheless eventually must, since 'Ich ertheli thinke hase ende'.

Any reader unacquainted with *The Avowing of Arthur* who may be prompted by this account to read it must be prepared for a certain degree of disappointment. The neglect of the poem is not, after all, absolutely unaccountable. Too often the poet allows himself to be satisfied with stock minstrelesque expressions such as Chaucer mocked in *Sir Thopas*; and the result, though vigorously and authentically narrative in character, offers rather few verbal felicities. Yet the poet's conception of his work, even partially realized as it is, displays an intelligence and moral imagination rare in medieval English romance. The *Avowing* could have been a masterly creation —if only the *Gawain*-poet had written it.

---

[15] *The Ages of Man: A Study in Medieval Writing and Thought* (Oxford, 1986), pp. 175–7.

Relatives at the Court of Heaven: Contrasted Treatments of an Idea in Piers Plowman and Pearl

IAN BISHOP

In the fourteenth century the word *court*, like its Latin counterpart, *curia*, carried two principal meanings. It referred to a court of law, and it could also denote the administrative, ceremonial and residential headquarters of the monarch. Since the monarch was regarded as the fountain-head of justice, the two senses were closely related. Langland exploits the closeness of this relationship in the episode of Lady Mede (*Piers Plowman*, B. II–IV). When Mede is 'attached' at the end of Passus II, she is brought before the king in the manner of one arrested on a criminal charge. But, when she arrives at Westminster, the king seems to regard her as a ward of court who is in danger of being 'disparaged' through marriage to the undesirable Fals Fikel-Tonge.[1] He proposes that she marry Conscience, a knight of his own retinue—one of his own 'courtiers'. When Conscience declines the offer of her hand, we are virtually transported back to the judicial court. For he speaks about her in the manner of a prosecuting counsel, accusing her (among other things) of causing kings to be murdered and popes to be poisoned (III. 127–8). Throughout the episode, the allegory shows how Mede possesses, and provides, access to the authorities in both kinds of court.

The inter-availability of these two senses of the word is no less evident when a visionary writer contemplates the court of heaven. It can be seen in Langland's very first reference to the heavenly court when he mentions the 'Consistorie' that Christ will hold on Doomsday (B. Prol. 98–9), and then proceeds to think of the cardinal virtues that are the hinges of the gates,

> There Crist is in kyngdom, to close and to shette,
> And to opene it to hem and hevene blisse shewe.
>
> (B. Prol. 105–6)[2]

[1] On the relevance of the legal notion of 'disparagement' to this passage, see Myra Stokes, *Justice and Mercy in Piers Plowman : A Reading of the B-Text Visio* (Beckenham, Kent, 1984), pp. 124 ff., and references in her n. 33.

[2] All quotations from the poem are taken from *The Vision of Piers Plowman: A Complete Edition of the B-Text*, ed. A. V. C. Schmidt (London, 1978).

These virtues are immediately dissociated from the officials at the Papal *curia*: 'the Cardinals at court that kaughte of that name'. But the only occasion when the poet gives us a glimpse of the interior of the court of heaven occurs in the visionary speech of Piers himself towards the end of Passus V. This is the passage from *Piers Plowman* with which I shall be especially concerned in this essay.

The two aspects of *court* also appear in *Pearl*, which is concerned exclusively with the court of heaven. At 701–2 the maiden warns the dreamer of his plight 'to corte quen thou schal com,/ Ther alle oure causes schal be tryed'.[3] If you are allowed 'to passe, when thou arte tryed', as innocent, you will be admitted into the community of 'The court of the kyndom of God alyve' (445), where Christ is the Prince, his mother is Empress, and all the inhabitants kings or queens.

The present essay is concerned with only one aspect of the question of access to the heavenly court; namely, the advantage of possessing relatives there. The idea is one that underlies the whole of the dramatic situation in *Pearl*; in Langland's poem it is treated with particular emphasis in the speech of Piers to which I have already referred. This speech has other affinities with the argument of *Pearl*,[4] but the differences between the two poems are even more interesting than the similarities. I shall consider the similarities first, using the passage from Langland as the basis of my discussion.

Piers enters the poem at the moment when the folk in the field, now turned pilgrims, are looking for a guide to the dwelling of Truth. This ploughman is the last candidate that any travel agent would choose to employ as a courier. His first speech implies that, throughout the 'fourty wynter' (V. 542) of his working life, he has remained on the same manor; in Passus VI his activities are centred upon a single half-acre. He is listened to only because the ostensibly well-qualified candidate—the widely-travelled Palmer—has been discredited as a guide to Truth. Piers calmly informs the company that Truth is, in fact, the lord of his manor. The directions he gives to Truth's 'place' (V. 555 ff.) read (if disburdened of their somewhat cumbersome allegorical tenor) like a description of the track that leads from the half-acre to the local manorial court. Piers is what the author of *Pearl* would call one of Truth's 'homly hyne' (cf. *Pearl*, 1211), one of God's household labourers—whether he works on his ploughlands or (as in *Pearl*) in his vineyard. Unlike most

---

[3] All quotations from *Pearl* are from *Pearl, Cleanness, Patience, Sir Gawain and the Green Knight*, ed. A. C. Cawley and J. J. Anderson (London, 1976). The standard edition, which contains detailed notes, apparatus and etymological glossary, is by E. V. Gordon (Oxford, 1953).

[4] A few verbal correspondences between the two poems are noted by J. A. W. Bennett in his edition: *Piers Plowman: the Prologue and Passus I–VII of the B-Text* (Oxford, 1972), p. 190 (note on V. 557–9). Bennett's commentary on the whole passage is invaluable.

terrestrial lords, Truth is 'as lowe as a lomb and lovelich of speche' (v. 553); and in *Pearl* it is as a lamb that the Prince of Heaven manifests himself. Langland shows that it is possible for man to enjoy a relationship with God similar to that described towards the end of *Pearl*:

> For I haf founden hym, bothe day and naghte,
> A God, a Lorde, a frende ful fyin.   (1203–4)

But, as Langland's passage proceeds, the relationship becomes even closer than that of friendship.

In Piers's speech the conventional landscape allegory (of the ten commandments) is replaced by a no less traditional architectural allegory when he describes the *manoir* of Truth as 'a court as cler as the sonne' (v. 585–6; see Bennett, pp. 191–2, note on v. 594). But, at the point where the conducted tour brings us to Truth's presence-chamber, the mode of expression is suddenly internalized from that of systematic allegorical exposition to that of poetic metaphor:

> Thow shalt see in thiselve Truthe sitte in thyn herte
> In a cheyne of charite, as thow a childe were,
> To suffren hym and segge noght ayein thi sires wille.
>
> (v. 606–8)

In Passus I, Holychurch had distinguished between transcendent and immanent Truth—between (on the one hand) God in Heaven and (on the other hand) the love of God and of one's neighbour, which dwells naturally in man's heart, and which makes him 'a god by the Gospel'. Jesus's statement that 'the Kingdom of God is within you' (Luke 17: 21) is implicit in these lines, as it is also in the argument of *Pearl*: in order to obtain the Kingdom of Heaven, the pearl of great price, it is necessary for us to undergo an internal transformation into pearls that will be pleasing to the Prince.[5] The figure of the child also stands at the centre of *Pearl*. In order to become pearls, adult Christians must re-acquire the innocence of the newly baptized child and be restored to the state of Grace through the sacrament of penance. Jesus declared that 'hys ryche no wyy myght wynne/ Bot he com thyder ryght as a childe':

> Quen such ther cnoken on the bylde,
> Tyt schal hem men the yate unpynne.
> Ther is the blys that con not blynne
> That the jueler soghte thurgh perré pres.   (727–30)

Similarly, Langland makes Grace the 'gateward' of Truth's *manoir*; the

---

[5] See Ian Bishop, *Pearl in its Setting: A Critical Study of the Structure and Meaning of the Middle English Poem* (Oxford, 1968), p. 96 and n. 58. See this study generally for the interpretation of the poem that is followed in the present essay.

assistant porter is called 'Amende-yow'; the password you must give him is 'I parfourned the penaunce that the preest me enjoyned' (v. 598). But the main entrance qualification is Humility. Hence the gate, which Eve closed through Pride and Mary (*ancilla domini*) re-opened in Humility, is described as a 'wiket'. This traditional image of the lowly entrance to heaven was still a living 'commonplace' in the seventeenth century, when Webster exploited it dramatically in *The Duchess of Malfi*. As the heroine stands with her executioners' cords already round her neck she addresses them:

> Pull, and pull strongly, for your able strength
> Must pull down heaven upon me:—
> Yet stay; heaven-gates are not so highly arch'd
> As princes' palaces, they that enter there
> Must go upon their knees.—[*Kneels*]. . . .[6]

In Piers's speech there soon follows one of Langland's sublime inconsistencies. Since the argument seems to have been insisting that the low wicket-gate provides the sole entrance to Truth's castle,[7] it is disconcerting to learn that the building has no less than seven posterns, each guarded by one of seven sisters, who are personified virtues. However that may be, it is with these sisters that I come to the central issue of this essay. Piers informs the pilgrims that anyone who is a relative of these sisters will be welcomed and handsomely received. He adds:

> And but if ye be sibbe to some of thise sevene—
> It is ful hard, by myn heed . . . for any of yow alle
> To geten ingong at any gate but grace be the moore!
>
> (v. 627–9)

On hearing this, three criminals among the folk begin to despair: ' "Now, by Crist!" quod a kuttepurs, "I have no kyn there." '[8] The force of the moral allegory here depends upon the sociological overtones of its 'vehicle'. 'We should have guessed', say the ordinary sinners, in effect, 'that it would be just like any other court. Only the gentlefolk have the entrée there.' But Piers reassures them:

> Mercy is a maiden there, hath myght over hem alle;
> And she is sib to alle synfulle, and hire sone also. . . .'
>
> (v. 635–6)

[6] *The Duchess of Malfi*, ed. John Russell Brown, The Revels Plays (London, 1964), IV. ii. 230–4.

[7] Piers continues the lesson in humility by warning (v. 609–17) against taking pride in one's good deeds ('bienfetes'). Cf. the argument in *Pearl* (617–708) about the danger of relying upon one's 'ryghte' (i.e. on one's 'rights' and 'righteousness').

[8] See Bennett's notes (pp. 195–6) on v. 640 and 641. On the disreputable activities of the 'wafrestre', see also Bennett's *Chaucer at Oxford and at Cambridge* (Oxford, 1974), p. 45.

The notion that, as a result of the Incarnation, God is related to all sinners, is a commonplace, at which Langland had already glanced at v. 504. The idea is explored with naïve explicitness in a lyric addressed to the Virgin by William Herebert:

> Thou my suster and my moder,
> And thy sone is my brother:
> Who shulde thenne drede?
> Whoso haveth the king to brother,
> And ek the quene to moder,
> Well aughte for to spede.[9]

Langland's lines benefit from their restraint; the identity of Mary remaining half-concealed in the personification, Mercy.

On this simple and sublime note the passus might well have ended. Indeed, in the corresponding passus in the A-text, it does. But the B-text concludes the passus with a satirical twist that introduces two characters who are so literal-minded that they cannot appreciate the spirituality of Piers's message:

> 'Bi Seint Poul!' quod a pardoner, 'paraventure I be noght knowe there;
> I wol go fecche my box with my brevettes and a bulle with bisshopes lettres.'
> 'Bi Crist!' quod a commune womman, 'thi compaignie wol I folwe.
> Thow shalt seye I am thi suster.' I ne woot where thei bicome.

The prostitute is, symbolically, the obvious companion for the simoniacal pardoner. But what interests me in these lines is the way in which she continues the theme of 'sib' that was developed in the previous passage. No doubt any prostitute would advise her client to claim (if questioned by patrolling authorities) that she was his sister. But this woman is thinking of the moment when the two of them arrive at the gate of Truth's court. She is in no position to utter the password that Amende-yow requires (cf. v. 596–600): she hopes that, by claiming kinship with the pardoner, she may enter on his passport. His indulgences are the officially sealed documents that are a recognized substitute for performing 'the penaunce that the preest . . . enjoyned'.

The author of *Pearl* is no less critical than Langland of those who adopt literal-minded attitudes towards *spiritualia*. Yet, if one believes (as I certainly do) that the maiden represents the beatified soul of the dreamer's dead daughter, there is one respect in which the poet's attitude is not so very unlike that of Langland's 'commune womman'. For he is aware of the possible advantages of having a close earthly relative placed in a privileged position

---

[9] Text from *Medieval English Lyrics*, ed. R. T. Davies (London, 1963), no. 28 (p. 96), lines 7–12.

within the court of heaven. However, before I discuss the particular situation in *Pearl*, something must be said about the medieval attitude generally to the question of friends and relations at the heavenly court.

Even though the Christian has 'the king to brother' and 'the quene to moder', there must have been times when individuals felt themselves to be overwhelmed by the sheer numbers of their brethren, and consequently looked for some kind of privileged access to the prince of heaven. A partial modern analogy to this situation is afforded by the National Health Service, under which everybody is entitled to receive treatment; nevertheless some, who can afford it, think it an advantage to pay for the privilege of private medical care. In the Middle Ages, access to an earthly monarch may sometimes have been expedited by bribing court officials, or through possessing genuine friends at court. But the most enviable position was that of the man whose own family was represented there.[10] When John Chaucer sent his son to be page to the countess of Ulster, his primary motive was no doubt to do well by the boy; but he probably also had in mind the advantages that would accrue to himself and his family generally. To judge from the fortunes of the Chaucer family in the fifteenth century, the investment paid off handsomely. It was undoubtedly felt that analogous advantages were available to anyone with an ancestor or other former earthly relative in the heavenly court. But how could one know whether any of one's kith or kin had been admitted to the celestial court? One might be informed directly in a vision. But one could not be sure that such a phenomenon was a genuine *somnium coeleste*. There were only two categories of persons about whom one could be certain: canonized saints and 'innocents'. We can appreciate how seriously the possession of a saint in the family was taken, if we observe how fourteenth-century English kings commemorated St Edward the Confessor and St Edward the Martyr. Across the Channel, Christine de Pisan observed that there have been a 'great host of kings and princes . . . queens and princesses who are saints in Paradise, like the wife of King Clovis of France'. These royal saints lived a long while ago. But Christine de Pisan also mentions among the saints in Paradise 'St Louis, King of France'.[11] Whereas the Anglo-Saxon saints were far removed from the Angevin kings of fourteenth-century England, the contemporary monarchs of the House of Valois (a cadet branch of the Capetian dynasty) had only to look back to the previous century to find a canonized relative. It was perhaps the memory of Louis IX that incited Richard II to conduct a sustained campaign for the canonization of his great-grandfather as a martyr. Edward II may seem to us an unlikely

---

[10] On the desire of families to have a son educated at court, see R. F. Green, *Poets and Princepleasers* (Toronto, 1980), esp. pp. 41 ff.

[11] Both quotations are from *The Treasure of the City of Ladies*, trans. Sarah Lawson (Harmondsworth, 1985), p. 46.

candidate for sainthood, but in 1395 a record of miracles attributed to him was sent to Rome.[12]

Although, strictly speaking, the age of innocence terminated when a child reached its seventh year, this did not prevent Edward III from regarding his daughter, Joan, who died when she was fifteen, as an innocent. I have elsewhere examined letters which the king sent, on the occasion of her death, to her fiancé, the Infante of Castile, and to his parents.[13] He imagines her 'in Choro Virginum', joined to the Heavenly Spouse and reigning there for ever—just as the maiden in *Pearl* is presented as a queen in Heaven, a bride of Christ, and a member of the company of the hundred and forty-four thousand virgins who follow the Lamb. Of particular interest in the present context is a diplomatic point that Edward (or his secretary) insinuates into the correspondence. He argues that, although the matrimonial alliance between the two royal families has been cruelly frustrated, an even more important and intimate bond between them has been established: both families will for ever share the same personal intercessor within the court of the prince of heaven.

Pearl is cast in the form of a *somnium coeleste*, in which the maiden appears in person to her earthly father. This 'veray avysyoun' (1184) is, of course, simply a poetic fiction. Nevertheless, it has its basis in what the poet regards as truth. He seems to believe that she has interceded with the prince of heaven for a special dispensation of prevenient Grace to set his thoughts upon the right road for his own salvation. Within the fiction of the dream, the point is not made explicitly until a late stage in the proceedings. At 965–6 the maiden tells the dreamer that God will not permit him to enter the heavenly city—but

> '. . . of the Lombe I have the aquylde
> For a syght therof thurgh gret favor.'

He may view it from the outside, but may not enter its streets unless 'thou wer clene wythouten mote' (972). Much of the poem's human appeal derives from the fact that the maiden finds it so difficult to make the dreamer understand the purpose behind her appearing to him. When he first recognizes her, he naturally hopes to restore their former relationship. Later, when she informs him that she is a queen in heaven, he disputes the justice of her reward and the propriety of her station. He then becomes so intent upon 'catching out' the maiden in what he fancies to be an academic disputation that he misses the lesson in humility that is embodied in her recounting, and in her interpretation of, the parable of the labourers in the vineyard. She has to bring the argument round in such a way as to warn him that he is himself in danger of being

---

[12] See J. W. Sherborne, 'Aspects of English Court Culture in the Later Fourteenth Century', in *English Court Culture in the Later Middle Ages*, ed. V. J. Scattergood and J. W. Sherborne (London, 1983), pp. 1–27, esp. p. 22 and ref. in n. 27.
[13] '*Solacia* in *Pearl* and in Letters of Edward III Concerning the Death of His Daughter, Joan', *Notes & Queries* 229 (1984) 454–6.

'caught out' (cf. *innome*, 703)—but in a much more serious sense—at the moment 'to corte quen thou schal com,/ Ther alle oure causes schal be tryed'.[14] Even when he beholds the procession of the Lamb, he still does not appreciate the purpose of the maiden's apparition. His desire at the end of the vision is still physically to cross the stream in order to be with his 'lyttel quene' just as it had been when he first recognized her. The maiden, having completed the mission for her earthly father's benefit, no longer notices him. Like her peers in the procession, she is thoroughly absorbed in her love for the Lamb.

The role of the maiden has several times been compared to that of Beatrice in her concern for the salvation of the poet who had adopted her as his Muse in his youthful poems of *fin' amors*, assembled in *La Vita Nuova*. The *Paradiso* concludes with the culminating vision of the heavenly court (cf. *Paradiso*, XXX. 96), to which Beatrice conducts Dante. Both poem and vision cease simultaneously, because the poet's *alta fantasia* (*Paradiso*, XXXIII. 142)—the human faculty that enables one to perceive a *somnium coeleste*—can no longer comprehend what it beholds. In the two English poems with which I have been concerned, the vision of the heavenly court is followed by an anti-climax. It is only after he wakes from his dream, and is cast 'Fro alle tho syghtes so quyke and queme' (1179), that the dreamer in *Pearl* begins to understand the purpose of what has been revealed to him. After Piers's description of the 'court as cler as the sonne', the poem descends, in Passus VI, to the unglamorous environment of the half-acre to begin a long and tortuous quest for the way to salvation. In both these poems the respective dreamers have looked in at the splendour of the heavenly court from the outside. Before they can themselves enter 'that fayre regioun', they have still to pass through that other aspect of the celestial court, 'Ther alle oure causes schal be tryed'.

---

[14] See Gordon's note (p. 71) on lines 703–4, and Bishop, *Pearl in its Setting*, Chapter 3, esp. p. 44.

Will's Pilgrimage in Piers Plowman B

MARGARET E. GOLDSMITH

The author of *Piers Plowman* presents himself to his readers as a fool. The man who dreams and recounts what he saw 'sleeping' is called a 'doted daffe' (stupid dolt) in his youth (B. I. 140), an 'ydiot' (ignorant simpleton) when he learns more about his own nature (B. XVI. 170) and a fool in a company of fools as he faces old age and death (B. XX. 74–7).[1] A fool obviously has licence to speak out on matters which the circumspect prefer to keep silent about, and the Dreamer takes advantage of that fact. However, his folly is not a simple authorial disguise. He shows himself eventually to be like the fool of St Paul's Epistles: *stultus fiat ut sit sapiens* ['he must become a fool so as to be wise'], and the 'fools' whose company he finally joins are fools in the eyes of the worldly-wise; they are *stulti pro Christi* (cf. 1 Cor. 4: 10).[2] The paradox that we may hear wisdom from a fool lies at the heart of the poem, and makes for considerable difficulty in interpretation. We do not know when we are to credit Will with clearer Christian insight than other characters show, and when to smile at his simple-mindedness. The author playing Will humorously plays upon our uncertainty, notably when he records without comment a priest's sarcastic remark that Piers the Plowman should preach on the text *Dixit insipiens* ['the fool hath said . . .'], or again, when he thanks Thought for telling him (among other things) that Dobet preaches St Paul's words, as translated,

> *Libenter suffertis insipientes cum sitis ipsi sapientes:*
> [Ye wise], suffreth the unwise with yow to libbe . . .   (B. VIII. 93)

thus apparently accepting Thought's complete perversion of 2 Cor. 11: 19.

---

[1] Quotations are from *The Vision of Piers Plowman: A Complete Edition of the B-Text*, ed. A. V. C. Schmidt (London, 1978).
[2] Biblical quotations are taken from the Vulgate, except in quotations from writers who may be using another version. The renderings are my own, being intended only as a guide to the non-Latinist.

Concerning the company of fools Will joins in the end there is seemingly no uncertainty: they are St Paul's *stulti pro Christi*, despised by the world, but obedient to Conscience in the house Piers has built for them. Their 'house' has no physical existence: it is acceptable as a model of reality only to those who can share Will's mature understanding of the nature of things:

> Animalis homo non percipit ea quae sunt Spiritus Dei; stultitia enim est illi, et non potest intelligere, quia spiritualiter examinatur.

> [Carnal man cannot take in the things of the Spirit of God, for they are foolishness to him and he cannot understand them, because they are discerned in the Spirit.]   (1 Cor. 2: 14)

A reader who holds the apostle's belief that commonsense intuitions about life on earth are far from true would expect the Dreamer seeking Truth, who starts by looking for some 'craft' in his 'cors' (B. I. 139), to need a personal conversion before his real quest could begin. It is indeed the gradual process of his conversion which makes the 'plot' of the poem. The author's problem in dramatizing his conversion must be to convey in words alone—the 'letter'— what living a life 'in the spirit' might be like. The problem is compounded by his obvious wish to induce his readers to take practical steps to put right social and political injustices and abuses; so the Dreamer cannot be allowed to become entirely absorbed in his own soul's health. The solution he found is a unique and extraordinarily complex blend of literary modes and styles. He avoids the dangers of abstraction by giving his personified vices and virtues companions with names like Robert and Hawkin. This works very well on the level of moral theology, but for the essence of his religious theme he must find other means. There can be no other recourse, given that he is writing for a wide Christian readership, than to employ the language of the scriptures as preachers up and down the country were wont to do. The biblical texts come to him caught up in webs of patristic teaching and already imbued with non-literal meaning, of which his more serious and perspicacious readers will need only to be reminded. The parables of the New Testament, instinct with moral and (as then thought) allegorical significance, are a natural source of inspiration; the familiar metaphors from the Epistles can be brought to life, and the 'spiritual' meanings which have accrued to the Psalms present the required contrast between secular and 'inward' understanding.

I surmise that St Paul's metaphor of sowing and reaping, which is used by him to distinguish 'carnal' and 'spiritual' ways of life, generates the central concept of a Plowman (cf. Gal. 6: 8–10). Piers the Plowman vows to give up his ordinary sowing of wheat in favour of a metaphorical 'sowing in tears'. Thus he can merge, in the dream-world, with the farmers of Ps. 125: 5 *Qui seminant in lacrymis*, and these in turn are figures of Moses and the prophets preparing for the harvest which the apostles would reap.[3] When a historical dimension is introduced, it is appropriate that the Plowman should also merge with the Sower of the gospel (cf. Marc. 4: 3–8) and the apostles who continue to spread the seed of God's word in the field of the world. Langland names his ploughman Piers, the English form of *Petrus*, so linking him both to his own time and place and to Peter of Galilee, the apostle charged to feed Christ's people and to administer the *lex Christi*.

Piers's conversion to an other-worldly set of values is figured in his tearing of Truth's letter. From then on, his progress to Jerusalem and beyond is in great leaps, out of sight of the Dreamer. Will, however, wanders about, asking questions of the wrong people, and cannot find his way until Anima leads him to meet Piers again. Though his steps are erratic, they are certainly not unforeseen by the author. As Schmidt points out, 'Study's striking reference to Ymaginatif [B. x. 117], who only appears at XI 408, shows Langland carefully planning his poem and using each of Will's interlocutors for a definite purpose in the task of bringing him to know Dowel' (p. 330). The reader is challenged to see ahead of slow-thinking Will and to recognize his shortcomings. The predictable *schema* of the three *Vitae* is realized in a fresh and contemporary milieu, but its course is based on the teaching of the apostles and the four Latin Doctors of the church.

In the body of this paper I attempt to show how a coherent substructure holds together what appears to some critics to be a somewhat rambling composition, incidentally taking a fresh look at one or two obscure passages. As I have already published my views on Piers, I concentrate here on matters which concern Will almost exclusively, looking first at the early stages of his quest and then at the outcome of all his endeavours. In writing about Piers I chose as an emblem of his changing person 'the Image on the coin':[4] if I were to choose an emblem for Will, it would be 'the Face in the mirror'. These patristic metaphors, only fleetingly and allusively mentioned by Langland, seem to me to present the two slightly different aspects of the doctrine of the restoration of the image of God in man, a doctrine which governs the course of Piers's transformations and Will's hard-won 'kynde knowynge'.

The mysterious mention of the face of Christ in a mirror comes in Will's

---

[3] Augustine, for example, quotes Ps. 125: 5 when commenting on Jn. 4: 35 ff. Jesus sends his disciples to reap where others have sown. Those who laboured in the past were Abraham, Isaac and Jacob; they were the 'sowers' in the cold:

> Moyses et ceteri patriarchae et omnes prophetae, quanta pertulerunt in illo frigore quando seminabant?

> [Moses and the rest of the patriarchs and all the prophets—how many things did they announce in that cold time when they were sowing?]
> (*Tract. in Ioh.* xv, CCSL 36, p. 163).

[4] In *The Figure of Piers Plowman: The Image on the Coin* (Cambridge, 1981).

dialogue with Anima, at the beginning of the *Vita de Dobet*, as he enquires about the nature of Charity:

'Clerkes kenne me that Crist is in alle places;
Ac I seigh hym nevere soothly but as myself in a mirour:
Hic in enigmate, tunc facie ad faciem.'   (B. xv. 161–2a)

The phrase 'in a mirour' obviously translates the words Langland *omits* from the Pauline text, namely *per speculum* (cf. 1 Cor. 13: 12), but 'myself in a mirror' also calls up St James's image of the man who looks into his mirror and then forgets, as he turns away, what his own face looks like. The man who forgets 'the face he was born with' [*vultum nativitatis suae*] represents one who is a 'hearer' but not a 'doer' of the word of God (cf. Ja. 1: 23–4). Will, up to this point a talker rather than a 'doer', has not, until he entered the domain of Dobet, been aware of seeing himself or his Maker in his looking-glass. From the time when he begins to listen to his own soul, Anima, he enters on an inward journey of self-discovery, as Wittig and others have shown:[5] but Langland never allows him to become totally self-absorbed. By various means Langland weights the poem's message towards *charitas in actu* rather than *charitas in affectu*, though Will's own spiritual journey is in *affectu* (affections, dispositions of the will).[6] It is noteworthy that both Jesus and Piers are presented as 'doers' more than preachers. This is most unmistakably evident in their combats with mankind's enemies, but there are unelaborated reminders along the way, and also in the final account of Jesus's ministry in terms of Dowel, Dobet and Dobest (B. xix. 108–88). One significant, though almost casual, reminder of Jesus as 'doer' is the mention that 'in his pilgrymes wedes' he went unrecognized on the road to Emmaus, until he performed the familiar act of blessing and breaking the bread.

The Glossa Ordinaria on Luc. 24: 30, quoted by Robertson and Huppé,[7] uses the incident of the breaking of the bread to reinforce St James's teaching

[5] See J. S. Wittig, ' "Piers Plowman" B, Passus IX–XII: Elements in the Design of the Inward Journey', *Traditio* 28 (1972) 211–80.

[6] For further discussion of these terms in Bernard's writings, see Goldsmith, 'Piers' Apples: Some Bernadine echoes in *Piers Plowman*' in *Leeds Studies in English*, NS 16 (1985) 309–25. In this article I have translated *affectus* 'affections' when the word occurs in quoted passages, but it is important to note that these are not secular feelings, but 'dispositions of the will', spiritual states, such as contrition.

[7] D. W. Robertson and B. F. Huppé, *Piers Plowman and Scriptural Tradition* (Princeton, 1951), p. 141. They also misleadingly refer to 'The *deceiving* mirror of James 1: 23 . . . in which only the fickleness of Fortune is perceived' (p. 130). They reach this unlikely equation by identifying Langland's 'mirour that highte Middelerthe' with James's mirror, on the strength of a comment in *Gl. Ord.* (PL 114, col. 673) which identifies the mirror with *Scripture*, albeit Scripture misread by the untutored (pp. 130–1, n. 52). For a different interpretation of 'looking into the mirror', see Wittig, p. 235.

about *auditores* and *factores*, and links it with the recognition of Truth. On Luc. 24: 31–2 a 'mystical' interpretation adds 'ut omnes intelligant se Christum non agnoscere, nisi fiant participes corporis ejus, id est Ecclesiae, cujus unitatem commendat Apostolus in sacramento panis, dicens *Unus panis, unum corpus multi sumus*' (PL 114, cols 352–3).[8]

> *Fregit, etc.* Quem in expositione Scripturae non cognoverunt in fractione panis noverunt, quia non auditores legis, sed factores justificabuntur, et veritas melius operando quam audiendo intelligitur.
>
> [He whom they had not recognized in the exposition of Scripture they knew through the breaking of bread, for it is not the hearers but the doers of the law who will be justified, and truth is perceived better through doing than through hearing.]

This gloss goes far to explain the course of Will's enlightenment. He remains confused and upset after listening to Scripture, principally because he shies away from the implication of her words. By the time he has progressed in Dobet, having become a pilgrim 'in the spirit', he comes very close to perceiving Truth in the Figure he sees as the communion bread is blessed at the Easter Mass.[9] Piers, the 'pattern of righteousness'[10] who reaches Truth before him, is finally praised as one 'that pursueth God *in doynge*' (B. XIX. 433, my italics).

What Will hears from Scripture endorses the uncompromising moral law promulgated by St James. I am persuaded that his Epistle was constantly in Langland's mind. It presents as a 'royal law' the commandment to love one's neighbour, and it will brook no smallest breach of God's commandments. Preachers anxious to stir people to repentance often quoted James's *offendat autem in uno, factus est omnium reus* (Ja. 2: 10), as Langland himself does elsewhere.[11] In Scripture's homily these words do not appear, but the passage

---

[8] The *Glossa* echoes Ja. 1: 22, incorporating *legis* from Ja. 1: 25 instead of the *verbi* of v. 22. The 'face in the mirror' image referred to in n. 4 follows, in Ja. 1: 23.

[9] For the idea of Truth as set before the communicant *in sacramento*, see Goldsmith, 'Piers' Apples', p. 320. The *Gloss. Ord.* gives a similar interpretation *mystice* of the Emmaus incident: only those who are part of his Body, the Church, whose unity the Apostle [Paul] commends in 1 Cor. 10: 17, will recognize Christ. In the middle of the Easter Mass, Will has a vision of Piers carrying a cross 'And right lik in alle lymes to Oure Lord Jesu' (B. XIX. 8), but he has to call on Conscience 'to kenne [him] the sothe' of what he sees.

[10] Augustine's theory of the *forma justitiae* ['pattern of righteousness'] which the apostles present to us is discussed fully in Goldsmith, *Figure*, pp. 15–16.

[11] At B. IX. 98 the verse *Qui offendit in uno* etc. reinforces Wit's agreement with St James that the man who 'does best' never offends with his tongue (cf. Ja. 3: 2), and similarly at B. XI. 308 it sentences the offender who speaks God's words improperly or scamps his liturgical offices.

from which this text comes underlies what she says about a Christian's duty. She comes to the 'royal law', as James does, in countering her hearers' tendency to treat rich people differently from poor people. She refers, as James later does, to the hoarded silver and moth-eaten cloaks which will bear witness against the uncharitable rich (cf. Ja. 5: 2–3) at the Judgement; she answers Will's questions about Dowel as James would have her do:

> Si tamen legem perficitis regalem secundum Scripturas Diliges proximum tuum sicut teipsum, bene facitis. (Ja. 2: 8)

> [If you perfectly obey the royal law *according to Scripture* 'Love your neighbour as yourself', you *do well*.]

The verb *perficitis* has its full force here, as the next verses show:

> Quicumque autem totam legem servaverit offendat autem in uno, factus est omnium reus.
> Qui enim dixit: Non moechaberis, dixit et: Non occides.
> (Ja. 2: 10–11)

> [Whoever has kept all the law, but offends in one point, makes himself guilty of all. For the One who said 'Do not commit adultery' also said 'Do not kill'.]

It can hardly be accident that Scripture's homily to Will also singles out these two commandments from the ten. Some scribes, and the editors, suppose that '*Non mecaberis*' (B. x. 364) is a plain error. Though we cannot now be certain of the original reading, I find it easier to credit that Langland is being intolerably cryptic, in his attempt to make Scripture speak 'derkliche', than that he could write *mechaberis* intending *occides*—and repeat the mistake in revising the passage for the B-text.[12] The point that both Scripture and St James are making in the end is that God's judgement will be merciful to those who have shown mercy. They both emphasize that the Law is not abrogated, but Scripture also reveals a more merciful dispensation when the legal death penalty for adultery is remitted by Christ and the transgressor is left to God's judgement. Langland describes this momentous event later (B. XII. 72–80), and I guess that he is here posing the paradox that the One who instituted the penalty of death also said 'Do not kill', a problem of justice and truth which slots into the overall theme of *Piers Plowman* that justice and love must

---

[12] Since Ja. 2: 11 is part of an exhortation to love one's neighbours without distinction of class or wealth, it was probably in Langland's mind when he wrote A. XI. 238–49. This would account for his singling out '*non mechaberis*, ne sle nou3t' from the 'ten hestis' (the one being an instance of 'harm', the other of 'destruction' of a creature 'in God's likeness'). The final words of Scripture's speech: 'but mercy it make' (A. XI. 249, B. X. 368) accord with the final words of Ja. 2: 13: *Superexaltat autem misericordia judicium* ['for mercy exalts judgement']. Some MSS read 'I slee' for 'Is slee' (365) which, taken with the parenthetic 'and seith *non mechaberis*', makes a riddling sense.

be reconciled. Whatever the explanation of these curious lines, Scripture obviously holds, with James, that doing *comparatively* well is not doing well enough, and every man needs God's mercy. She imposes an impossible task on fallible man: Will cannot 'do well' without the help of Grace, whose 'prowor' is Piers the Plowman, as will be disclosed later in the poem.

His studies having brought him face to face with the exigencies of the Law, Will takes refuge in the notion that study is useless. For a time he gives up, comforting himself with the thought that nothing he can do will alter what Providence has ordained. He decides to cast his lot with 'lewed men and of litel knowyng' (B. x. 469), since even the great scholar Augustine envied the simple faith of 'idiotes'. He recalls that 'the doughtieste doctour' of them all said, *Ecce ipsi idiote rapiunt celum ubi nos sapientes in inferno mergimur* (B. x. 450, 452a).

Will is misquoting and is vague about his source: once more the reader must charge Langland with slackness or alternatively credit him with subtlety. Since much of the poem is imbued with Augustinian thought, it is likely that the vagueness is feigned, to give a further impression that Will is a careless student. The point which Will's misquotation obscures is that learning *without charity* does not profit the soul.[13]

Scripture, vexed with Will's stupidity, next invokes St Bernard to chasten him, hinting at a way out of his present negative frame of mind:

Multi multa sciunt et seipsos nesciunt.[14]   (B. xi. 3)

Langland's attitude to book-learning is no more ambivalent than that of Augustine or of Bernard. All agreed that the Church cannot exist without 'Clergy', but that, since Adam fell because of his desire for knowledge, to pursue knowledge to enhance oneself can be spiritually dangerous. Both Augustine and Bernard teach that humble introspection can tell a man more about his Maker than he can learn from an objective reading of books.

Will, however, is not yet ready to face what he really is. He slips back into the carnal world, keeping company with those familiar temptresses, *Concupiscentia Carnis* and 'Pride of Parfit Lyvynge' in his early years, and 'Coveityse of Eighes' in his middle age. This period of his life is described

---

[13] The sentence in Augustine's *Confessiones* (VIII. 8) has the synonym *indocti* for Langland's *idiote*, and importantly includes the phrase *sine corde* ['without heart']. Augustine is deploring his own purely intellectual attitude to learning, which could not raise him out of the carnal world. It is significant, as Wittig has noted (pp. 245–8), that this outburst occurs when Augustine accuses himself of a wounded and divided will, holding back from the commitment to God which he desires: immediately after the outburst, he falls to weeping in contrition, and after a sign from heaven finds that his irresoluteness and doubt have left him. See *Confessionum Libri XIII*, ed M. Skutella (Stuttgart, 1969).

[14] As is well known, these words are the opening of a treatise not now ascribed to Bernard: to Langland they no doubt carried the stamp of his authority.

very conventionally, except for his disappointment with the friars, who let him down when the ladies do, just when he needs some support. The chief point of interest in this episode is 'the lond of longynge and love' (B. XI. 8) in which he dallies.[15] In view of the reference to the *Confessiones* and the implication of Scripture's quotation from 'Bernard', there can be no doubt that Will is now being painted as the Prodigal of the parable who wasted his substance in 'a distant land' [*regio longinqua*].[16] Having 'come to himself' [*reversus in se*], the Prodigal determined to offer himself as a servant to his father, and returned to his home. Augustine and Bernard both relate the parable to the theory of the restoration of God's image in man. The relevance of the Prodigal's repentance to Will's pilgrimage can be seen in the commentaries on the Psalms quoted below. In Ps. 119, the singer mourns his long absence from home:

> Heu me quod incolatus meus longinquus factus est . . .
> Multum peregrinata est anima mea. . . .   (vv. 5, 6)

> [Alas, my sojourn has been a long way off . . .
> Far has my soul travelled. . . .][17]

Augustine, putting aside the literal meaning, interprets this exile as a separation from God:

> Ne peregrinationem corporalem intellegeres, animam dixit peregrinari. Corpus peregrinatur locis, anima peregrinatur affectibus. Si amaueris terram, peregrinaris a Deo; si amaueris Deum, adscendis ad Deum. In caritate Dei et proximi exerceamur, ut redeamus ad caritatem.[18]

[15] The Three Lusts of 1 Jn. 2: 16, representing 'all that is in the World', are commonplace in religious writings: it is, however, of interest that in the chapter of the *Confessiones* from which Will quotes, Augustine's fleshly temptations are personified as his 'old mistresses'; and when, two chapters later, he looks back on his 'carnal' life he analyses the temptations he has experienced under these three heads, associating *concupiscentia oculorum* (Langland's 'Coveitise of Eighes') with vain and curious learning through the senses. Langland's Will likewise desires to 'see wonders' (B. XI. 10), which put his quest out of mind—

> That of Dowel ne Dobet no deyntee me thoughte.
> I hadde no likyng, leve me, [o]f the leste of hem ought to knowe.
> Coveitise of Eighes com ofter in mynde
> Than Dowel or Dobet among my dedes alle.   (B. XI. 48–51)

Langland does not develop this aspect of the second Lust and its relation with the third, *Superbia vitae*, but Will's besetting sin is certainly curiosity, and because of this Anima accuses him of being 'oon of Prides knyghtes' (B. XV. 50).

[16] For the parable, see Luc. 15: 11–32, and on the *regio longinqua* see Wittig, p. 234, and references in Goldsmith, 'Piers' Apples', p. 323.

[17] For *multum peregrinata est*, the Vulgate reads *multum incola fuit*, emphasizing the sojourn abroad rather than the travelling.

[18] *Enarrationes in Psalmos*, CCSL 40, p. 1785.

[Lest you should understand this as a bodily journeying, he has put 'the soul travelled'. The body travels in places, the soul travels in affections. If you have loved the earth, you travel away from God; if you have loved God, you ascend towards God. Let us be active in love of God and our neighbour so that we return to Love.]

Attracted by terrestrial delights, Will the Dreamer, like the Prodigal, moves his affections away from Truth, and only starts his journey back to God when he begins to feel the *affectus* of shame.[19] Then, as Dame Study foresaw, he is moved by Ymaginatif to take stock of his forty wasted years and to resume his search for Dowel, which leads him 'back to Love'. His companion on the pilgrimage is Patience, whose 'lemman' is Love (B. XIII. 138–9).

Augustine in the passage I have just quoted, like James in the passage on the 'royal law', exhorts us to be active in loving one another. It is at first sight odd that Will the Dreamer is not pictured helping a neighbour, or indeed interacting with people, as he journeys: he has, it seems, no friends or human companions. All the emphasis is on his inner life, and his waking life is hardly fleshed out at all. His spiritual progress is outwardly signalled, paradoxically enough, by his refusal to bow politely to lords and ladies (B. XV. 5–9); in this fashion he shows that he will not transgress the 'royal law' by being 'a respecter of persons' (cf. Ja. 2: 1–10). His 'return to Love' is accompanied by a brief mention of a wife and child, but they do not emerge as characters in their own right. His *affectus* are marked by tears, the blush of shame, a wiping of the eyes, by a world-weariness, but not by tenderness towards individuals. The whole picture is consistent with his role as an allegorical figure representing the will of Everyman in its peregrinations towards true and false loves. It is Will's innate desire to conform himself to the will of God, to restore the image in which he was made, but his longing for the apple of knowledge turns him from his purpose for many years.

St James's epistle ends with exhortations to his disciples to wait with patience for the last days of earth. He reminds them how patiently a farmer waits for the harvest. He reminds them of the patience of the prophets. He tries to draw back those who have strayed from the path of truth (cf. Ja. 5: 7–11, 19–20). There is no need for me to spell out comparisons with the lives of Piers and Will, but I do wish to draw attention to the patience of the prophets. In the brilliant dinner-party scene which contrasts the carnal behaviour of the Doctor with the asceticism of Patience, Clergy reappears and concedes his authority to Piers the Plowman (B. XIII. 123–9). The horizon recedes as Will goes forward, and the conversation at the dinner-table reveals that in reaching Dobet Will is only at a halfway stage in his journey. The scene

---

[19] See Wittig, pp. 221–9, for a theory that the three 'Do's' are three states of *affectus*, and Will 'the reluctant *affectus* who bears the responsibility of supplying precisely what Wit cannot' (p. 226). This seems to me too exclusive a definition in both cases.

hints in many enigmatic ways that Will is retracing the steps of God's people from the wilderness and out of bondage: the meal with its sour dishes recalls the Jewish Passover, as Conscience implies: 'Thanne, passe we over til Piers come and preve this in dede' (B. XIII. 132). The scene also humorously, but somewhat ominously, portrays Conscience as transgressing the 'royal law' by showing such marked respect and honour to the great man and putting the poor pilgrims at a lower table.

Patience sustains his friends with a piece of the Paternoster, *fiat voluntas tua* (B. XIV. 49), a sign that Will is learning to conform himself to the will of God. In Augustine's metaphorical language, he is returning home from 'the land of longing' which is also 'the region of unlikeness':

> Non ergo loco quisque longe est a Deo, sed dissimilitudine. Quid est, dissimilitudine? Mala uita, malis moribus. Si enim bonis moribus propinquatur Deo, malis moribus receditur a Deo. Vnus ergo idemque homo corpore stans uno loco, et amando Deum accedit ad Deum, et amando iniquitatem recedit a Deo; nusquam pedes mouet, et tamen potest et accedere et recedere. Pedes enim nostri in hoc itinere, affectus nostri sunt.
>
> (*En. in Ps.* 94, CCSL 39, p. 1331)

> [For a person is not far away from God spatially, but in 'unlikeness'. What is it—this 'unlikeness'? It is in evil living, in evil practices. For if through good practices he is brought near to God, by bad practices he is separated from God. Thus a man standing in one place, both draws near to God by loving God, and by loving wickedness draws away from God: his foot does not move anywhere, and yet he can draw near and draw back. For our 'feet' on this journey are our affections.]

Will, having started back from 'the region of unlikeness', is now capable of seeing in his looking-glass 'the face he was born with', but he is not yet ready to do so. When he has come to recognize the old Adam in himself, as he does when he stands under Piers's mysterious apple-tree watching the consequences of his own pride and curiosity, he will be humbled sufficiently to see the Son of Justice, whose coming is heralded in the last book of the prophets. Then he will 'wipe his eyes' and come in sight of the Samaritan, a parable figure identified by the exegetes with Christ.[20] He did not learn from Scripture and Clergy, in the days when he was merely curious, and his curiosity nearly got the better of him again, when he saw the three staves holding up the Tree of

[20] See e.g. Bernard's *Sermones in Cantica*, XXI. 4 (PL 183, col. 874), which also includes 'and I will run after Thee', adapting *post te curremus* (*Cant.* 1: 3), a text which Langland probably had in mind when he had Will *run*—for the first time—after the Samaritan (B. XVII. 85). Bernard describes how the soul when warmed from its cold torpor by the *Sol Justitiae* will run towards God (ibid. 4–5). For the significance of Langland's pun on 'justice(s) sone', see Goldsmith, 'Piers' Apples', pp. 317–19.

Charity, but with the Samaritan he learns 'bi his werkes' about God's redemptive love for man, and through his words what God is like. He offers himself (like the returning Prodigal) as a servant to Christ the Samaritan: in *affectus* he is drawing nearer to God. On Easter Day he comes very close to recognizing Truth as he participates in the blessing of the Eucharistic bread at Mass, but his pilgrimage is not yet over.

The visions which make up the *Vita de Dobet* have brought Will through the eras of prophecy and of the Redemption which seals Truth's promises to mankind. He has still to move into the last age of the world, the era of grace. The goal of his earthly pilgrimage is not, as some critics have thought, the holy city of Jerusalem. Characteristically, Langland invites his readers to recall the phrase he refrains from writing—the phrase which really defines what it means to 'do best'. At the climax of Will's most sublime vision, Love sings the opening words of Ps. 132,

> *Ecce quam bonum et quam iocundum &c.*   (B. XVIII. 426)

The words which that *et cetera* silently sounds are *habitare fratres in unum* ['brothers to dwell in unity']. Will's quest will not end until he and all his neighbours are in the living temple imagined by St Peter as made by the 'in-comers and pilgrims' [*advenas et peregrinos*] who have 'tasted the goodness of the Lord' (cf. 1 Pet. 2: 3–12). St Peter tells his disciples, 'Once you were like sheep going astray, but now you have been brought back to the shepherd and overseer [*episcopus*] of your souls' (1 Pet. 2: 25). Will the Dreamer who once wandered, 'as I a shepe were', finally

> comsed to rome
> Thorugh Contricion and Confession til I cam to Unitee.
>   (B. XX. 212–13)

Piers, in Passus XIX openly identified with St Peter, the overseer of Grace, has built the house Unity, which is in its different aspects the Sower's grange, the Samaritan's inn, and the Prodigal's Father's house. It is called 'Holy Chirche on Englissh' (B. XIX. 330).

Psalm 132, the psalm Love sings, is a peculiarly Jewish psalm, celebrating the unguent on the beard of Aaron and the dew upon Mount Sion. I think it is important for Langland's general purpose that it should be so. The holy charge laid upon Aaron and Moses descends upon St Peter: when the Jewish 'letter' of the psalm is 'spiritually' interpreted by Augustine the unguent is revealed as a figure for the blessing which flowed down to the disciples at Pentecost. Those disciples were the first *Christians* to hear 'Ecce quam bonum et quam iocundum, etc.', Augustine says, and he quotes:

> Et erat illis anima una et cor unum in Deum.
>   (Act. 4. 32; *En. in Ps.*, CCSL 40, p. 1927)

129

Significantly for our understanding of another feature of the *Vita de Dobest*, he goes on to say that this *unitas* joins together all those who dedicate themselves to God and render to God what they have promised. He quotes a psalm which brings in the familiar command *reddite*:

> Vovete, et reddite Domino Deo vestro.   (Ps. 75: 12)

> [Vow, and render to the Lord your God.]

He adds, 'Plane numquam reddet, si de suo se putauerit redditurum [Plainly no-one will render, if he has thought that he will render out of his own resources].' This is the thought that haunts the penitent sinners in *Piers Plowman*. Piers can pardon and absolve only the soul who *redit quod debet—*

> Paieth parfitly, as pure truthe wolde.   (B. XIX. 195)

Natural justice plainly demands that the penitents pay their debts to their wronged brethren, but Holy Church demands more:

> '*Reddite Cesari*,' quod God, 'that *Cesari* bifalleth,
> *Et que sunt Dei Deo*, or ellis ye don ille.'   (B. I. 52–3)

When Augustine quotes this text in his Discourse on Ps. 94 he observes:

> Tamquam diceret 'Si Caesar quaeret in nummo imaginem suam,
> Deus non quaerit in homine imaginem suam?'

> [It was as if he said 'If Caesar looks for his image on the coin, will not God look for his own Image in man?']

The relevance of Holy Church's text to the course of Will's pilgrimage is plainly expressed in Augustine's amplification of this thought:

> Ergo si dissimilitudine recedimus a Deo, similitudine accedimus ad Deum. Qua similitudine? Ad quam facti sumus, quam in nobis peccando corruperamus, quam peccatorum remissione recepimus, quae in nobis renouatur intus in mente, ut tamquam resculpatur in nummo, id est, in anima nostra imago Dei nostri, et redeamus ad thesauros eius.   (*En. in Ps.* 94, CCSL 39, p. 1332)

> [Therefore, if through 'unlikeness' we draw away from God, we draw near to God through 'likeness'. Through what 'likeness'? To that in which we were made, which we marred in ourselves by sinning, which we have received again in the remission of our sins, which is renewed in us within our soul as if on the coin—that is, our soul—the Image of our God is formed again, and we may go back into his treasury.]

In order to restore the Image of God in ourselves, Augustine concludes, we must love our enemies, imitating God the Father, who sends his rain and sun equally upon the just and the unjust (cf. Matt. 5. 45–6). Langland portrays Piers, the god-like man, similarly working towards this ideal:

> A[c] wel worthe Piers the Plowman, that pursueth God in doynge,
> *Qui pluit super iustos et iniustos* at ones.   (B. XIX. 433–4)

I have been quoting from Augustine's Discourse on Ps. 94, *Venite exsultemus Domino*. This well-known psalm contrasts the forty years of estrangement from God, the years spent wandering in the wilderness, with the present joy of the congregation kneeling *in confessione* before their Lord and Saviour.[21] The 'plot' of *Piers Plowman* traces the return of a single soul to his Father's house, but concurrently, through the transformations of Piers, and in sundry riddling ways,[22] we are made aware that this one Will typifies the wills of all God's people who have received the divine revelation from the time of Abraham onwards. The disruption of their peace in *Unitas* goes back in history: even the apostles had to warn their followers against false brethren, and a thousand years before Langland wrote Augustine was both celebrating *fratres in unum* and at the same time exhorting fellow-Christians not to fight each other, but to do battle against the Devil. He reminds his readers that the blessing given to Moses and Aaron descends like an unguent on those only who love their enemies. Langland, expressing the like belief, does not want to expel the unruly friars from Piers's house, though he exposes the appalling harm that they can do. He shows Will finding his way into Unity only to discover a crowd of fearful and sick people and an unregistered number of quack doctors.

Will's question to Holy Church 'How may I save my soul?' is answered by Langland through the voices of the apostles and the great monastic teachers of the past: and they give but one answer: 'From your own resources, you cannot.' There has to be an infusion of the Holy Spirit into the questing soul: this is why the Christian needs 'Piers'. Bernard answers the great question in a sermon which pictures the operation of the Spirit in restoring a wounded man to health. In Passus XX of the poem, Langland presents a black parody of such an image, with his groping friar as an obscene caricature of the Divine Physician. Bernard quotes the psalmist:

> Putruerunt et corruptae sint cicatrices meae a facie insipientiae meae.   (Ps. 37: 6)

> [My wounds stink and fester because of my foolishness.]

[21] The psalmist's *in confessione* prompts Augustine to expatiate on confession in praise and confession in penitence, both of which he finds apt here: he believes that the tongue does nothing more worthy than employ itself so (*En. in Ps.* 94, CCSL 39, p. 1333).
[22] The most notable enigmas are Patience's riddle, and the Tree of Charity, both of which carry moral significance for the single soul and allegorical significance for the congregation of God's people in every century.

He then describes how the Physician draws near to the wounded soul, cuts away the diseased ulcer and anoints the wound; then follows a strenuous convalescence:

> Deinde apponitur medicamentum poenitentiae, malagma jejuniorum, vigiliarum, orationum, et si qua sunt alia poenitentium exercitia. In labore cibandus est cibo boni operis, ne deficiat. Quod opus sit cibus, inde doceris: *Meus cibus est*, inquit, *ut faciam voluntatem Patris mei* (Joan. IV, 34). . . . Sumpto cibo potuque, quid jam restat, nisi ut pauset aegrotus, et quieti contemplationis post sudores actionis incumbat? Dormiens in contemplatione Deum somniat; per speculum siquidem et in aenigmate, non autem facie ad faciem interim intuetur.[23]

> [Then are applied the medicament of penitence, the plaster of fasts, vigils, prayers, and other exercises of the penitent. He needs to be nourished in his exertions with the food of good works, so that he does not become worn out. What food is needful, you may learn from what Christ says, 'My food is to do the will of my Father'. . . . When the sick man has taken food and drink, what remains for him to do but to rest and recline in the quiet of contemplation after the fatigues of activity? Sleeping in this contemplation he sees God in a dream: though only in a mirror and obscurely, and not as yet face to face.]

Bernard's image shows the Holy Spirit at work in the souls of Christian people, and the glorious hope that animates him and his followers. Langland's dismal simulacrum shows the 'fools' having their wounds dressed, not with penitential exercises, but with soothing words which cover up the festering in pretending to cure it. It is this which enervates Contrition, 'the soverayneste salve' (B. XX. 373), and brings Conscience to the point of leaving Unity. In the end, Conscience, crying out for Grace, proposes to walk out of the house, though the whole import of the poem implies that he is wrong to do so. Somehow Contrition ought to be reinvigorated within the catholic and apostolic Church. But the last words of the poem leave the reader to guess what sort of a fool the old poet thought himself to be for having invested a lifetime of hope in church unity.

[23] *Sermones in Cantica*, XVIII. 5–6, PL 183, col. 862.

Piers Plowman *B. XVIII. 371:*
'right ripe must'

HANNEKE WIRTJES

Quod myrrha enim tristificat, vinum laetificat.
(*Glossa Ordinaria* in Cant. 1: 13)

I

When, in Passus XVIII of *Piers Plowman*, Christ harrows Hell, he outwits
Satan in a legal argument and says triumphantly:

> The bitternesse that thow hast browe, now brouke it thiselve;
> That art doctour of deeth, drynk that thow madest!
> For I that am lord of lif, love is my drynke,
> And for that drynke today, I deide upon erthe.
> I faught so, me thursteth yet, for mannes soule sake;
> May no drynke me moiste, ne my thurst slake,
> Til the vendage falle in the vale of Josaphat,
> That I drynke right ripe must, *resurreccio mortuorum*.
> And thanne shal I come as a kyng, crouned, with aungeles,
> And have out of helle alle mennes soules.
>
> (B. XVIII. 364–73)[1]

The general meaning of these lines is clear: they refer to the Last Judgement,
which it was believed in the Middle Ages would take place in the vale of
Jehoshaphat (see Joel 3: 2, 12–13), as the commentators point out.[2] The
opposing forces of life and death, Christ and Satan, are conceived of in terms
of drink: Satan, 'doctour of deeth', is called upon to swallow his own poison
(364–5), whereas Christ, whose drink is love and who died for love's sake,
will not be able to slake his thirst until the Day of Judgement, when he will
raise the dead and drink 'right ripe must' (366–73).

---

[1] References are to *The Vision of Piers Plowman: A Complete Edition of the B-Text*, ed.
A. V. C. Schmidt (London, 1978).
[2] See, for instance, Skeat's note in *The Vision of Will Concerning Piers the Plowman*, ed.
W. W. Skeat, 2 vols (Oxford, 1886), II. 263; Schmidt, p. 352; *English Verse
1300–1500*, ed. John Burrow (London, 1977), p. 142.

To the modern producer or knowledgeable drinker of wine *must* would mean 'grape juice in the process of becoming wine',[3] and because it is still fermenting it is certain to make anyone who is foolish enough to drink it very drunk very quickly. This was well known in the Middle Ages: Peter Comestor writes, 'Vehementior est ebrietas de musto quam de vino defecato',[4] and Hildegard of Bingen advises against drinking it: 'Sed et novum et crudum mustum, quod nondum in fervore ebulliendo sordes eiecit, non bibat.'[5] To associate Christ with this sort of drunkenness would surely be inappropriate, and the definitions *OED* and *MED* give are broader than Schoonmaker's: *OED* s.v. *must* sb.[1], sense 1, states that *must* is 'new wine; the juice of the grape either unfermented or before the fermentation is completed', and *MED* s.v. *must* n., sense 1 (a), describes *must* as 'the juice of grapes, unfermented or undergoing the process of fermentation; new wine, must'. Is 'ripe must' then simply a poetic synonym for 'wine' in a line that alliterates on *m*? *MED*'s gloss on the phrase, 'fermented must', which would logically equal 'wine', suggests that it might be; the phrase is not attested elsewhere.

The earliest recorded instance, from the Alfredian translation of Boethius, does not unambiguously distinguish between 'must' and 'wine': 'Ne meaht þu win wringan on mide winter, þeah ðe wel lyste wearmes mustes', although 'mustes' may be 'young wine' here. The remaining occurrences in Old English are also translations of Latin *mustum*, except for a gloss noted in Bosworth-Toller s.v. *must*: *isomellum*, 'must mid hunig gemenged', where 'must' is unlikely to be fermenting grape juice. Bosworth-Toller further gives a quotation from Ælfric's *Homilies*, 'Ðas men sindon mid muste fordrencte', which renders Acts 2: 13, 'musto pleni sunt isti'. In the *Paris Psalter*, Ps. 103: 14, 'must and windrinc' translates *vinum*, 'et vinum laetificet cor hominis' becoming 'heortan manna/ must and windrinc myclum blissað'.[6]

All the citations given by *MED* s.v. which connect must and intoxication are translations or paraphrases of Acts 2: 13: *Lambeth Homilies*, 'mid miste fordrencte' (Pentec. 91); *Southern Passion*, 'Þeos men beoþ dronke of mostʒ; hi ne conne hare tonges holde' (2480); Wycliffite Bible, 'ful of must'; *Cursor Mundi*, 'Drunken . . . o must ar þai' (18968); and *Ludus Coventriae*, particularly scornfully, 'Muste in here brayn so sclyly doth creppe/ þat þei chateryn And chateryn As they jays were' (353/18). The association with advanced intoxication may suggest that 'must' is the still fermenting grape

---

[3] Frank Schoonmaker, *Encyclopedia of Wine*, ed. Hugh Johnson (London, 1974), s.v. *must*.

[4] *Historia scholastica*, PL 198, col. 1653.

[5] *Causae et curae*, ed. P. Kaiser (Leipzig, 1903), p. 168. The context is cures for disorders of the lung.

[6] *The Paris Psalter and the Metres of Boethius*, ed. George Philip Krapp, Anglo-Saxon Poetic Records 5 (New York, 1933; repr. 1972), p. 77; the other Old English quotations are from *OED*.

juice here, but Pentecost is not the time of the vintage; besides, the Greek has 'ἕτεροι δὲ διαχλευάζοντες ἔλεγον ὅτι γλεύκους μεμεστωμένοι εἰσίν', γλεύκους from γλεῦκος, meaning 'sweet new wine', not 'fermenting grape juice'. 'New wine' is indeed one of the meanings of Medieval Latin *mustum*, though it is not generally recorded as a separate sense, as it should be.[7] The Latin word was certainly used in England to denote 'new wine'. An example can be found in a royal account of 1243 detailing expenditure on wine: 'Et pro xx doliis musti Gallici, xxx l.'[8] This cannot have been fermenting grape juice, because, even if the royal household had wanted to drink it, this *mustum* would not have been safe to transport; on the other hand, since the price is similar to that of the other items on the list, the *mustum Gallicum* must have been wine, not verjuice, which, being unfermented, was much cheaper.

The modern sense, 'grape juice in the process of becoming wine', is attested by John Lydgate: 'Must lesyth his name toward seint martynes' (*Secreta Secretorum*, 1440), i.e. November 11th, which is in fact the earliest approximate date when the wine of the new vintage is of a reasonable alcohol content and ready for drinking. Today it is mainly the Beaujolais Nouveau which is made to be drunk so early, and normally even the most ordinary wine is left to mature at least until the following spring; this was not the practice in the Middle Ages.

Returning to Langland's phrase, we have two possible meanings for 'must': 'new wine' and 'grape juice in the process of becoming wine'. The former would produce a tautology: 'new wine' is already 'right ripe' in the sense that fermentation has been completed. Alternatively, 'right ripe must' could be an oxymoron, 'old new wine', but Langland does not, as far as I know, use oxymoron, and the context makes it clear that what Christ will drink is the wine of the new vintage. Indeed, he will not be able to quench his thirst 'til the vendage falle in the vale of Josaphat' (370), when he will drink the new wine as soon as the fermenting grape juice has been turned into wine: then the must is 'right ripe' and will no longer produce the violent effects noted by Hildegard and the Comestor. By calling it 'right ripe must', Langland suggests that the wine Christ drinks is produced miraculously quickly— Christ does not need to wait until the feast of St Martin—and hence it has all the freshness of newly pressed grapes.

Freshness was highly prized, and the arrival of the new wine was something

---

[7] For instance, *Novum glossarium mediae latinitatis*, fasc. M–N (Copenhagen, 1959–69), s.v. *mustum*. Du Cange, *Glossarium mediae et infimae latinitatis* (Niort, 1883–7), has no entry *mustum*; the *Revised Medieval Latin Word-List from British and Irish Sources*, ed. R. E. Latham (London, 1975), s.v. *mustum*, has no more than 'grape-juice', which is quite inadequate.

[8] André L. Simon, *The History of the Wine Trade in England*, 3 vols (London, 1907), I. 110 and note. The reference is to Mag. Rot. 29 Henry III, ult. m. 1a. Simon translates *musti Gallici* 'of new or sweet French wine' without further explanation.

of an event in medieval England. By the fourteenth century, most of the English vineyards had been grubbed, because it made more sense economically to grow more profitable crops and import wine from countries where the vine yielded sweeter and more abundant fruit than in England. For obvious political reasons, most wine drunk in England came from France.[9] Wine was shipped to England twice a year in wooden casks, in the autumn and in the spring. Even if the vintage had been early, the new wine did not usually reach England before November; the wines that arrived in the spring were the wines 'of rack', which were so called because they were not racked off their lees (i.e. 'drawn') until the spring. Corks and glass bottles were unknown, so wine was kept in wooden casks, which inevitably were porous. Without a reliable means of preserving the wine, it deteriorated fast and was soon undrinkable without a liberal addition of spices and honey: this explains why the wine of the previous year was sold off cheaply as soon as the new vintage appeared on the market and why fresh and new wine was always preferred to old (Simon, I. 264–6).

To the modern palate, most of these wines would have been excessively 'hard' if they were red, for being young they were still high in tannin, but in the Middle Ages people may well have had a taste for 'hard' wines,[10] which is not surprising in view of the alternative: months of drinking wine that was getting progressively more like vinegar must have made people look forward eagerly to the new vintage. This, then, is the reason why Langland's 'right ripe must' is so much more evocative than simply 'wine', but there is more to

[9] Edward Hyams, *The Grape Vine in England* (London, 1949), p. 40. Hyams says that until about 1300 Worcestershire, Langland's native county, 'was a sort of English Bordeaux' (p. 40). See also Simon, I. 268: 'Ever since Rouen had been lost to the Plantagenets, Gascony had become the chief source of supply of the English wine trade'; German wine was scarce and hence expensive. Langland mentions both: 'Whit wyn of Oseye [Alsace] and wyn of Gascoigne,/ Of the Ryn and the Rochel [la Rochelle] the roost to defie' (B. Prol. 229–30).

[10] Simon, I. 261–3. 'Glass bottles being then unknown, and the proper treatment of wine in casks only very imperfectly comprehended, wines were mostly drunk new, and custom had engendered a taste for their natural harshness. The stronger the wine the better it would keep, although the longer it would remain on tap the worse it would become, so that either light or old wines were always considered the worst by mediaeval customers' (p. 261). See also Hugh Johnson, *Wine* (London, 1974; updated reprint, 1978), p. 26. Nevertheless there are numerous references in Greek and Latin literature to prove that the ancients loved old wines, e.g. Homer, *Odyssey*, III. 390–2 and Horace, *Odes*, III. 21. The Greeks preserved their wine in earthenware jars, which were non-porous and acted as airtight containers in which the wine was able to mature. This would not have been possible in wooden (and hence porous) casks: see H. Warner Allen, *A History of Wine* (London, 1961), p. 18. The Romans had less skill in pottery and therefore needed an inner coating of pitch, which would keep the *dolia* airtight and also act as a preservative. Not all their wine was pitched, however: Allen, referring to Pliny, *Naturalis Historia*, XIV and Columella, *De re rustica*, XII. 19, 2, says that the best Roman wine was not (pp. 83–4).

the phrase than this: an examination of Langland's use of the biblical imagery of wine and the vintage in these lines, taking into account the traditional medieval interpretations of the material alluded to, will reveal just how complex and interesting this short passage from *Piers Plowman* is.

II

Although the vintage was a popular image of eternal life in late antique funerary art, deriving from the Dionysiac belief in eternal bliss,[11] it does not, as far as I know, appear as a symbol of the resurrection of the dead in the early Fathers of the Church: Tertullian, for instance, in his treatise on the subject, takes the changing of the seasons, the natural cycle of death and rebirth, as an indication that the dead shall be raised, but he does not mention the vintage.[12] The image of Christ drinking 'right ripe must' at the Last Judgement is in all likelihood Langland's own, but his use of wine and the vintage has a long history, going back to the Bible and patristic commentary.

A number of mentions of grapes and wine in the Old Testament were interpreted in the Middle Ages as types of Christ's Passion. The most important of these are the bunch of grapes from the Promised Land (Num. 13: 24), the cluster of Cyprus grapes (Cant. 1: 13; the Vulgate has 'botrus cypri', the Authorized Version, more correctly, 'a cluster of Cyprus blossom'), the mystical winepress (Isa. 5: 1–7) and the treading of the grapes (Isa. 63: 1–6). In Isa. 63: 1–6 the second speaker was taken to be Christ, his clothing spattered with the blood of the Passion. The winepress of Isa. 5: 1–7 was seen as an instrument of torture in which Christ was pressed like a grape (compare Cant. 1: 13, where the beloved was allegorized as Christ).[13] In the passage

---

[11] See Corrado Leonardi, *Ampelos: il simbolo delle vite nell'arte pagana e paleocristiana*, (Rome, 1947), pp. 41–60, esp. p. 60: 'Orbene, quelle scene di vendemmia che fanne parte esclusiva dell'arte funeraria classica profana, esprimono il caraterre dionisiaco della felicità eterna, e la preparazione del vino, la bevanda d'immortalità.'

[12] See *De resurrectione mortuorum*, in *Tertulliani Opera, Pars II: Opera Montanistica*, CCSL 2, pp. 912–1012: 'Reuoluuntur hiemes et aestates, et uerna et autumna cum suis uiribus moribus fructibus. . . . Semel dixerim: uniuersa conditio ricidiua est. Quodcumque conueneris, fuit; quodcumque amiseris, erit. Nihil non iterum est; omnia in statum redeunt cum abscesserint, omnia incipiunt cum desierint. Ideo finiuntur, ut fiant; nihil deperit nisi in salutem. Totus igitur hic ordo reuolubilis rerum testatio est resurrectionis mortuorum' (p. 935). Bromyard's *Summa praedicantium* s.v. *resurrectio* does not mention the vintage and neither does Augustine in his treatment of the resurrection of the dead (*De civitate Dei*, XX and XXII); Tertullian, however, has a striking metaphor of the resurrection of the dead as a refreshing drink: 'Cuius si hauseris fontem, nullam poteris sitire doctrinam. nullus te ardor exuret quaestionem: resurrectionem quoque carnis usquequaque potando refrigerabis' (p. 1012).

[13] See Alois Thomas, *Die Darstellung Christi in der Kelter* (Düsseldorf, 1935; repr. 1981).

from Numbers the bunch of grapes and the staff on which they were carried were held to prefigure Christ and the Cross. The traditional allegorical explanations of these texts would have been familiar to Langland and his contemporaries from a variety of sources: directly, from biblical commentary and exegesis, but also from the liturgy, from art and from literature.

The winepress of the Passion was not used in art in England, but numerous representations of the bunch of grapes from the Promised Land exist.[14] The winepress is particularly frequent in Latin hymns (Thomas, pp. 68–77); the two passages from Isaiah appear in a few Middle English lyrics (Woolf, pp. 199–202). In the liturgy for Palm Sunday (Sarum Use) the clergy say the verse, 'Hic est qui de Edom venit tinctis Bosra vestibus, in stola sua formosus, gradiens virtutibus, non in equis bellicosis nec in altis curribus' (which is based on Isa. 63: 1) during the Procession of Palms: Langland refers to the service on Palm Sunday at the beginning of Passus XVIII (lines 6–9). On Wednesday of Holy Week Isa. 62: 11–63: 7 is one of the Old Testament readings at Mass. Isa. 5: 1–7 forms the basis of the second *tractus* at Mass on Holy Saturday. Isa. 62: 11–63: 7 is the first lesson at Mass on Wednesday of Holy Week.[15] These are not the only texts used in the liturgy for Holy Week that link wine, vines or the vintage and Christ's Passion. On Good Friday, Jer. 2: 21 forms the basis of a responsory, and a following versicle in the second Nocturn—'Vinea mea electa ego te plantavi. Quomodo conversa es in amaritudinem: ut me crucifigeres et Barrabam dimitteres'—is followed by, 'Ego quidem plantavi te vinea mea electa omne semen verum'. The first Nocturn has as its second Lesson Lam. 1: 13–15, which ends, 'torcular calcavit Dominus: virgini filiae Juda'.[16] Lam. 1: 12 appears throughout on Good Friday: 'O vos omnes qui transitis per viam, attendite et videte si est dolor sicut dolor meus: quoniam vindemiavit me, ut locutus est Dominus in die furoris irae'.[17] It occurs in its entirety as the first reading of the second Nocturn; the first part (O . . . dolor meus) is repeated in the versicle after the third reading, and again on Holy Saturday after the ninth reading of the third Nocturn. It is also the first antiphon at Lauds on Holy Saturday (*Missal*, p. 113). The vineyard of Jer. 2: 21 is explicitly linked with the vinegar mixed with gall offered to the suffering Christ in the chant of the clergy at Mass on Good Friday before the Adoration of the Cross: 'Qvid ultra debui facere tibi et non feci ego quidem plantaui te uinea mea fructu decora et tu facta es michi

---

[14] Rosemary Woolf, *The English Religious Lyric in the Middle Ages* (Oxford, 1968), pp. 201-2. For illustrations, see Thomas; also Rosamund Tuve, *A Reading of George Herbert* (Chicago, 1952). Tuve, passim, draws attention to the *Biblia pauperum* and the *Speculum humanae salvationis* with their pictorial representations of types of Christ.
[15] *The Sarum Missal*, ed. J. Wickham Legg (Oxford, 1916), pp. 95, 120, 100.
[16] *Breviarium ad usum insignis ecclesiae Sarum*, I, *Kalendarium et Ordo temporalis*, ed. F. Proctor and C. Wordsworth (Cambridge, 1882), cols 787–8.
[17] *Breviarium*, cols 787–8, col. 801.

satis amara aceto namque mixto cum felle sitim meam potasti et lancea perforasti latus saluatori tuo' (ibid.).

The mention of the Good Friday Mass at the beginning of Passus XVIII and the reference to the Adoration of the Cross at the end (lines 430–4) suggest that Langland had the liturgy firmly in mind when he composed his account of his vision of the events of Good Friday. Actual quotations from the liturgy in Passus XVIII confirm this: 'Ars ut artem falleret' (line 161) is from Venantius Fortunatus' hymn *Pange lingua*, which was sung at Mass on Good Friday during the Adoration of the Cross (ibid.), and it provides a conceit that is central to Langland's legalistic conception of the Harrowing of Hell, that of 'bigile the gilour' (lines 159–61).[18] Ps. 23 was part of the Second Nocturn on Holy Saturday and is quoted in line 261 ('Attolite portas') and lines 316, 317 and 319 ('Quis est iste? . . . Rex glorie . . . Dominus virtutum');[19] it could be argued that the description of Christ's triumphant entry into Hell is constructed around these references to Ps. 23.[20] Although the connection of wine and the Day of Judgement derives from commentaries on Joel,[21] the frequent association of wine and the Passion in the liturgy is important here because Passus XVIII grew out of Langland's familiarity with the liturgy for Holy Week. But however crucial the liturgy is here, it is to the patristic tradition of exegesis, which links certain mentions of wine and grapes in the Bible with Christ's Passion, that we must now turn, for that is where we will find the key to the meaning of lines 364–73 of Passus XVIII.

A note of warning needs to be sounded first. Little is known of Langland's life and less still of his reading. It may by now, as Judson Boyce Allen says, be 'a presumption of criticism that Langland thought in concordances and

[18] Note that there are textual problems here. Line 161 is supplied from the C-Text by Schmidt and by Kane and Donaldson (*Piers Plowman: The B Version*, ed. George Kane and E. Talbot Donaldson, London, 1975): for a discussion of the corruption in lines 160–1, see Schmidt's Textual and Lexical Commentary, p. 297. Line 159 is regarded as metrically deficient by Schmidt and by Kane and Donaldson because in their view it lacks a stave in the second half-line. Whether or not the line is acceptable as it stands—and it reads the same in all B-MSS—depends on how strict Langland's metrical practice in the B-Text is considered to be.

[19] *Breviarium*, col. 797.

[20] Ps. 23 is widely used in medieval plays dealing with the Harrowing of Hell; see, for instance, the York Play on the subject; also Karl Young, *The Drama of the Medieval Church*, 2 vols (Oxford, 1933; repr. 1962), I. 149–77. The Psalm is quoted in the Gospel of Nicodemus, so it is conceivable that Langland is here referring not to the liturgy but to the apocryphal Gospel.

[21] See the *Glossa Ordinaria* on Joel 2. The Gloss on Joel is not in Migne (PL 113–14). As Beryl Smalley tartly remarks of Migne's edition of the *Glossa Ordinaria*, 'Anyone who has tried to use it knows how worthless it is' (*The Study of the Bible in the Middle Ages*, 3rd edn (Oxford, 1983), p. 56). References to parts of the Gloss which are not in Migne are to the glossed Bible in four volumes (Bodleian Library Auct. 5. Q. Infra. II. 6–9) printed in Venice in 1495. Joel 2 is on f. 923r.

distinctiones',[22] but there is no way of finding out which ones he had access to. Moreover, Passus XVIII is a narration of events rather than a disquisition on a moral or theological problem which takes a verse from the Bible for its text: Langland was less likely here than elsewhere to turn to books intended as aids for sermon writers in need of dictionaries of scriptural quotations with appropriate allegorical interpretations—a critical approach that works for Haukyn's coat (see Alford) does not work for the Harrowing of Hell. The *distinctiones* are useful, however, in that they indicate which of the Bible texts containing images of grapes, wine and the vintage were commonly linked together by preachers, and what the generally favoured allegorical interpretations were. The *Glossa Ordinaria* may serve a similar purpose: in the absence of specific and unambiguously identifiable sources, the modern commentator needs a guide to tell him which glosses from the Fathers were widely current and hence known to Langland and his fourteenth-century readers.

In none of the Old Testament texts referred to which use images of grapes, wine and the vintage is there any mention of thirst or drinking. For texts which do mention these things, we have to go to the New Testament. Langland's picture of Christ thirsting recalls Christ's cry from the Cross, 'Sitio' (John 19: 28), which is quoted in the corresponding passage in the C-Text (C. xx. 408), though not in B.[23] What Christ was offered (but refused to drink: Matt. 27: 34, Mark 16: 23) was vinegar. The *Glossa Ordinaria* gives various interpretations, all of which are relevant. The glosses on John 19: 28 and Luke 23: 36 suggest that the vinegar symbolizes the Jews 'a vino patriarcharum degenerantes' (f. 1141^v), the 'false Jewes' of B. XVIII. 92–109. The gloss on Mark 15: 36 quotes St Jerome, connecting the vinegar with the apple from which Eve and Adam ate. One kind of sour juice cancels out another: 'Hoc aceto succus letalis pomi abstergitur. Et non accipit id pro quo patitur. Unde de eo quod non rapui tunc exoluebam' (f. 1095^v). But according to Matthew the vinegar is mixed with gall (Matt. 27: 34) and according to Mark with myrrh (Mark 16: 23), both of which would have made the vinegar, sour in itself, bitter. The *Glossa Ordinaria* cites Bede on Mark 16: 23: 'Mattheus: cum felle mixtum: quod idem est. Fel enim pro amaritudine posuit. Myrrhatum enim uinum est amarissimum quodque fieri possit ut & fel & myrrha amarissimum redderunt uinum' (f. 1095^v). Bitterness appears also in the gloss on John 19: 29, which refers to Jer. 2: 21, 'Dominus plantavit vineam Soreth: et quomodo conversa es in amaritudinem vitis alienae: et

[22] 'Langland's Reading and Writing: *Detractor* and the Pardon Passus', *Speculum* 59 (1984) 342–62 (p. 343). See also John Alford, 'The Role of the Quotations in *Piers Plowman*', *Speculum* 52 (1977) 80–99, and Jill Mann, 'Eating and Drinking in *Piers Plowman*', *Essays and Studies*, NS 32 (1979) 26–43.

[23] References to the C-Text are to *Piers Plowman: An Edition of the C-Text*, ed. Derek Pearsall (London, 1978).

exspectavi ut faceres uvas, et fecisti spinas' (PL 114, col. 239). As we have seen, Jer. 2: 21 is part of the Second Nocturn on Good Friday (see p. 138 above). The 'bitternesse' (B. XVIII. 364) that Satan has brewed is not just the traditional 'bitter cup of death',[24] but also the vinegar that was offered to the crucified Christ. Vinegar is wine gone bad, which is why, when the dead have been raised and God's judgement under the Old Law—condemning mankind to everlasting death because of the sin of our first parents—has been overturned, Christ will drink not vinegar, which symbolizes the 'false Jewes' and their refusal to acknowledge Christ, but 'right ripe must'. Wine, the *Allegoriae in Sacram Scripturam* point out, can stand for love and for vengeance: 'dilectio, ut in Cantico (VIII. 2): "Et dabo tibi poculum ex vino condito", id est, dabo tibi laetitiam ex amore vero . . . vindicta, ut in Apocalypsi (XIV. 10): "Et hic bibet de vino irae Dei", id est sentiet vindictam Dei, antequam judicium Dei inferat'.[25] Thanks to God's mercy and the New Law, this is not the vintage of Joel or the Apocalypse. Lucifer, whose speech to the other devils, in which he insists on the Old Law (B. XVIII. 272–84), echoes the words of Righteousness with her legalistic conception of God's justice (B. XVIII. 187–201), gets his just deserts:

> 'Thus by lawe,' quod Oure Lord, 'lede I wole fro hennes
> Tho [leodes] that I lov[e] and leved in my comynge.
> And for thi lesynge, Lucifer, that thow leighe til Eve,
> Thow shalt abyen it *bittre*!'—and bond hym with cheynes.
> (B. XVIII. 401–4; my italics)[26]

But of course wine, in real life as well as in scriptural exegesis, also means joy, and that surely is what the image of Christ drinking the new wine conveys. The gloss on Cant. 1: 13, 'Botrus cypri dilectus meus mihi in vineis Engaddi', which is one of the Old Testament texts that was commonly associated with the Passion (see p. 137 above), runs:

> Quia morti Mediatoris mox resurrectionis gloria successit, recte subditur, *Botrus*, qui fuit fasciculus myrrhae [Cant. 1: 12] in amaritudine passionis, in dulcedine resurrectionis exstitit botrus cypri. Quod myrrha enim tristificat, vinum laetificat.
> (PL 113, col. 1134)

---

[24] On which see Carleton Brown, '*Poculum Mortis* in Old English', *Speculum* 15 (1940) 389–99 and G. V. Smithers, 'Five Notes on Old English Texts', *English and Germanic Studies* 4 (1951–2) 65–85 (pp. 67–75). Smithers quotes two examples from Bede on John 2 of Christ's drink of life (PL 94, cols 72, 73) and draws attention to a passage in the *Ormulum* where Orm contrasts the Devil's mortal drink (15356 ff.) with that dispensed by Christ (15402–7).

[25] Ascribed to Hrabanus Maurus; PL 112, cols 849–1088 (col. 1079).

[26] 'leodes' is not in any of the B-MSS; again, it depends on one's view of the metre of the B-Text whether one agrees with Schmidt here: see his Textual and Lexical Commentary, p. 298, and compare note 18 above.

The bitter myrrh of the Passion is opposed to the sweet wine of the Resurrection, because Christ has outwitted the Devil and turned the 'bitternesse' (364) that the 'doctour of deeth' (365) had prepared for him into the 'right ripe must' (371) of the Resurrection, his own and that of the dead, who will be raised through God's grace under the New Law.

The other place in the New Testament where Christ is offered drink but will not take it is the account of the Last Supper: Matt. 26: 29, Mark 14: 25 and Luke 22: 18. Luke has, 'Dico enim vobis, quod non bibam de generatione vitis, donec regnum Dei veniat'. Ps. 8, which has the heading 'In finem pro torcularibus psalmus David', was generally associated with Christ's Passion through the symbol of the winepress.[27] In his *Enarrationes in Psalmos*, the standard commentary on the Psalms in the Middle Ages, Augustine links the wine of Luke 22: 18 with the vinegar the Jews offered to the crucified Christ. Like wine, one's understanding of God's word improves with age 'si negligentia non acuerit':

> Acuit namque in Judaeis, et hoc aceto (*Joan.* XIX. 29) Dominum potaverunt. Nam illud vinum quod de generatione vitis Novi Testamenti bibiturus est cum sanctis suis Dominus in regno Patris sui (*Luc.* XXII. 18), suavissimum atque firmissimum sit necesse est.   (PL 36, col. 110)

Perhaps it is not being too fanciful to suppose that Langland, following Augustine, connected the wine of the Last Supper and the vinegar of the Crucifixion.

If he did, it would explain something else. Both Matthew and Mark add a striking detail:

> Dico autem vobis: Non bibam amodo de hoc genimine vitis usque in diem illum, cum illud bibam vobiscum novum in regno Patris mei.   (Matt. 26: 29)

> Amen dico vobis, quia iam non bibam de hoc genimine vitis usque in diem illum, cum illud bibam novum in regno Dei.
> (Mark 14: 25)

Could it be that Langland, not here using the *Glossa Ordinaria* (which contrasts the Old Adam and the New),[28] seized on the word 'novum' in the knowledge that the new wine that is *suavissimum atque firmissimum*, the best wine imaginable in the Middle Ages, is 'right ripe must', drunk immediately after the long-awaited vintage—in this case, in the vale of Jehoshaphat?

---

[27] As, for instance, in *S. Melitonis clavis, Spicilegium solesmense*, ed. J. B. Pitra (Paris, 1855), 4 vols, II, s.v. *torcular*; *torcular* is allegorized as, among other things, 'crux, Passio Christi'.

[28] See the gloss on Matt. 26: 29: 'Dicens illud *novum*, hoc vetus, ostendit corpus: scilicet, de veteri Adam quod immortalitate immutabitur' (PL 114, col. 169).

Whether or not Langland made this connection cannot be proved, but at least it has, I hope, become clear that 'right ripe must' is more than just a poetic locution for 'wine' and that these lines from Passus XVIII are far richer in symbolic associations than has hitherto been realized. Langland's method of composition here was, in his own words, to drink not from 'deep clergyse' but from 'comune coppes' (C. XX 405–6), not resorting to specialist theological learning, as he does in the Pardon Passus, but using sources known to everybody in his fourteenth-century audience, the liturgy and standard interpretations of familiar Bible texts.

Chaucer in the Suburbs

JOHN SCATTERGOOD

I

One of the most poignant incidents in Chaucer's *Troilus and Criseyde* occurs when, on the tenth day after Criseyde's departure, Troilus and Pandarus await her return to Troy. They are 'on the walles of the town' (v. 1112) early,[1] in an optimistic mood, but as the day progresses their confidence that she will arrive diminishes. Though 'fer his hed over the wal he layde' (1145), Troilus is never rewarded with the sight of his returning mistress (though he mistakes others coming to the city for her). All hope, on that day at least, disappears when the gates of the city close at nightfall:

> The warden of the yates gan to calle
> The folk which that withoute the yates were,
> And bad hem dryven in hire bestes alle,
> Or al the nyght they moste bleven there.   (1177–80)

The warden's proper sense that there are occasions when that which is within the city has to stay in and that which is outside has to stay out provides a powerful analogy for the separation of the lovers. This is something of a special case, of course: the sense of inclusion and exclusion is the greater because the city is under siege. Nevertheless, the physical and psychological importance of the city wall and gates must have been clear to Chaucer. From 1374 to 1386 (the period of his service at the Custom House) he leased a house over Aldgate, beneath which ran the main route in and out of London in an easterly direction.[2] Daily experience as much as anything else must have provided him with a sharp sense of the limits of cities, and no medieval author writes better on this subject.

It is almost axiomatic among historians of western civilization that the city is of immense importance, not simply as an economic entity but as an idea:

[1] All Chaucer references are to *The Complete Works of Geoffrey Chaucer*, ed. F. N. Robinson, 2nd edn (London, 1957).
[2] See *Chaucer Life-Records*, ed. M. M. Crow and C. C. Olson (Oxford, 1966), pp. 144–7.

The city, as one finds it in history, is the point of maximum concentration for the power and culture of a community. It is the place where the diffused rays of many separate beams of life fall into focus, with gains in both social effectiveness and significance. The city is the form and symbol of the integrated social relationship: it is the seat of the temple, the market, the hall of justice, the academy of learning. Here in the city the goods of civilization are multiplied and manifolded; here is where human experience is transformed into viable signs, symbols, patterns of conduct, systems of order. Here is where the issues of civilization are focused: here, too, ritual passes on occasion into the active drama of a fully differentiated and self-conscious society.

Thus writes Lewis Mumford.[3] But the stability that he describes so enthusiastically and evocatively was one that emerged gradually by means of a process at once hesitant and interrupted yet also dynamic and inevitable. According to Mircea Eliade, the earliest cities were reflections of the cosmic order.[4] A common plan was to group buildings around a cultic establishment adorned with the features of the heavens and representing them. These cities were the earthly embodiments of cosmological order, and for an enemy to destroy the cultic establishment made defeat likely: the safety of Troy depended upon the preservation of the palladium. But as ancient cities became also the seats of kings the identification of them with another type of order emerged—social order. This has been defined as consisting in 'the deliberate regulation of human relationships through custom corrected by law and by the royal power over a territory that had limits'.[5] The destruction of this sort of city was perceived as being the overthrow of a sort of order, the giving over of civilization to social desolation. So Isaiah predicts of Babylon 'the glory of kingdoms' (13: 19–22): 'wild beasts of the desert shall lie there; and their houses shall be full of doleful creatures . . . the wild beasts of the islands shall cry in their desolate houses, and dragons in their pleasant palaces'. Out of a combination of cosmological order and social order came something distinct— perfect order, an amalgam of the properly desirable relations between God and man and the authoritative relations between men on earth: in the Western Christian tradition this manifested itself in the idea of heaven as a city—the heavenly Jerusalem.

These ideas, and variations on them, were powerful and persistent even during the so-called 'age of migrations': in the literature of this period the foundations of cities were still celebrated, and their destruction lamented.

---

[3] Lewis Mumford, *The Culture of Cities* (London, 1938), p. 3.
[4] See *City Invincible*, ed. C. Kraeling *et al.* (Chicago, 1960), pp. 363–6.
[5] Sylvia Thrupp, 'The City as the Idea of Social Order' in *Society and History: Essays by Sylvia L. Thrupp*, ed. R. Grew and N. H. Steneck (Ann Arbor, 1977), p. 90. I am much indebted to this fine essay.

The *encomium urbis* was a well-established type of poem: there are examples dealing with Milan and Verona; Alcuin wrote on York, and an anonymous Anglo-Saxon poet on Durham.[6] But well established too was the *de excidio* tradition, in which the ruin of cities was mourned, and the implications of their ruin set out.[7] The destruction of Rome and Roman civilization was, of course, the great example but not the only one. As the Anglo-Saxon author of *The Ruin* (which is probably about Bath) makes clear, a city was identified with an ordered mode of civilized life, which tended to disappear if that city was destroyed:

> Hryre wong gecrong,
> gebrocen to beorgum, þær iu beorn monig,
> glædmod ond goldbeorht, gleoma gefrætwe[d],
> wlonc ond wingal, wighyrstum scan;
> seah on sinc, on sylfor, on searogimmas,
> on ead, on æht, on eorcanstan,
> on þas beorhtan burg bradan rices.   (31–7)[8]

The implication of this sort of poem is that cities are fragile things, and so too are the ordered, civilized life and the value system which maintain it. All, in one way or another, are constantly under threat.

Chaucer does not write an *encomium urbis* or a *de excidio* poem. Nevertheless, it is clear that the stability and instability of cities was something which he had thought seriously about, if only because it was a subject raised by several of the stories he chose to tell. In *The Knight's Tale* he presents unforgettable images of a city and a civilization destroyed by war—'Thebes with his olde walles wyde' (I 1880). But, perhaps more interestingly, in *The Second Nun's Tale* and *The Canon's Yeoman's Tale* he deals with more subtle threats posed to two other cities—Rome and London. Here it is not the destruction of the fabric which is at issue, but the subversion of the value systems and ideologies which sustain these cities, and which they represent.

What threatened medieval cities was disorder, usually from outside, though that disorder was not a product of the countryside, which had its own sort of order and its own systems. And, in any case, in the late Middle Ages the differentiation between the country and the town or city was by no means absolute. The two were economically interdependent and intercourse between them was normal: countrymen brought their produce to the markets which

[6] For a brief account of this tradition see Margaret Schlauch, 'An Old English *Encomium Urbis*', *JEGP* 40 (1941) 14–28.
[7] See G. W. Dunleavy, 'A "De Excidio" Tradition in the Old English *Ruin*', *Philological Quarterly* 38 (1959) 112–18.
[8] The text is from *Three Old English Elegies: The Wife's Lament, The Husband's Message, The Ruin*, ed. R. F. Leslie (Manchester, 1961), p. 52. ['Destruction brought it to the ground, smashed to rubble, where formerly many a warrior, glad-minded and gold-adorned, gleaming splendidly, proud and flushed with wine, shone in his war gear, gazed on treasure, on silver, on gemstones, on wealth, on property, on jewellery, on this bright city and its broad domains.']

grew up in towns and purchased the manufactured goods and services which towns provided in order to improve their own ways of life. Nothing shows this better, in its ideal state, than Ambrogio Lorenzetti's fresco of 'good government' in the Palazzo Pubblico, Siena.[9] But rural villages had never been devoted to purely agricultural concerns: handicrafts had flourished there from an early date. Nor were towns purely industrial and commercial: some of the population practised rural occupations, and gardens and orchards, occasionally fields and pastures, were sometimes found in towns. But the rapid development of towns and cities and the sense of inclusiveness and exclusiveness that they promoted gave rise to a number of ideas about the relations between rural as opposed to urban ways of living. The idealization of the country as a place of simplicity and repose, a reflection of some lost earthly paradise, begins to appear, as does the equally inaccurate notion that towns are characteristically places of moral wickedness, sharp practice, and dissipation. Those who flee urban situations for the safety of the country,[10] and countrymen who find themselves faced with the disturbing, unfamiliar complexity of towns and cities become subjects for literature.[11] Urban sophistication and country

[9] For a reproduction see Frederick Hartt, *A History of Italian Renaissance Art*, rev. edn (London, 1980), Colorplate 14 and Figs 119 and 120.

[10] See particularly the Anglo-Norman 'Outlaw's Song of Trailbaston' (c. 1350) from British Library MS Harley 2253 in *Political Songs of England*, ed. Thomas Wright, Camden Society OS 6 (1839), pp. 231–6:

> Pur ce me tendroi antre bois sur le jolyf umbray;
> La n'y a faucete ne nulle male lay;—
> En le bois de Belregard, ou vole le jay,
> E chaunte russinole touz jours santz delay.   (17–20)

['For this reason I will keep within the woods, in the beautiful shade, there where there is no falseness nor any bad law, in the wood of Belregard, where the jay flies and the nightingale sings without ceasing.']

> Vus qy estes endite, je lou, venez a moy,
> Al vert bois de Belregard, la ny a nul ploy,
> Forque beste savage et jolyf umbroy;
> Car trop est dotouse la commune loy.   (53–6)

['I advise you who are indicted to come to me, to the green wood of Belregard, there where there is no annoyance, only the wild beast and the beautiful shade; for the common law is too uncertain.']

'Belregard' appears to be a fictional name; the poem was probably written in the south-west of England. Like other outlaws, the speaker would prefer to be back in his proper place in society, though the country provides a refuge (see lines 93–6). See further *Rymes of Robyn Hode: An Introduction to the English Outlaw*, ed. R. B. Dobson and J. Taylor (London, 1976), pp. 250–4, and Maurice Keen, *The Outlaws of Medieval Legend* (London, 1961), pp. 204–5.

[11] See, for example, 'London Lickpenny' in *Historical Poems of the XIVth and XVth Centuries*, ed. Rossell Hope Robbins (New York, 1959), no. 50.

boorishness begin to be set against each other. What receives very little attention, however, except by Chaucer in *The Second Nun's Tale* and *The Canon's Yeoman's Tale*, is that area which is properly speaking neither country nor town—the suburbs, although by the late Middle Ages most towns show a certain amount of suburban development.

It is difficult to generalize about the suburbs of medieval towns and cities. In part, pressure of space within the urban settlements caused suburbs to be developed: in the thirteenth century, when the population of England as a whole was increasing, suburbs tended to grow. Neither natural boundaries (such as rivers) nor man-made boundaries (such as walls) prevented this. Bristol rapidly became built up in the thirteenth century and had suburbs to the south across the Avon, as well as to the east and north. The main suburbs of Gloucester were outside the north gate. The earliest development outside Worcester was towards Northwick before the end of the eleventh century, and later there was more building in that area as well as on the south side and over the bridge on the west bank of the Severn. The suburbs of Warwick lay mainly beyond the walls to the east.[12] The development of suburbs was unsystematic, but generally they tended to grow up along the main routes in and out of the city, 'clustering in particular about the enlarged open spaces that were usually to be met with at the gates'.[13] The characteristic late medieval spread of the suburbs can be seen most easily on Speed's maps (though they date from the early seventeenth century).[14] In the late fourteenth century London was by far the biggest city in England and it, of course, was ringed with suburbs. John Stow, writing in 1598, contrasts Fitzstephen's description of the suburbs with his own observations:

> 'On all sides, without the houses of the Suburbs, are the citizens gardens & orchards, planted with trees, both large, sightly, & adioyning together. On the north side, are pastures, & plain medows, with brooks running through them, turning water mils, with a pleasant noise. Not far off, is a great forrest, a well wooded chase, having good covert for Harts, Buckes, Does, Boores & wild Bulles. The corne fields are not of a hungrie sandie mould, but as the fruitfull fields of Asia: yeelding plentifull encrease, & filling the barnes with corne. There are near London on the north side, especiall welles in the Suburbes, sweet, holesome, and cleare. . . .'
> Thus farre out of Fitz Stephen, for the Suburbs at that time. The 2. of H. the 3. the Forest of Midlesex and the Warren of Stanes

---

[12] For a good brief description of the development of suburbs in some West Midland towns see R. H. Hilton, *A Medieval Society: The West Midlands at the End of the Thirteenth Century* (London, 1966), pp. 183–7.

[13] Colin Platt, *The English Medieval Town* (London, 1976), p. 49.

[14] See the reproductions in Platt of Speed's map of Chichester (Fig. 10), Winchester (Fig. 16) and Stamford (Fig. 17).

were disaforested: since the which time, the suburbs about London hath bin also mightily increased with buildings. . . .[15]

According to Stow, some of this building was recent, but much of it was medieval.

Suburbs appear to have existed in an uneasy relation to the cities and towns to which they belonged. Citizens or freemen, of course, enjoyed advantages and privileges (and also bore responsibilities) to which the unenfranchized had no access; as Sylvia Thrupp says, 'they alone, for example, could exercise the local political rights, and they alone were legally entitled to buy in the city with the intention of reselling and to keep shops for selling at retail'.[16] And the granting of citizenship was something which the ruling oligarchies kept a strict control over and exploited for political reasons. But there were also physical factors which emphasized the exclusiveness of cities and towns. A city or town was very much identified by its walls, and the walls frequently appear on seals (as with, for example, Canterbury, Colchester, London, Oxford, Shrewsbury).[17] The principal function of a wall was, of course, defence. In the late Middle Ages English cities and towns were not threatened frequently, so the often elaborate and costly walls which enclosed them were not put to their main use. But it is fairly clear from continental examples that, in extremity, suburbs were regarded as expendable; in 1418–19 no attempt was made to defend the suburbs of Rouen against Henry V's invading army, and they were devastated.[18] What is more, it was outside the walls of cities and towns that space was provided for establishments which might be inconvenient or dangerous: leper hospitals were sited just outside the walls of Exeter, Gloucester, Grimsby, Leicester, London, Stamford and elsewhere (for details see Platt, pp. 45–6). Occasionally, trades which were considered to be antisocial because they caused pollution of the water supply—butchering, tanning, and dyeing—were banished beyond the walls downstream.[19]

There did come a time, in the comparative security of Elizabethan England, when it could seriously be proposed that the suburbs provided the best places for a gentleman to live, because they combined the civilization of urban centres with the peace and wholesomeness of the countryside:

[15] See John Stow, *A Survey of London*, ed. C. L. Kingsford, 2 vols (Oxford, 1908), II. 70.
[16] *The Merchant Class of Medieval London* (Ann Arbor, 1948), p. 3.
[17] See Platt, pp. 49–55; Mumford, pp. 15–16; Hilton, pp. 186–7.
[18] See John Page's account in 'The Siege of Rouen', ed. J. Gairdner in *Collections of a London Citizen*, Camden Society NS 17 (1876), pp. 3–4.
[19] On this interesting subject see Jacques Le Goff, 'Licit and Illicit Trades in the Medieval West' in *Time, Work and Culture in the Middle Ages*, trans. Arthur Goldhammer (Chicago, 1980), pp. 58–70; Jean Gimpel, *The Medieval Machine: The Industrial Revolution of the Middle Ages* (London, 1977), pp. 85–7; Platt, pp. 57–8.

The manner of the most Gentlemen and Noble men also, is to
house them selves (if possible they may) in the Subburbes of the
Cittie, because moste commonly, the ayre there beeinge somewhat
at large, the place is healthy, and through the distaunce from the
bodye of the Towne, the noyse not much: and so consequently
quiet. Also for the commoditie we finde many lodginges, both
spacious and roomethy, with Gardaines and Orchardes very
delectable. So as with good government, wee have as litle cause to
feare infection there, as in the verye Countrey: our water is
excellente, and much better then you have anye, our ground and
feeldes most pleasaunte, our fier equall with yours.

So argues one of the characters in *Cyvile and Uncyvile Life* (1597), a dialogue
concerning the respective merits of life in the town as opposed to life in the
country.[20] In the late Middle Ages it is doubtful if many would have agreed
with him. It is true that, on occasions, the rich chose to live outside cities
and towns; as Colin Platt says, 'In fourteenth-century Warwick, as the tax
records clearly show, it was in the suburbs that the wealthy chose to establish
themselves, attracted there by the borough's extensive suburban fields' (p.
46). But generally it seems fairly clear that the suburbs housed many of the
less well-off. Studies based on the taxation returns relating to Winchester and
Leicester show this, and Colin Platt, basing his conclusions on the *terrier* of
1454, writes of Southampton: 'the small total of cottages recorded there can
suggest only that the labouring poor lived, for the most part, outside the
defended *enceinte* of the borough, and that the very poorest, unidentifiable in
any surviving record, are likely to have done the same. On this and other
evidence, the rich in medieval Southampton, at least from the building of
its first systematic defences, undoubtedly avoided the suburbs' (p. 48).
Obviously, some suburbs were more opulent and attractive than others. In his
description of 'The suburbes without the Walles' of London, John Stow
sometimes speaks of 'large and strong houses', but more often he describes
'small cottages', 'small and base tenements', 'many tenements of poore
people'; the route outside Aldgate was 'so incroched upon by building of
filthy Cottages, and with other purprestures, inclosures and Laystalles . . .
that in some places it scarce remaineth a sufficient high way for the meeting
of Carriages and droves of Cattell, much lesse is there any faire, pleasant or
wholsome way for people to walke on foot: which is no small blemish to so
famous a city, to have so unsavery and unseemly an entry or passage
thereunto' (p. 72). Stow also speaks of theft, piracy, and murders in these
areas (see particularly pp. 71–2). When Chaucer writes about the suburbs it

---

[20] Quoted by Platt (pp. 229–30) from *Inedited Tracts: Illustrating the Manners, Opinions
and Occupations of Englishmen during the Sixteenth and Seventeenth Centuries*, ed. W. C.
Hazlitt (London, 1868), p. 78.

is in terms of the poverty of their inhabitants and in connection with furtive and criminal activities.

II

Because the *Canon's Yeoman's Tale* does not appear in the Hengwrt MS, which is by common consent the earliest *Canterbury Tales* manuscript, it has been argued that it is not Chaucer's.[21] But it appears in the Ellesmere MS, where it is linked to the *Second Nun's Tale*, and the two stories are probably meant to be seen together for comparison and contrast.[22] In material and in form they differ considerably. The *Second Nun's Tale* is a retelling, in noble rhyme-royal stanzas, of the life and martyrdom of St Cecilia, based on some version of the *Legenda Aurea*; the *Canon's Yeoman's Tale*, written in fairly plain couplets, has no known source and can scarcely be called a story, since it does little more than recount three tricks perpetrated by an alchemist upon a gullible but greedy dupe. But though the *Second Nun's Tale* is set in imperial Rome and the *Canon's Yeoman's Tale* in late medieval England, both are located in a sort of suburban underworld. And both tales concentrate on some of the ways in which unorthodox behaviour relates to orthodoxy. The early saints and the modern alchemists find the world of material observable facts unsatisfactory, and both are zealously and obsessively engaged in a search for what is hidden:

> . . . we seken thilke divinitee
> That is yhid in hevene pryvely.   (VIII 316–17)

> But that science is so fer us biforn,
> We mowen nat, although we hadden it sworn,
> It overtake, it slit away so faste.   (680–2)

Both belief in the Christian religion in imperial Rome and the search for the philosopher's stone in fourteenth-century England involved challenges, and

---

[21] See N. F. Blake, 'The Relationship between the Hengwrt and the Ellesmere Manuscripts of the *Canterbury Tales*', *Essays and Studies* NS 32 (1979) 1–18, and further his edition of *The Canterbury Tales by Geoffrey Chaucer* (London, 1980), pp. 3–13. This view has not found general acceptance among scholars: see, for example, my review in *Hermathena* 132 (1982) 64–6. But Blake has restated his views, with some modifications, in *The Textual Tradition of the Canterbury Tales* (London, 1985).

[22] See, for example, J. E. Grennan, 'Saint Cecilia's "Chemical Wedding": the Unity of the *Canterbury Tales*, Fragment VIII', *JEGP* 65 (1966) 466–81; Bruce A. Rosenberg, 'The Contrary Tales of the Second Nun and the Canon's Yeoman', *Chaucer Review* 2 (1968) 278–91; Glending Olson, 'Chaucer, Dante, and the Structure of Fragment VIII of the *Canterbury Tales*', *Chaucer Review* 16 (1982) 222–37.

the desire to make converts sharpened the conflict with orthodoxy. The unorthodoxy of both the early saints and the modern alchemists had a price in the stigma of illegality and poverty which rightly or wrongly ostracized them from a more comfortable urban existence.

Cecilia chooses to leave her family, which was one of some social consequence in Rome: she 'was comen of Romayns and of noble kynde' (121). She sets aside her material ease and security: 'The world and eek hire chambre gan she weyve' (276). Instead she devotes herself to an illegal religious movement which has its headquarters three miles outside the walls of the city along the Via Appia, in the Catacombs—the underground passages which provided the early Christians with both refuge and a burial site. She and her fellow converts live out a furtive existence: they move about the city only at night (379, 547), or lurk in the Catacombs, 'Among the seintes buryeles lotynge' (186). Their leader, 'this hooly olde Urban' (185), is an outlaw who lives under sentence of death. So too does anyone who seeks to join him, as Tiburce makes clear to Valerian, his brother:

> 'Ne menestow nat Urban,' quod he tho,
> 'That is so ofte dampned to be deed,
> And woneth in halkes alwey to and fro,
> And dar nat ones putte forth his heed?
> Men sholde hym brennen in a fyr so reed
> If he were founde, or that men myghte hym spye,
> And we also, to bere hym compaignye.'   (309–15)

Urban has his natural allies among 'poure folkes' who live outside Rome, and he and his disciples do their work 'prively' (547) and 'softely' (408) lest they be detected by the authorities.

The *Second Nun's Tale*, therefore, concerns unorthodox belief in a hostile environment—its acquisition, understanding and dissemination. The Second Nun modestly describes herself as 'unworthy' (62) to engage in testifying to her belief, and this finds an echo in Cecilia's particular situation: she is not the leader of a movement, but simply one of Urban's disciples (176–8). Nevertheless, she has a discernment which she can communicate: her name, in the Second Nun's etymologizing, is a dynamic symbol giving rise to a wealth of meanings—'wey to blynde' (from *caecus via*) and 'wantynge of blyndnesse' amongst others (92–106), because of the clarity of her perception of the divinity. The acceptance of Christianity, in this tale, is a prerequisite for spiritual sight: Valerian explains to the unconverted Tiburce that he and Cecilia wear crowns of roses and lilies 'whiche that thyne eyen han no myght to see' (255); yet after his conversion Tiburce 'saugh, in tyme and space,/ The aungel of God' (355–6) every day. He acquires a full understanding of the Christian faith and when 'parfit in his lernynge' (353) he can, in his turn, disseminate the word and make converts. Before they are martyred he and his

153

brother preach the word to Maximus who, before his own execution, acquires spiritual insight and transmits it:

> This Maximus, that saugh this thyng bityde,
> With pitous teeris tolde it anonright,
> That he hir soules saugh to hevene glyde
> With aungels ful of cleernesse and of light,
> And with his word converted many a wight.   (400–4)

Men die, but the insight is not lost and the work continues.

The Second Nun opens her story with some moral advice on the concept of 'bisynesse' (5). What she calls 'leveful' or 'feithful bisynesse' (24) is that which enables the sin of 'ydelnesse' (14) to be avoided and which produces beneficial effects in that it testifies to the faith.[23] She interprets her 'werk' as the translation and retelling of the life of Cecilia, who in her turn is 'Ful swift and bisy evere in good werkynge' (116) in her task of spreading the Christian religion in unfavourable conditions. In this story there is a direct correlation between activity and faithfulness. Cecilia, paradoxically sown with 'the fruyt of thilke seed of chastitee' (193), is 'lyk a bisy bee' (195), a common symbol of activity,[24] who fertilizes the flowers of the field because her abstinence is fruitful (159–61). Most of those with whom she comes into contact are pollinated and the Christian movement in Rome grows and flourishes: it spreads from her to her family (351–7), through the ranks of the army (367–78), and even into the senior members of the government (411). The vital catalyst of conversion is the sense of smell, the pervasive perfume of lilies and roses, blossoming out of season, which symbolize purity and martyrdom, and give assurance of the ability of faith to make magical transformations:

> 'The sweete smel that in myn herte I fynde
> Hath chaunged me al in another kynde.'   (251–2)

Conversion allows the Christian to transcend the conditions of earthly life which corrupt and hinder the aspirations of the soul, which, as the Second Nun says, 'troubled is by the contagioun/ Of my body' (72–3). Baptism cleanses the convert (300) and is a guarantee of spiritual health.

Cecilia's ultimate testing comes by way of a confrontation with the authorities of the city of Rome and an argument about the contingency of the material world. The confrontation is set out in terms which suggest the stability and complacency of the representatives of urban culture. The writing is full of words denoting rank: 'sergeantz of the toun of Rome' (361), 'prefect'

---

[23] See Richard Hazleton, 'Chaucer and Cato', *Speculum* 35 (1960) 357–80, especially 365–7, where he derives Chaucer's wording from Cato and *glossulae* on Cato.
[24] 'As busy as a bee' was a fairly common proverbial expression in the Middle Ages; see B. J. and H. W. Whiting, *Proverbs, Sentences, and Proverbial Phrases from English Writings Mainly Before 1500* (Cambridge, Mass., 1968), B165.

(362), 'ministres' (411), 'princes' (444, 449), 'officer' and 'justise' (497). And Almacius insists on his official capacities with respect to eradicating Christianity and maintaining worship of the pagan Gods: the Roman 'princes' have 'comanded and maad ordinaunce' (445) on the matter and have given him 'power and auctoritee' (471) over life and death. He seeks to overbear her belief by reminding her how far his 'myght may strecche' (469). She does not deny his power, but argues that he uses it to maintain what is false. Because of his 'nycetee' Almacius attributes divinity to what is simply stone:

> 'Ther lakketh no thyng to thyne outter yën
> That thou n'art blynd; for thyng that we seen alle
> That it is stoon,—that men may wel espyen,—
> That ilke stoon a god thow wolt it calle.
> I rede thee, lat thyn hand upon it falle,
> And taste it wel, and stoon thou shalt it fynde,
> Syn that thou seest nat with thyne eyen blynde.'   (498–504)

Her obduracy provokes the wrath of the urban authorities, who preserve their own view of things and resist the challenge of Christianity by martyring Cecilia. The end of the tale appears to be little more than a bland, updating summary, but it does in fact extend the story's meaning. After her burial in the Catacombs her house outside the city becomes 'the chirche of Seint Cecilie' where 'into this day' people 'doon to Crist and to his seint servyse' (550–3). The early saints may be martyred, but the ideas and the movement continue: their testimony has a tangible permanent effect—such is the implication of the last lines quoted. Even the Second Nun can set forth her own commitment to the faith, in her own modest way.

The *Canon's Yeoman's Tale* exists in something of a burlesque relation to the saint's legend: the same themes are addressed, but in the alchemist's story they acquire a different dimension. The lifestyle of the Canon and the Yeoman is a distorted image of the pious lives of the early saints. They do not simply live among the poor, but are poor themselves. Devotion to a craft which is supposed to be able to produce riches has only impoverished both master and servant: the Canon 'caried lite aray' (568) and what he did have was in bad condition; the Yeoman is 'so bare' of possessions and so 'endetted' through borrowing that he doubts his capacity ever to repay everything (723–36). He describes their fugitive existence in the suburbs:[25]

> 'In the suburbes of a toun', quod he,
> 'Lurkynge in hernes and in lanes blynde,

---

[25] In Ben Jonson's *Alchemist* I. i. 19 Subtle says that Face has been a 'suburb-Captayne', and Face then proceeds to describe Subtle's impoverished condition when they met (24–47).

> Whereas thise robbours and thise theves by kynde
> Holden hir pryvee fereful residence,
> As they that dar nat shewen hir presence;
> So faren we, if I shal seye the sothe.'   (657–62)

They are constantly on the move, and find it necessary, like the early saints, to be unforthcoming about their activities. In part this is because alchemists held that practitioners of the art should be secretive about their scientific processes: 'kepeth it secree', says one alchemist to his dupe, lest men have 'greet envye' of him and kill him because of his knowledge (1368–74). But other, less creditable, reasons for the secrecy of alchemists emerge—the 'sorwe and shame' (702) some of them feel at the deceits they practise, and the ever-present need to avoid those whom they have swindled.

Like the saint's legend, the *Canon's Yeoman's Tale* concerns the acquisition and dissemination of arcane knowledge. Like the Second Nun the teller of the story is an underling: he admits that he does not know 'al' about the craft he follows, but he knows 'somewhat'—for he is in charge of blowing the fire (924). He opens his story with a declaration about his service in the craft:

> With this Chanoun I dwelt have seven yeer,
> And of his science am I never the neer.   (720–1)

Seven years was the customary length of a normal apprenticeship in an urban trade, after which a young man may be 'free' and deemed expert. But the apprentice alchemist—though he has sacrificed both money and health (722–8)—is no closer to understanding his trade: 'of my swynk yet blered is myn ye' (730) he complains. The image is significant because, though it operates on a literal level in that the Yeoman has ruined his eyes with his work around the alchemical furnaces, 'to blear the eye' also means, on a metaphorical and proverbial level, 'to blind' or 'to deceive' (Whiting, E217). Among the early saints acceptance of the Christian faith brought a sight of what was hidden, but exposure to alchemy brings blindness, not illumination. 'This multiplying blent so many oon,' says the Yeoman (1391), and his cautionary story of the deceived London priest demonstrates this:

> O sely preest! o sely innocent!
> With coveitise anon thou shalt be blent!
> O gracelees, ful blynd is thy conceite. . . .   (1076–8)

The priest is deceived by three sleight-of-hand tricks and the alchemist's 'termes' or jargon. Part of the falseness of alchemy resides, according to the Yeoman, in its appearance of learning. Though their 'termes been so clergial and so queynte' (752), and though when they are together 'Every man semeth a Salomon' (961), the alchemists have no real insight into the subject: the Yeoman can give impressive lists of materials, equipment and processes (754–861), but he is no nearer to finding the philosopher's stone. No matter

156

how learned a man may be, though 'he sitte at his book bothe day and nyght' trying to learn 'this elvysshe nyce loore', 'Al is in veyn' (838–43). Like the proverbial blind horse Bayard (Whiting, B71) the alchemists blunder about not knowing what they do (1413–16). The Yeoman's arduous apprenticeship has given him access to no coherent body of knowledge, and provided him with no insight except that his chosen craft, alchemy, is a failure.

But though the subject has no secure intellectual basis, this does not prevent the alchemists, like the early saints, from working hard at it or from seeking converts. Gower, in that book of *Confessio Amantis* which deals with sloth, classifies the original alchemists with discoverers and inventors as figures of intellectual labour: they 'soghten besinesse/ Of vertu and of worthinesse' (IV. 2603–4).[26] Chaucer's alchemists labour continually at high temperatures around their furnaces, and in studying the right combination of ingredients and the right methodology which might lead to a major discovery,

> Oure lampes brennyng bothe nyght and day,
> To brynge aboute oure purpos, if we may.   (802–3)

They are certainly not slothful, but theirs is a case of misdirected energy: 'Noght helpeth us, oure labour is in veyn' (777); 'lost is al oure labour and travaille' (781). The suburban backstreet laboratory has something of the appearance of a more ordinary place of work, with its equipment and materials, but it leads to no product: 'The pot tobreketh, and farewel, al is go' (907). In consolation, they compare the riskiness of their enterprises with the notion of 'aventure' which underlay mercantile capitalism: 'A marchant, pardee, may nat ay endure' (947).[27] But the analogy is false, because these alchemists never make a profit—not a legal one anyway. Around their furnaces, working among toxic fumes, the labouring alchemists appear not to belong to the urban scale of things: they seem diabolic, and though the devil cannot be seen the Yeoman thinks that 'he with us be, that ilke shrewe' (917). Certainly, there is something diabolic in the way in which those who have lost their 'owene good thurgh jupartye' are keen to provoke others to do the same so that they may have company in their misery (746–7).[28] Alchemists, moreover, betray the infernal nature of their activities by the pervasive stench of brimstone, and this very malodorousness, in contrast to the smell of lilies

---

[26] *Confessio Amantis* is quoted from *The English Works of John Gower*, ed. G. C. Macaulay, 2 vols, EETS ES 81–2 (1900–1).

[27] Compare *The Canterbury Tales* VII 224–38; and for the theory that the risks they took justified the profits that merchants made see R. H. Tawney, *Religion and the Rise of Capitalism* (London, 1926), pp. 32–3.

[28] Compare Mephistophilis's explanation of why Lucifer seeks to 'Inlarge his kingdome': 'Solamen miseris socios habuisse doloris' (*Dr Faustus*, 472–4). The idea was common and may derive ultimately from Seneca's *De Consolatione ad Polybium*, XII. 2.

and roses which announced the sanctity of the early Christians, is the
principle by which moral corruption spreads through the atmosphere:

> Men may hem knowe by smel of brymstoon.
> For al the world they stynken as a goot;
> Hir savour is so rammyssh and so hoot
> That though a man from hem a mile be,
> The savour wole infecte hym, trusteth me.   (885–9)

And the alchemist of the Yeoman's cautionary tale 'wolde infecte al a toun'
(973). The disease Chaucer has in mind is probably plague. Medical ignorance
about the true causes of plague allowed a plethora of theories to gain some
currency—among them the notion that it was transmitted by a corrupted
atmosphere. In this story, disease, probably plague, is a metaphor for the
spread of alchemy: the 'elvysshe craft', like plague, is the scourge of
cities—stinking, corrupting, deadly, and equally to be shunned. The early
saints purified and cleansed their converts through baptism; in this story
alchemists, conversely, are agents of infection, bringing moral and physical
degeneration. In Canto XXIX of Dante's *Inferno* 'infallibil giustizia' (56)
punishes the shades of the alchemists (and other counterfeiters) with excruci-
ating disease: the air is filled with the stench from their 'marcite membre'
(51).[29] Chaucer's alchemists suffer something of this punishment on earth:
their particular smell goes with them everywhere; the Yeoman's eyes have
been 'blered' and his face 'discoloured' (664).

The urban authority confronted by the Yeoman takes the form of Harry
Bailly, who, if he is to be identified with 'Henri Bayliff ostyler' of Southwark,
was a considerable and prominent citizen—an M.P. in 1376–7 and 1378–9,
and a holder of several other responsible civic offices. As in the previous story
the argument here concerns the intractability of matter:[30] the Yeoman claims
that his master is endowed with such 'subtilitee' (620) that he can turn
upside-down the ground on which they are riding and 'pave it al of silver and
of gold' (626). Harry Bailly does not dispute this philosophically, but puts a
simple but devastating practical question: why, if the alchemist is so clever,
do they not lead more affluent lives? The Yeoman has no answer and instantly
admits that their science is defective: 'we faille of oure desir' (671) and 'evere
we lakken oure conclusioun' (672). His confrontation with Harry Bailly's
urban self-interest and self-assurance provokes the Yeoman to abjure his
profession and admit that the tradition of learning to which he hoped to
belong is a fractured one: no authoritative knowledge on the subject can be

---

[29] Dante's *Divine Comedy* is quoted from the edition by John D. Sinclair, 3 vols
(London, 1971). The phrase *marcite membre* means 'festered limbs'.
[30] On this aspect of *The Canon's Yeoman's Tale* see the fine account of Charles
Muscatine in his *Chaucer and the French Tradition: A Study in Style and Meaning*
(Berkeley and Los Angeles, 1957), pp. 213–21.

passed on.[31] The Yeoman ends with an exemplary story. A 'disciple' asks Plato 'the name of the privee stoon' and the following conversation takes place:

> And Plato answerde unto hym anoon,
> 'Take the stoon that Titanos men name.'
> 'Which is that?' quod he. 'Magnasia is the same,'
> Seyde Plato. 'Ye, sire, and is it thus?
> This is *ignotum per ignocius.*
> What is Magnasia, good sire, I yow preye?'
> 'It is a water that is maad, I seye,
> Of elementes foure,' quod Plato.
> 'Telle me the roote, good sire,' quod he tho,
> 'Of that water, if it be youre wil.'
> 'Nay, nay,' quod Plato, 'certein, that I nyl.
> The philosophres sworn were everychoon
> That they sholden discovere it unto noon,
> Ne in no book it write in no manere.'   (1453–66)

In a completely orthodox way Chaucer appears to believe that the science of alchemy may at one time have had a firm basis, but that the original secrets had been lost. Unlike the Second Nun the Yeoman cannot testify to a continuing tradition: he curses the man who 'me broghte first unto that game' (708) and vows to have nothing more to do with him. He forsakes what he comes to realize is probably a ruined belief.

There are marked contrasts between these two stories, the major one being that Christianity is a continuing faith whereas alchemy, in its medieval form at least, was a science without a basis. But the similarities are important too. In these two stories, Chaucer seems to me to be interested in the ways in which stable urban organizations and their representatives confront the challenges of unorthodoxy. Assured by an unadventurous certitude, the representatives of the urban culture use, in one instance, somewhat arbitrary and tactless force, in the other an unshakeable conviction that any aspiration should manifest itself in material well-being and improvement. Neither the authorities of imperial Rome nor the substantial London citizen take much trouble to understand what is challenging their view of the world and threatening to change it. Both are concerned simply to bring the outsiders back into the fold, and their refusal to countenance any other way of looking at things is almost instinctive. The monoliths of conventional belief are hard to move. Both stories suggest that it is possible to make converts, but difficult—the early Christians have to be prepared to lose their lives; the modern alchemists have

[31] For the idea that the Yeoman undergoes a conversion see Bruce L. Greenberg, 'The Canon's Yeoman's Tale: Boethian Wisdom and the Alchemists', Chaucer Review 1 (1966) 37–54; John Gardner, 'The Canon's Yeoman's Prologue and Tale: An Interpretation', Philological Quarterly 46 (1967) 1–17.

to be ready to lose their property, risk their health, swindle and cheat so that they can continue their experiments. In unfavourable circumstances commitment is not easy to maintain: Cecilia has no doubts and persists in her belief; the Yeoman falters, loses faith in a craft he realizes is defective, and to a certain extent conforms. Yet firmly based or not, new ideologies constantly present a challenge to the establishment.

III

There is a disagreement about the broad social effects of urbanization in the late Middle Ages. Colin Platt puts the matter plainly and declares his preference:

> It has been one recent view that the 'structure of urban society in the later Middle Ages became, not less flexible, but more so'; admissions to the franchise had come to include the weavers and the fullers, and governing councils were very frequently enlarged. Yet it would be hard to ignore the evidence, everywhere abundant and compelling, of a closing down rather than a widening of opportunity. If admissions to the franchise rose in many late-medieval boroughs, it was because the ruling elite could not rightly afford to restrict them, gaining more than it lost from such expansion. Likewise, if a governing council grew in size, the electorate, just as often, might narrow. In borough society at many levels, the same restrictive pressures were felt. Ineluctably, they fenced that society in.[32]

There is plenty of evidence, some of which is reflected in fifteenth-century verse, of conflicts between the ruling oligarchies of towns such as Cambridge in 1418 and Coventry in 1494–6 and those who sought to dispute their power.[33]

But Chaucer was not essentially a controversialist: disputatious contemporary questions tend to become attenuated in his work. In the *Second Nun's Tale* and *Canon's Yeoman's Tale*, however, the confrontation between an established, powerful and self-assured urban ruling order and the unorthodox denizens of the suburbs is not far below the surface. When Chaucer, in the *General Prologue*, describes the urban establishment—five members of a London religious fraternity—what emerges is their somewhat absurd pomposity and complacency. They are concerned with their dress: 'Ful fressh and

---

[32] Platt, p. 144. (He is quoting A. R. Bridbury, *Economic Growth: England in the Later Middle Ages* (London, 1962), p. 58).
[33] For these disputes and the verses generated by them see my *Politics and Poetry in the Fifteenth Century* (London 1971), pp. 367–8, 371–6.

newe hire geere apiked was' (I 365), and their knives, belts and pouches are elaborately ornamented. They have social ambitions within the city:

> Wel semed ech of hem a fair burgeys
> To sitten in a yeldehalle on a deys.
> Everich, for the wisdom that he kan,
> Was shaply for to been an alderman (369–72)

—though elevation to this status was unlikely considering the insignificance of their trades.[34] They are wealthy both of 'catel' and 'rente' (373). Their wives are interested in being called 'madame' and in the niceties of social precedence. Their ambitions, though real, are limited and safe; they exist within the context of acceptable orthodoxy. Outside, in the suburbs, among the alchemists, the striving is more desperate:

> A! nay! lat be; the philosophres stoon,
> Elixer clept, we sechen faste echoon;
> For hadde we hym, thanne were we siker ynow.
> But unto God of hevene I make avow,
> For al oure craft, whan we han al ydo,
> And al oure sleighte, he wol nat come us to.
> He hath ymaad us spenden muchel good,
> For sorwe of which almoost we wexen wood,
> But that good hope crepeth in oure herte,
> Supposynge evere, though we sore smerte,
> To be releeved by hym afterward.
> Swich supposyng and hope is sharp and hard;
> I warne yow wel, it is to seken evere.
> That futur temps hath maad men to dissevere,
> In trust therof, from al that evere they hadde.
> Yet of that art they kan nat wexen sadde,
> For unto hem it is a bitter sweete,—
> So semeth it,—for nadde they but a sheete,
> Which that they myghte wrappe hem inne a-nyght,
> And a brat to walken inne by daylyght,
> They wolde hem selle and spenden on this craft.
> They kan nat stynte til no thyng be laft. (VIII 862–83)

This too, of course, is absurd. But when Chaucer writes like this it is hard to escape the conclusion that in his view the potential for growth and change and the energy to turn the world upside-down lay beyond the comfortably reassuring town walls in the suburban tenements of those who were by choice and necessity outsiders. Chaucer was not essentially unorthodox but he knew

[34] See Sylvia Thrupp, *The Merchant Class of Medieval London*, Appendix A, for a table of aldermanic families. Most aldermen were mercers, grocers, drapers, fishmongers and goldsmiths. There are a few examples of haberdashers, but carpenters, weavers, dyers, and 'tapycers' are not represented.

how change worked. It depends often on a willingness to suffer present discomforts in the hope that something better may emerge: in the alchemists' terms, it 'hath ymaad us spenden muchel good' for which they 'almoost . . . wexen wood', but they are willing to do this in the hope that they may be 'releeved . . . afterward' in the 'futur temps'. They are willing to mortgage the present because they believe that they may be able to create a different world. Even against the evidence and against the odds that is what the prospective changer of the status quo has to believe.

Characteristically, of course, Chaucer does not declare himself on either the desirability for change or on its likelihood—he merely sets one example of a shift in belief that was successful against another which to all intents and purposes had failed. There may be a sense in which, as an artist, he should not declare himself. What he does make clear, however, is his perception of the way in which orthodoxy maintains and defends itself and what, on the other hand, the compulsion for change might be.[35]

---

[35] In a slightly different form this paper was given as the ninth Annual Tucker-Cruse lecture at the University of Bristol on 12 February 1985.

Lexicography
and Semantic History

Defining Daftness

T. L. BURTON

dafte adj. Also **defte**. [OE **dæfte** & *****defte** gentle; cp. OE **dafenian** be seemly, fitting.]

1. (a) Well-mannered, gentle, modest, humble; (b) ? noble, exalted.

(a) ?c1200 *Orm.* 2175: ӡho [Mary] wass . . Shammfasst, & daffte, & sedefull, & þwertt ut wel bifundenn. *Ibid.* 4610: Maggdennhad . . ӡiff þatt itt iss . . meoc & daffte & sedefull I þæwess & i lusstess. a1300(a1250) *Bestiary* 23: Ne wu he dennede him in ðat defte meiden . . ðe him bar to manne frame. c1450 *Alph.Tales* 440/14: þer was a fayr yong man . . he was so pratie & so defte, at yong wommen wex evyn fond on hym. (b) a1450 *Yk.Pl.* 4/92: I sall be lyke vnto hym þat es hyeste on heghte; Owe! what I [Lucifer] am derworth and defte.

2. Dull, uncouth, boorish, awkward [prob. by way of 'humble, good-natured'].

c1300 *Body & S.* (5) p.37: Ne wist i ӡwat was guod nor il, Bote as a wretche dumb and daft. ?c1450 *St.Cuth.* 443: Bot to make it I am daft, For I can noӡt of potter craft. ?a1475 *PParv.* (Win) 123: Defte or dul: Obtusus: Agrestis.

So reads the entry for *dafte* and *defte* in *MED*. It contains two evident uncertainties: the queried sense 1. (b) '? noble, exalted', for which there is only one example; and the tentative suggestion that the pejorative senses 'dull, uncouth,' etc. developed 'prob[ably] by way of "humble, good-natured"'. It will be noted further that 'skilful', the usual sense of *deft* in modern English, is not entered in *MED* at all. A comparison of this single entry with the two separate entries under *Daft* and *Deft* in *OED* (too long for reproduction here) reveals a surprising disagreement about the semantic development of the word (or words), beside the underlying agreement on the origin. That *daft* and *deft* are two forms of what was originally one word and that the two spellings in time became attached to two different branches of the semantic tree, the one pejorative, the other ameliorative, is not in dispute; but on two important points the lexicographers do not agree: the stage at which the sense 'skilful' arose and attached itself to the form *deft*; and the process by which the sense 'stupid' developed for the form *daft*. It is these two points I wish to address

165

here, in an attempt to solve some of the questions prompted by the entry in *MED* quoted above. I shall be asking specifically (i) concerning the 'good' senses: (a) is there any justification for the sense '? noble, exalted'? (b) does the sense 'skilful' originate in the Middle English period (and should it therefore be included in *MED*)? (ii) concerning the 'bad' senses: can the quotations for sense 2 in *MED* ('dull, uncouth,' etc.) be re-arranged in such a way as to give a more convincing explanation of the development of the current sense 'stupid' than by the unlikely way of 'humble, good-natured'?

I   THE 'GOOD' SENSES

Although the sense 'skilful' is not recorded in *MED*, *OED* has two quotations for this sense from the Middle English period, one from the *York Plays* under *Deft* (sense 2), one from the *Chester Plays* under *Daft* (sense 5), the latter indicating (if correct) that 'skilful' has not invariably been associated with the form *deft*. Of these two quotations in *OED*, the first, from Lucifer's self-adulatory monologue in the Barkers' play from the York cycle ('Owe! what I am derworth and defte'), does in fact appear in *MED*: as may be seen from the entry reproduced above, it is the one quotation adduced in support of the queried sense 'noble, exalted'. What are we to make of this disagreement between the historical dictionaries? Is it dexterity (*OED*) or is it nobility (*MED*) that Lucifer is claiming? It is, of course, quite impossible to tell from the few words to which the dictionaries are restricted by the exigencies of space: this is unfortunately not one of those examples so judiciously sought by Johnson where the word to be defined is 'so combined as that its meaning is apparently determined by the tract and tenour of the sentence'.[1] I therefore quote here the two complete stanzas of Lucifer's speech, to supply a fuller context:

> Owe! certes! what I am worthely wroghte with wyrschip, i-wis!
> For in a glorius gle my gleteryng it glemes,
> I am so mightyly made my mirth may noghte mys,
> Ay sall I byde in this blys thorowe brightnes of bemes.
> Me nedes noghte of noy for to neuen,
> All welth in my welde haue I weledande,
> Abowne ȝhit sall I be beeldand,
> On heghte in þe hyeste of hewuen.
>
> Ther sall I set my selfe, full semely to seyghte,
> To ressayue my reuerence thorowe righte o renowne,

---

[1] Quoted from the 'Preface to the English Dictionary' in *Johnson: Prose and Poetry*, selected by Mona Wilson, 2nd edn (London, 1957), pp. 314–15.

I sall be lyke vnto hym þat es hyeste on heghte;
Owe! what I am derworth and defte.—Owe! dewes! all goes
   downe!
My mighte and my mayne es all marrande,
Helpe! felawes, in faythe I am fallande.[2]

Even this, however, is insufficient to settle the issue: it is clear enough that Lucifer is puffed up with pride in his appearance and with ambition, and in that context each of the proposed meanings makes some sense; neither, however, can claim to be self-evidently correct. In such a case the lexicographer ought certainly to choose a sense that the word in question is known to have elsewhere rather than to postulate a new sense for which there is no support in other contexts. And on those conservative grounds the speculative sense 1. (b) in *MED*, '? noble, exalted', must, I think, be summarily dismissed: there is no evidence that *daft* or *deft* ever has such a meaning elsewhere, and no necessity for that to be the sense here. The short answer to our first question, 'Is there any justification for the sense "noble, exalted"?', must, then, be 'No'.

But does it therefore follow that we must accept the definition in *OED*, 'Apt, skilful, dexterous, clever or neat *in action*' (my italics)? Perhaps; yet the context contains no action to which Lucifer's deftness could be linked (unless it be the verb *set* in the first line of the second stanza, which is rather distant). In such cases of doubt one can do worse than appeal to the etymology of the word in question; and here *OED*'s discussion (under *Daft*) is particularly helpful: 'The primary meaning of the adj. must have been "becoming, fit", cf. the adv. *gedæftlice* fitly, suitably, seasonably, and the vb. *gedæftan* to make fit or ready, to prepare.' *MED*'s etymological comment, making comparison with OE *dafenian* 'be seemly, fitting', though not quite the same, is similar in import: the dictionaries agree that the underlying sense of *daftness/deftness* is simply 'fitness, suitability'. A second look at Lucifer's speech will suggest, I believe, that this is precisely the sense required here: he is speaking of his aspirations towards Godhead; he gives the reason why he sees himself in the highest position—'I am derworth and defte'—and in that very moment he is cast down. Although it is quite possible, semantically, that these alliterating adjectives amount to no more than a Jack-Hornerish boast ('How noble and clever I am!'),[3] it is proper that they should here have a stronger force; and so indeed they have if they carry their primary senses in this passage. The root meaning of *derworth* is, transparently, '(very) worthy' (see *OED*, s.v. *Dearworth, derworth*, a.), that of *deft*, as we have just seen, 'fit'. If these senses are allowed here, Lucifer's last words before his fall are, 'I

---

[2] *York Plays*, ed. Lucy Toulmin Smith (Oxford, 1885), p. 4.
[3] *Everyman and Medieval Miracle Plays*, ed. A. C. Cawley, rev. edn (London, 1974), p. 6, gloss for line 92.

shall be equal to the highest in heaven: I am worthy [of it] and fit [for it]' (cf. the equivalent passage in the *Ludus Coventriae*, where Lucifer claims three times within the space of three lines that he is worthier than God)[4]—and what could be more appropriate, both theologically and dramatically, than that he should be struck down in the moment of his highest blasphemy?

I submit, then, that the sense 'fit, suitable' is more convincing contextually than either of the meanings proposed for this occurrence in the historical dictionaries, and that it accords with the etymology and early sense development outlined in *OED*. The present instance would then be a late survival of the primary sense 'apt, fit, suitable' (without specialized application); and it would be from this sense that the specialized meaning 'apt, skilful, etc. *at some action*' (*OED*, *Deft*, 2) naturally developed.

But at what stage (to turn to the second of our questions concerning the 'good' senses) did this specialized application, 'skilful', become current? If we accept the evidence of *OED*'s citation from the *Chester Plays* under *Daft*, sense 5, we will place this sense firmly within the Middle English period, before 1500; if, on the other hand, we accept the negative evidence of *MED*, we must believe that the sense 'skilful' did not develop until the modern English period. To the questionable example from the *Chester Plays*, then, we must now direct our attention.

The situation in the Painters' play of the shepherds is as follows: the three shepherds have wrestled, one after the other, with the boy, Garcius, and each in turn has been worsted; the bright star has appeared; the angel has sung his 'Gloria in excelsis Deo et in terra pax hominibus bonae voluntatis'. There follows an argument amongst the four humans as to the wording and meaning of the angel's song, in these terms:

TERTIUS PASTOR
. . . hit was 'grorus glorus' with a 'glee.'
Hit was neyther more nor lasse.

GARCIUS
Nay, yt was 'glorus glarus glorius';
methinke that note went over the howse.
A seemely man hee was, and curiouse;
but soone awaye hee was.

PRIMUS PASTOR
Nay, yt was 'glorus glarus' with a 'glo,'
and mych of 'celsis' was therto.
As ever have I rest or woo,
muche he spake of 'glas.'

---

[4] See *Ludus Coventriae*, ed. K. S. Block, EETS ES 120 (1922 for 1917), p. 18, lines 53–5.

SECUNDUS PASTOR

Naye, yt was neyther 'glas' nor 'glye.'
Therfore, fellowe, nowe stand bye.

TERTIUS PASTOR

By my fayth, hee was some spye,
our sheep for to steale.
Or elles hee was a man of oure crafte,
for seemely hee was and [wounder] defte.

GARCIUS

Nay, hee came by night—all thinges lefte—
our tuppes with tarre to teale.[5]

This passage is a lexicographer's nightmare. The latest editors of the *Chester Cycle* gloss *defte* in the penultimate speech as '*skilful*' (following *OED*); but their unease with this gloss is indicated by the addition of a note saying, 'The line . . . involves a play on the two words, *deft*, "apt, skilful, dexterous, clever", with a sense of "neat, trim, handsome" especially appropriate here but recorded only from 1579; and *daft* "silly, wanting in intelligence, stupid".'[6] This suggestion, however, seems to me to raise more problems than it solves. The third shepherd is giving reasons why the mysterious singer may have been a shepherd, like himself and his fellows ('a man of *our* craft'): his reasons (indicated by the word *for*) are that the singer was 'seemely' and 'defte'. But I am not persuaded that either neatness (a sense not recorded till the late sixteenth century) or stupidity on the singer's part would lead to the deduction that he was a shepherd: on the contrary, these senses fit *less* comfortably than 'skilful' itself.

Almost the only observation that may be made without argument is the purely syntactic one that *defte* (in some manuscripts *dafte*) is coupled here with *seemely*, as is *curiouse* in a similar pairing eleven lines earlier. That said, there remains an alarming number of semantic uncertainties: are *defte* and *curiouse* more or less synonymous, as their syntactic parallelism may imply, or do they pick out different attributes? Do they merely reinforce the general sense of *seemely*, or do they add something (or some things) significantly different? To what quality or qualities of the angel do they in fact allude? It looks as if *seemely* is used of his appearance (*OED*, sense 1, 'of a pleasing or goodly appearance, fair, well-formed, handsome, "proper"'); but the same can hardly be said of the words coupled with *seemely*, since both *curiouse*, with its overtones of sumptuousness and sophistication (*MED*, senses 2–4), and

---

[5] *The Chester Mystery Cycle*, ed. R. M. Lumiansky and David Mills, 2 vols, EETS SS 3 (1974), 9 (1986), I. 142–3, lines 382–99.
[6] Ibid., II, note to line 397. I am grateful to Professor Mills for his generosity in allowing me access to this note—in the knowledge that it was likely to provoke disagreement—while the volume was still in press.

defte, with its suggestion of neatness (if admissible at this early date), would suggest an appearance too refined to lead the shepherds to the conclusion that the singer is one of their kind. Could the words be used, then, of his manner—'solicitous, concerned, eager' (*MED, curious*, 1. (c); *OED*, 1, 1. b); 'well-mannered, humble, etc.' (*MED, dafte*, 1. (a); *OED, Daft*, 1 and *Deft*, 1)? Or of his singing, which is the chief point of interest? Or of the stealth with which he seems to have appeared and disappeared? Or of his supposed expertise in shepherding?—In any of these last three cases both words might mean 'skilful, expert' (*MED, curious*, 1. (b); *OED, Deft*, 2); but there are just too many possibilities to allow the meanings to be pinned down with any confidence. On such slippery evidence it would be dangerous indeed to claim a new sense for any of the doubtful words (and if the argument above concerning Lucifer's speech is accepted, the current example becomes the earliest use of *deft* in the sense 'skilful', antedating the next example by a clear hundred years).

One needs grounds more relative than this: the establishment of a new sense depends on an unambiguous context. In the present instance it must be safer (though no doubt less imaginative) to take both *curiouse* and *defte* as alluding to the angel's demeanour in the sense most closely allied to that of *seemely*, i.e. respectively, 'solicitous' and 'humble': the singer was very eager to give them his news, but he behaved humbly enough to be taken for a shepherd. In this case *defte/ dafte* must take its place as a fifth example under sense 1. (a) in *MED* ('well-mannered, humble,' etc.); and it is not, indeed, until 1592, well into the modern English period, that the sense 'skilful' can unhesitatingly be claimed. This is the date of what now becomes the earliest quotation for the sense 'skilful' in *OED* (s.v. *Deft*, 2): 'Whether the Deft Writer be as sure a workeman as the neat Taylor'; it now appears, moreover, that the sense 'skilful' has from the first been associated with the form *deft*. If this reasoning holds good, it gets rid of the awkward anomaly whereby the one word, in either of its forms, could at the same time mean both 'awkward' and 'dexterous', 'stupid' and 'clever', since the senses implying skill or specialized knowledge become restricted to one form, *deft*; moreover, they do not arise until the other form, *daft*, has quite lost its originally 'good' senses and has come to mean 'stupid, etc.'.

II THE 'BAD' SENSES

The second major disagreement between the historical dictionaries concerns the path by which the pejorative senses 'dull, uncouth, boorish, awkward' (*MED*, 2) or 'silly, foolish, stupid' (*OED, Daft*, 2; *Deft*, 5) arose for a word earlier expressive of high approbation, as in the use of *daft* and *deft* in the *Ormulum* and the *Bestiary* to describe the Virgin Mary (see the quotations under sense 1. (a) in the entry for *MED* at the head of this essay). *MED* suggests, as we have seen, that the passage was probably 'by way of "humble, good-natured"'; but the leap from good nature to boorishness is difficult. *OED*, in its more discursive treatment of the semantic history, proposes a development from 'becoming, *decens*' (of persons) to 'meek, mild, innocent' to 'innocent, inoffensive' to 'irrational' (of animals), and so to 'silly, foolish, deficient in sense' (of persons), comparing this development to that of the words *innocent* and *silly*. This is attractive but purely hypothetical, since no evidence is adduced that *daft* was in fact ever used in the intermediate sense 'innocent': what is needed to verify the argument in *OED* is an example of the word's use in a context implying lack of knowledge, but doing so in a neutral, non-judgemental way.

I believe that the reasoning in *OED* is substantially correct and that the evidence for it is in fact present in both *OED* and *MED*, although it remains unused in both through misdefinition. In the first quotation under sense 2 in *MED* ('dull, uncouth,' etc.) and sense 2.a in *OED* ('silly, foolish, stupid'), from *Þe desputisoun bitwen þe bodi and þe soule*,[7] the body, having been accused by the soul of bringing about their mutual perdition, counterattacks with the argument that the soul is to blame, since the soul was endowed with reason and should have guided them both better:

> . . . And ȝif þou wolt me þerof wyte
> Þat boþe schul we ben ispilt,
> Mid þi self scholdest þou furst flyte,
> For al was hit þyn owne gilt.
> Þat schewe ich þe wiþ wordes luyte
> And wiþ riȝt resun, ȝif þou wilt;
> Þou art to blame, and ich al quite,
> For boþe schuldestou vs from schome han schilt.
>
> For god þe schop aftur his schaft,
> And ȝaf þe boþe *wit and skil*;
> And in þi lokyng al was ich laft,
> To wissen after þyn owne wil.
> *Ne couþe i neuere of wikked craft,*
> *Ne wuste what was good or il,*
> *But as a beest doumbe and daft,*
> And as þou tauhtest me þertil.
>
> For ich was betauȝt þe to ȝeme,
> A *witles þing* as ich was boren,
> And set to seruen þe to queme,
> Boþe an euen and at moren.

---

[7] Ed. W. Linow, Erlanger Beiträge zur englischen Philologie und vergleichenden Litteraturgeschichte 1 (1889).

Ac þou þat deedes couþest deme
Scholdest ha ben war beforen
Of my folye, as hit now seme;
And þus art þow þi self forloren.

Vernon MS, stanzas 24–6 (my italics)

The contrast is between one entity which has *wit and skil* (i.e. a rational faculty), enabling it to distinguish between right and wrong, and another which has not, and which cannot therefore be held responsible for its actions. In such a context *witles* (st. 26, line 2) must mean not 'stupid or dull-witted' but 'devoid of understanding, lacking a rational faculty'. The same applies to *daft*, here plainly synonymous with *witles*. The body is protesting its innocence on the grounds that it cannot distinguish between good and evil because, like an animal, it lacks the faculties of speech and reason (see the three italicized lines in the second of the stanzas quoted: the Vernon reading, *beest*, as above, is clearly more appropriate than *wretche*, the Laud version quoted in *MED*). Here, plainly, we have a use of *daft* entirely without trace of the pejorative senses 'stupid, boorish,' etc., a wholly neutral use in the intermediate sense 'innocent' or 'irrational' (i.e. 'not possessed of the faculty of reason'), exactly as postulated by *OED* in its introductory essay.

Somewhat similar comments may be made on the second quotation under *MED* sense 2 (the first under sense 2.b in *OED*), from *The Life of St. Cuthbert in English Verse*.[8] Here the child Cuthbert, distressed by the breaking of 'a litil bell þai kalled a kelym' (426), which was a gift from his relatives, takes the bell to a smith to be repaired. The smith wants to help but lacks the necessary expertise:

Dere childe, he says, I walde fayne
For godes sake make þi bell agayne,
Bot to make it I am daft,
For I can noȝt of potter craft.   (441–4)

If the smith is upbraiding himself for stupidity, boorishness, etc., as suggested in the dictionaries, he is being unduly hard on himself. But there is no need to suppose that this is what he is doing: the probability must be that he is merely lamenting his inability to repair the bell because *he has not had the requisite training*. As a smith he will be experienced in general metalwork; but the making of bells and pots (whether earthen or metal)[9] is a highly specialized craft, and one of which he 'can noȝt' ['knows nothing']—like Guildenstern with the recorders, he has not the skill; and he has not the skill because (presumably) he has not been taught it. The editor's gloss, 'unskilful', though overlooked by *OED* and *MED*, is just right.

---

[8] Ed. J. T. Fowler, Publications of the Surtees Society 87 (1891 for 1889).
[9] See ibid., note to line 444; also *OED*, s.v. *Potter*, sb.¹, 1 and 1.†b

This example may be supported by a very similar one (previously unnoticed) from the Middle English encyclopaedic dialogue, *Sidrak and Bokkus*.[10] In answer to King Bokkus's question, 'Which ffolke be tho, as þou wenys,/ Thatt the world most sustenys?', Sidrak replies:

> Oon is these men of crafte,
> That techeþ other þat ben dafte
> Konnyng here lyvelode to wynne
> And God to serue withoute synne.   (Laud MS, 6539–42)

We have here the same rhyme as in the two previous quotations, *craft/ daft*, making the same contrast between those who have a particular kind of knowledge (whether of right and wrong or of a given occupation) and those who do not. It might be argued that the lack of this knowledge indicates stupidity (and that, of course, is how words like *ignorant* came to develop pejorative senses), but the neutral tone of all three passages is against such an interpretation in these specific instances. In the case of the last passage it might equally be argued that the people being taught a craft are apprentices who have been specially selected on the grounds of their aptitude (i.e. that *daft* here means 'deft' in the current sense); but there is nothing in the passage to indicate positively that this is so: the lines speak in general terms about people being taught a craft so that through occupying themselves with it they may make an honest living and stay free from sin (cf. *Piers Plowman*, B. XIX. 230–52).[11] The only necessary quality of daftness in all three passages discussed here is *lack of knowledge*; in none of them are pejorative overtones apparent.

III   A REVISED ENTRY FOR *MED*

I suggest, then, a revision of the entry for *dafte* in *MED* along the following lines:

1. Apt, fit [illustrated by Lucifer's claim from the *York Plays*: the present 1. (b), redefined and re-positioned. Presumably this is the earliest sense, although this, the only surviving example of it, is relatively late.]
2. Well-mannered, humble, etc. [The present 1. (a), illustrated by the same four quotations, from the *Ormulum* (two), the *Bestiary*, and *An alphabet of*

---

[10] For brief details of this work see *A Manual of the Writings in Middle English 1050–1500*, III, ed. Albert E. Hartung (New Haven, 1972), 744–5, 900–1. Quotation and line numbering follow my parallel-text edition (in preparation) of MSS Laud Misc. 559 (Bodleian) and Lansdowne 793 (British Library).

[11] Ed. A. V. C. Schmidt (London, 1978), pp. 242–3. I am grateful to Dr Myra Stokes for drawing my attention to this parallel, and for her helpful comments on an earlier draft of this essay.

tales; and with the addition of a fifth, the description of the angel from the *Chester Plays*.]

3. (a) Not endowed with the faculty of reason; innocent, guileless [illustrated by the quotation from *Body and Soul*]. (b) Untaught, ignorant, lacking a specialized knowledge or skill, unskilled, inexpert [illustrated by the quotations from *St. Cuthbert* and *Sidrak*].

4. Dull, stupid, boorish, etc. [illustrated only by the quotation from *Promptorium parvulorum*, the quotations from *Body and Soul* and *St. Cuthbert* having been moved to 3. (a) and (b) respectively].

This arrangement, beginning with the primary sense 'fit' and supplying (under sense 3) the hitherto missing or misplaced links later in the semantic chain, gives us a perfectly coherent sense development: from 'apt, fit' to 'well-mannered, humble' to 'innocent'; hence to 'ignorant, lacking *specialized* knowledge'; and so at last to 'ignorant *in general*', hence, with the addition of pejorative connotations, 'stupid'. It is a development very close to that postulated (but not shown) in *OED*, and similar, as *OED* remarks, to that of such words as *innocent* and *silly* (to which might be added *lewd*).

Thomas Warton and the Waxing of the Middle Ages

PAT ROGERS

In any age, Basil Cottle would have been a notable scholar. But it is only within the last century and a half that he could possibly have held a distinguished post in Medieval English. The prime reason for this has nothing to do with the belated appearance of departments of English within universities (Dr Cottle could, in any case, have survived happily under the aegis of 'classical studies' (to use an anachronistic form), such are his attainments in the ancient languages). But the middle ages, as a linguistic entity, were not fully to dawn until the nineteenth century. Prior to 1800, anyone who wished to specialize in, say, Middle English (not many did) would have had to describe himself or herself as a Goth of one kind or another.

The lexical history of terms such as 'middle age' and 'medieval' has been explored on a few occasions, although never for the purposes I shall adopt in this essay. When the original *OED* reached the letter M in about 1905, the editors were unable to find any examples of *middle age(s)* earlier than 1722, with two further citations from the eighteenth century—the more interesting from Chambers's *Cyclopaedia* (1753 edition). The illustrations show that the usage took off properly in the next century, and it was probably Henry Hallam's work entitled *A View of the State of Europe during the Middle Ages* (1818) which confirmed the currency of the phrase as a historiographical marker. The recent supplement to *OED* has found earlier citations, from a Donne sermon and from the historian Henry Spelman: both date from the first quarter of the seventeenth century, but neither seems to be the easy use of a widely recognizable or accepted label. The locution existed, but it did not trip off the tongue: it had still to acquire the force of a technical term. As for the entry *mediæval, medieval*, *OED* finds nothing prior to 1827. The second instance given is dated 1856, and comes from Ruskin; he provides the first example for both *mediævalist* (1874) and *mediævalism* (1853). The supplement cannot antedate these cases: so recent is the adoption of expressions which seem so necessary and natural in the scholarly world today.

In a recent essay in *Speculum*, Fred C. Robinson has considered both these key terms, though in a highly personal manner. His article has two centres of interest: first, the earliest appearance of the terms in major European languages, and second, their current linguistic fate. Robinson ends by deploring the 'sorry semantic state of *medieval* and *Middle Ages*' today—by this he means such distorted usages as 'medieval torture'. His complaint is ostensibly on grounds of historical accuracy (medieval warfare was not conducted with the ferocity which careless modern speakers and writers assume). But on a deeper level it can be seen as part of a long campaign to distance these words from associations of barbarity and uncivilized crudity. This 'anti-medieval mischief' has been going on in the language for centuries, and it is a pity that Robinson's account leaps over a truly crucial phase in the evolution of both expressions. What he says about the emergence of the terms is highly important; Robinson shows, for example, that there was a separate development of the phrase 'Middle Age' (and its equivalents) in modern languages, independently of the supposed root form *medium aevum*. Alongside this neo-Latin version there were competing expressions such as *media aetas*. In addition, Robinson has some useful comments on such matters as the preference in various languages for singular or plural in the noun *age/s*: and he even has time to say something about the Anglo-American split on the medial vowel in *mediæval/medieval*. It is, in short, a stimulating discussion of an intrinsically important topic.[1]

But there is a black hole at the centre of this cosmography. One cannot understand the current semantic state of the keywords under review, whether it be sorry or otherwise, without some understanding of what happened to them in their lexical adolescence. As far as English goes, this is intimately tied up with a complex set of historical, political, cultural and social factors. The story carries a sub-plot, in the form of the fortunes of the Gothic. Our neutral and technical use of *medieval* in the present century, just as much as our casual or journalistic application of the word as a loosely condemnatory term, goes back to developments in the language two hundred years ago. It was the eighteenth century which institutionalized the study of Old and Middle English, though it did not invent such study. For its own purposes the age increasingly came to feel the need for labels and descriptive terminology: the shorthand of historical analysis. In my submission, it was the intellectual needs which manifested themselves around the 1770s which explain, more than any other comparable data, the course which *middle ages* and (indirectly) *medieval* have taken in subsequent use. According to this view of the matter, it was that curious marriage between old and new, the enlightenment and the antiquarian movement, which produced the first literary history and the first ideological typing of the medieval. The key figure in this process is Thomas Warton, though he must be seen in a context which displays to view Samuel

---

[1] Fred C. Robinson, 'Medieval, the Middle Ages', *Speculum* 59 (1984) 745–56.

Johnson, Thomas Gray, Richard Hurd, Thomas Percy, Warton's own brother Joseph, and others.

I

Thomas Warton is celebrated as the author of what is generally considered the first major work of literary history in the language: the *History of English Poetry, from the Close of the Eleventh to the Commencement of the Eighteenth Century*, which appeared in three volumes between 1774 and 1781. Part of a fourth volume was left incomplete at Warton's death in 1790, and was printed in subsequent editions, notably that of Richard Price in 1824. Two dissertations were placed in the first volume, a third, on the *Gesta Romanorum*, followed in the third. Price puts all three at the head of the entire work.[2] Warton had corresponded with Gray in 1769–70, at a time when the poet was finally resigning himself to the fact that his own planned history would never go beyond 'fragments, or sketches of a design'. Through the intercession of Hurd and William Mason, Warton sought to discover what Gray's 'scheme' for his work had been. After some delay Gray sent Warton his outline of the history of English poetry, 'in some measure taken from a scribbled paper of *Pope*'. The only relevant feature of this draft for our present purposes is that it is divided into 'schools', but has no term remotely corresponding to *medieval*. There is a reference to the poetry 'of the Goths', but this is a loose racial categorization, not any sort of cultural marker and not really a period designation as such.[3]

Warton's plan is different in significant ways. After the dissertations, it is almost entirely a chronological account; the notorious digressive quality of the text does not affect that fact. The narrative is chiefly organized under reigns of the various English monarchs, even where Warton can find nothing specially characteristic in the writing of that reign. A typical opening to a chapter will take the form, 'We have seen, in the preceding section, that the character of our poetical composition began to be changed about the reign of the first Edward' (I. 111). Warton is not seeking to create wholly discrete phases of 'Edwardian' and 'Ricardian' poetry and the like, but his method does directly involve a mode of periodization which is central to the development of literary history. Such temporal organization is so natural to us that it takes an effort to appreciate how avoidable such a course was for Warton. In the vogue work of

---

[2] Thomas Warton, *History of English Poetry*, ed. [Richard Price], 4 vols (London, 1824). All references are to this edition. Subsequent quotations are given in the text within parentheses.

[3] *Correspondence of Thomas Gray*, ed. P. Toynbee and L. Whibley, rev. H. W. Starr (Oxford, 1971), III. 1092–3, 1125–7.

criticism from the previous decade, Warton's friend Richard Hurd had set out his ideas in a series of *Letters on Chivalry and Romance* (1762). Similarly, Edward Young had offered *Conjectures on Original Composition*, 'in a letter to the author of *Sir Charles Grandison*' (1759). Such forms of words indicate that the discursive will prevail over the temporal. Literature will be viewed *sub specie aeternitatis*, or at least under aspects which only incidentally correspond with time divisions. Warton made a celebrated claim to the effect that he was undertaking something unattempted yet, a history 'at large, and in form'. The claim is justified in more than a purely formal sense. Few books, as a matter of fact, had actually specified their subject matter by reference to 'centuries': the word, as applied to a period such as 1500–1600, did not enter English until the 1630s and was quite rare until Warton's time (Adam Smith employs it in *The Wealth of Nations*). And no treatment of literature had been on a wide enough scale to make an overarching concept such as the middle ages fully intelligible between a single pair of covers. This concept was later adopted in the service of various Whig versions of literary history; Warton helped to initiate the Whig versions, not because of the specific teleology which his argument enshrines (although there is one), but because he laid foundations large enough for others to construct their own intellectual edifices on.

There are two seminal modern accounts of the nature of Warton's achievement. One is the culminating chapter in René Wellek's magisterial *Rise of English Literary History* (1941; 2nd edn, 1966). The other is the section devoted to the *History* in Lawrence Lipking's *The Ordering of the Arts in Eighteenth-Century England* (1970): this brilliant panoptic volume sets Warton alongside the historical surveys and summations of men like Johnson, Horace Walpole, Reynolds, John Hawkins and Charles Burney. Both are remarkably illuminating, and deserve careful study.[4] But Lipking seems to me to exaggerate the 'thoroughly compromised' form of the *History*. He speaks of a 'surrender' by Warton to the materials, the blurring of 'any clear line of interpretation', the inability to contrive any 'permanent order for English poetry'. According to Lipking, Warton was defeated by his vacillation on the issue of progress:

> Earlier historians of poetry like Pope and Spence and even Gray could believe in a progress of poetry that had led to their own times; later historians could believe that all great poets join in a single community of genius which acknowledges no progress or

---

[4] R. Wellek, *The Rise of English Literary History* (1941; rptd. New York, 1966), pp. 166–201; L. Lipking, *The Ordering of the Arts in Eighteenth-Century England* (Princeton, 1970), pp. 352–404 (quotations which follow are from pp. 354–5, 371, 395–6). A more specialized but informative treatment will be found in Joan Pittock, *The Ascendancy of Taste: The Achievement of Joseph and Thomas Warton* (London, 1973), pp. 167–214.

division. Warton could believe both, or neither. At times he applies the idea of progress dogmatically, at times he dogmatically contradicts it.

As a result, Warton has no true principle guiding his work: 'Politely turning his back on schools and systems, [he] opens his history to the full complicated play of illimitable information.' But Lipking's last observation is based on what Warton says in his preface, and the subsequent text does not altogether bear out that statement of intent.

Though not systematic, Warton's historicism is endemic to his book. It is seen as clearly as anywhere at the start of the dissertation on the *Gesta Romanorum*:

> Tales are the learning of a rude age. In the progress of letters, speculation and enquiry commence with refinement of manners. Literature becomes sentimental and discursive, in proportion as a people is polished: and men must be instructed by facts, either real or imaginary, before they can apprehend the subtleties of argument, and the force of reflection.   (I. clxxvii)

What is apparent here, and it is a crucial quality which Lipking and others have missed, is a strong tincture of enlightenment thought and jargon (especially seen in words such as 'refinement of manners', 'sentimental', 'polished'). Warton is indeed writing the progress of romance, a decade before Clara Reeve undertook that task. Later on, we find Warton remarking of minstrelsy, 'as the minstrel profession became a science, and the audience grew more civilised, refinements began to be studied, and the romantic poet sought to gain new attention, and to recommend his story, by giving it the advantage of a plan' (II. 14–15). Later still, the narrative reaches Stephen Hawes, and Warton controverts the opinion of Antony Wood regarding the *Passetyme of Pleasure*:

> Wood, with the zeal of a true antiquary, laments, that 'such is the fate of poetry, that this book, which in the time of Henry the seventh and Eighth was taken into the hands of all ingenious men, is now thought but worthy of a ballad-monger's stall!' The truth is, such is the good fortune of poetry, and such the improvement of taste, that much better books are become fashionable.
>
> (III. 54)

The received view of Warton would place him as one actuated by 'the zeal of a true antiquary'. What such passages show is that he could take a more independent line. The entire work is studded with comments along these lines:

> The antiquaries of former times overlooked or rejected these valuable remains ['fables of chivalry']. . . . But in the present age

179

we are beginning to make ample amends: in which the curiosity of
the antiquarian is connected with taste and genius, and his
researches tend to display the progress of human manners, and to
illustrate the history of society.   (II. 41–2)

The key word here, along with 'progress', is obviously 'taste'. A sentence
like the last one quoted could hardly have been written without the tutelary
presence of Hume. And indeed the Scottish enlightenment underlines the
entire work—not surprising for any book entitled a 'history' in the 1770s, but
a totally disregarded fact up till now. A long shadow is cast over the work by a
classic text of the previous decade: Adam Ferguson's *Essay on the History of
Civil Society* (1767), with its seminal discussion of the nature of a 'polished'
society. Ferguson considers the use of such expressions as 'barbarian' in the
light of conquest and colonization; he anatomizes the idea of progress in terms
of organic metaphor; and he plots the stages by which civilizations move from
the 'rude' to the 'refined'. I do not know whether Warton read this actual
work, but its currency was sufficient for its message to spread through to him
by osmosis. Warton can hardly have missed the ideas of Hume, or those of
Adam Smith—even though what appears to have been Smith's classic
statement of the four stages of human development remained in the form of
unpublished lecture notes until recently, and did its work through the
advocacy of Smith's pupils and acolytes.[5]

This is, needless to say, not an attempt to recruit Warton to the ranks of the
Edinburgh literati. But no one writing at this precise juncture, on issues of
historical evolution, could fail to be influenced at some level by the ferment of
thought in this area. Even a timid Oxford don would have gleaned from his
literary contacts something of what had been happening in ideas. Warton was
not so blinkered as to have avoided reading and citing, several times, the
historical work of Voltaire. Meetings with Burke at the Club, not to mention
the appearance of *The Wealth of Nations* and the first part of the *Decline and
Fall* in 1776, would further have opened his mind. The source of such
contamination of an old-style antiquarian sensibility by fashionable philosophic
history can only be a matter of conjecture, in the absence of published records
of Warton's reading at the time he was engaged on writing the *History*. But the
fact of this influence is visible throughout: an example occurs in the discussion
of the effect of the 'cultivation of an English style' during the Renaissance—
another omnipresent modern term not available to Warton, who speaks of 'the
general restoration of knowledge and taste' (IV. 154). Few later generations
would specify 'taste' in delimiting this epoch. Warton's idiom at such

[5] Smith's lecture notes are printed in *The Origins of the Scottish Enlightenment
1707–1776*, ed. Jane Rendall (London, 1978), pp. 141–3. Quotations from Ferguson
relevant to my argument appear on pp. 137–9, 187–9, 201–3; for Hume, Robertson,
John Millar *et al.* see Rendall, passim.

moments is often close to that in which Johnson contemplates raw nature in the Hebrides and places it in the scale of values against 'civilization'. The idea of literacy is central to both authors. But the point of making such collocations is not to give Warton a precise intellectual ancestry; it is rather to indicate that Warton's novel enterprise had its parallels among the social and political enquiries of the time. Ragged as its final effect may sometimes be, Warton's book is far more than a thoughtless accumulation of detail (a fault he imputes to the early chroniclers). It is in fact an attempt to *range* facts, to make sense of a series of events by imputing connection, contrast, development. Warton is constantly explaining features of literature by reference to its historically determined quality: thus, 'It is in vain to apologise for the coarseness, obscenity, and scurrility of Skelton, by saying that his poetry is tinctured with the manners of his age. Skelton would have been a writer without decorum at any period' (III. 167).

Warton seeks 'a general literary history of Britain' (III. 161), and to this end follows 'the progress of modern letters in the fifteenth century' (III. 257). His habit of periodization results at times in what may now seem a blatant kind of historicism: 'I consider Chaucer, as a genial day in an English spring. . . . But winter returns with redoubled horrors . . . and those tender buds . . . which were called forth by the transient gleam of a temporary sun-shine, are nipped by frosts' (II. 361). In other words, 'most of the poets that immediately succeeded Chaucer seem . . . relapsing into barbarism'. The point is not how persuasive such views are, but how intelligible they make history. I wish to suggest that Warton, more than anyone else, gave a shape and entelechy to the course of literature. Johnson's *Lives of the Poets* (1779–81) could not do this, since they began in the seventeenth century. Gray had characteristically ducked out. Percy could editorialize, Mason could biographicize, Hurd and Joseph Warton could criticize—but none of these was able to realign the great historical categories. It took a maggoty old fellow to construct a usable past. Like another seemingly credulous guardian of a cabinet of curiosities, John Aubrey, he was to show that what looked like antiquarian jottings could lay the groundwork of a serious and organized human science.

II

'The progress of romance and the state of learning in the middle ages', wrote Gibbon in the *Decline and Fall*, 'are illustrated by Mr Thomas Warton with the taste of a poet, and the minute diligence of an antiquarian.'[6] This is one of Gibbon's very infrequent uses of the term at the centre of this inquiry. It was by no means a familiar or natural expression, even at the height of a decade which saw unparalleled activity in historiography. For example, it scarcely

---

[6] Cited by Price, *History of Poetry*, I. i[n].

ever occurs in Charles Burney's *General History of Music*: I have noted a fitful instance, in the second volume (1782): 'With respect to the music of the middle ages in Italy. . . .' Burney, of course, has the standard concerns of the age; his attitudes are made manifest in a passage earlier in this same volume:

> If it be true that the progress of music in every country depends on the degrees of civilization and culture of other arts and sciences among its inhabitants, and on the languages which they speak . . . great perfection cannot be expected in the music of Europe during the middle ages, when the Goths, Vandals, Huns, Germans, Franks, and Gauls, whose ideas were savage, and language harsh and insolent, had seized on its most fertile provinces.

The role of Italy was to 'civilize and polish [its] conquerors'; whereas it is inconceivable that the Welsh, 'a rude, and uncivilized people, . . . without commerce or communication with the rest of Europe, should *invent counterpoint*'. Burney also refers to a 'dark and Gothic period'.[7]

A rapid scan suggests that Joshua Reynolds's *Discourses* contrive, not surprisingly, to get by without any mention of the middle ages. But the term is also rare, more unexpectedly, in William Robertson's *History of the Reign of the Emperor Charles V* (1769). This work enjoyed great celebrity in its day, and was at the peak of its renown when Thomas Warton was engaged on his *magnum opus*. Robertson begins with 'A View of the Progress of Society in Europe, from the Subversion of the Roman Empire, to the Beginning of the Sixteenth Century' (note the parallel in form to Warton's title). He makes reference to 'the martial spirit of Europe, during the middle ages', and to 'the first literary efforts . . . of the European nations in the middle ages'. But his concern is avowedly philosophical, that is, analytic rather than chronological; it is a review of such matters as feudalism, rather than a century-by-century chronicle of the dark ages.[8] This is very different from Warton, who organizes his work on narrative rather than discursive lines. The discursive episodes are, formally speaking, inadvertent.

A comparison might also be drawn with Percy's *Reliques*. The very first sentence of the 'Essay on the Ancient Minstrels in England', which Thomas Percy set at the head of his *Reliques of Ancient Poetry* (1765), states that 'The Minstrels were an order of men in the middle ages, who subsisted by the arts of poetry and music'. But the concept of the middle ages drops from attention as Percy goes on to compile a 'slight history' of minstrelsy from the 'scanty materials' available. In his Preface, Percy evinces the usual desire to 'exhibit the progress of popular opinions', and seeks to display the 'many artless

[7] C. Burney, *A General History of Music*, ed. F. Mercer (London, 1935), 2 vols: I. 457, 458, 487, 622, 631.
[8] W. Robertson, *The History of the Reign of the Emperor Charles V*, 7th edn (London, 1792), I. 61, 87.

graces' of primitive poetry for the delight of 'a polished age, like the present'.[9] Five years later, Percy wrote a preface to the translation of Paul-Henri Mallet's *Introduction à l'histoire du Danemarck*, entitled *Northern Antiquities*. This is mainly devoted to dispelling the confusion which had arisen concerning the notions 'Gothic' and 'Celtic', and although it reveals the usual pre-occupations ('refinement of manners' as a source of linguistic change, for example), it does not reach the medieval era proper.[10]

None of these writers, whatever his contribution, seems to me to have foregrounded the 'medieval' as Warton does, though he cannot yet do this *eo nomine*. His employment of the expression 'middle ages', though more regular than that of his colleagues, is equally casual and unemphatic on most occasions. Thus we are told that 'Statius was a favourite writer with the poets of the middle ages' (II. 197). *Confessio Amantis* is a miscellany of the tales which delighted 'readers of the middle age' (Warton makes no distinction between singular and plural forms). Just over the page, there is mention of collections of the marvellous 'which in the middle ages multiplied to an excessive degree' (II. 313, 315). But on at least one occasion the defining role of the term is crucial, for it is precisely on its 'historical' function that this characteristic passage of the *History* relies:

> We are apt to form romantic and exaggerated notions about the moral innocence of our ancestors. Ages of ignorance and simplicity are thought to be ages of purity. The direct contrary, I believe, is the case. Rude periods have that grossness of manners which is not less friendly to virtue than luxury itself. In the middle ages, not only the most flagrant violations of modesty were frequently practised and permitted, but the most infamous vices. Men are less ashamed as they are less polished.

All this derives from the belief that 'Chaucer's obscenity', in the fabliaux naturally, 'is in great measure to be imputed to his age' (II. 266–7). We need not enter here into the question of how much—if any—historical under-standing Warton actually commands when writing in this vein. The point is that he seeks to make sense of the past specifically by allowing for the situation of earlier writers. The evolution of a definable 'middle age' was essential to his purposes. Sometimes he can make do with a more narrowly delimited temporal span: 'Many classic authors were known in the thirteenth century, but the scholars of that period wanted taste to read and admire them' (II. 175).

But the sweep of the *History* is such that Warton often feels the need for broader categories. It is the 'age' at large, not a temporary fashion, which

---

[9] T. Percy, *Reliques of Ancient English Poetry* (London, 1857), I. xvi, xxv, xxxv.
[10] P.-H. Mallet, *Northern Antiquities*, tr. T. Percy [*et al.*], ed. I. A. Blackwell (London, 1847), pp. 1–21.

explains the lack of any 'just idea of decorum' in the miracle plays (II. 76). Even in his moments of near-Gibbonian irony, Warton is especially prone to the word 'age' to adumbrate historical change. On the subject of Stonehenge, he remarks, 'That the Druids constructed this stupendous pile for a place of worship, was a discovery reserved for the sagacity of a wiser age, and the laborious discussion of modern antiquaries' (II. 466). Irony is perhaps not the right word here: Warton does not doubt for a minute that his is a wiser age, and his faint self-mocking amusement rests on a clearcut view of the 'progress' from one age to another. No previous generation of writers had such constant occasion for the terminology of ages, eras, epochs. A self-consciously 'refined' culture needs to naturalize its prejudices, and the ideological function of 'middle ages' is to give essentially normative terms the force of neutral historic markers. Warton's book is the most important single document in the literary sphere to perform this task.

III

The question may well be asked, were there no preceding terms which the new expressions came to supplant? The answer is yes and no. None of the possible synonyms or alternative concepts could fill exactly the same role as 'middle ages'. Expressions like 'our feudal ancestry' or 'the spirit of chivalry', used by Warton's editor Price, are too specialized for general use.[11] The fact is that the commonest epithets in the eighteenth century are simply 'ancient' writers, 'older' literature, and the like. Warton himself has 'our elder English classics' (II. 41). But words like 'older' have a double ambiguity. First of all, they can lead to confusion with a quite different group of ancient writers, that is, those of classical antiquity. Second, the usage works in opposition to the common verbal habit which alludes to the 'infancy of society', a key notion in the enlightenment critique (as in Smith and Ferguson), explicitly or implicitly. People of Warton's generation saw their own culture as mature and developed; they did not really want expressions which suggested that their predecessors were older than themselves. There is a bit of an ambiguity with 'middle age', but it was a less worrying one for Warton and his friends.

This is to leave aside the other key term, 'Gothic', which is a topic too large to enter upon in any detail. It is enough to say that Warton uses the expression a dozen or more times in his *History*, but generally in a 'neutral' fashion. The word is employed sometimes in an architectural or artistic sense (e.g. III. 394, 462). Sometimes it is quasi-ethnological, used in the sense Percy attempted to make distinctive. But sometimes it does appear to be a kind of historical label, as when Warton says, 'The very devotion of the Gothic times was romantic'

[11] Price, ed., *History of Poetry*, I. 12–13.

(III. 285). The commonest usage is 'Gothic romance' or 'Gothic fiction', an indeterminate form.

Plainly, the overtones of the word were so complex, and for the most part so obviously hostile, that it could not seriously hope to survive as a bland historical term. One student has distinguished three principal senses of 'Gothic' in the period.[12] The first is the opprobrious expression meaning barbarous or uncivilized. The second, in time, is the plain sense 'medieval' (neither is in the first edition of Johnson's *Dictionary* in 1755, though the former appears in the 1773 revision). A third and more specialized sense is the one found in 'Gothic novel', that is, 'grotesque' or 'supernatural'. The student argues that the first two senses 'marched on' their separate ways, without any mutual influence. He suggests that it was Hurd who neutralized the term for general historical use, in his famous *Letters on Chivalry and Romance*. But the term is as much an aesthetic categorizer as a simple temporal marker; when Hurd distinguishes a Gothic poem from a classical one, he is not really pointing to any closely defined epoch. Hurd speaks without any embarrassment of the 'Gothic language and ideas' in *Paradise Regained*, and this is more like the third sense than the second. It was only with the *History* of Warton, in my judgement, that the expression loses all its emotional overtones. Famously, in his poem on Reynolds's window at New College, Oxford (1782), Thomas Warton frees himself of 'visionary rapture' and with the help of Reynolds's classic art breaks the 'Gothic chain'. In fact, most commentators believe that his fundamental adherences remained unaffected up to his death.[13] But it could be said that in the *History* he had done much to break the Gothic chain, in the sense of supplying an alternative model of cultural development, which meant there was less need for an overtly normative term such as 'Gothic' had always been, in Hurd as much as anywhere else. (That Hurd approves where others had disapproved does not affect the point.)

Warton was never to complete the task he set himself. In 1790, as Isaac D'Israeli rather heartlessly put it, he expired amid his volumes.[14] But he had done much already to codify, as well as to chronicle, English poetry. There are two passages of surpassing eloquence which stuck in the English mind for generations: all the major Romantic poets knew these paragraphs. One concerns the reign of Elizabeth, in Section LXI: here Warton asserts that the reformation did not manage to 'disenchant all the strong holds of superstition':

> A few dim characters were yet legible in the mouldering creed of tradition. Every goblin of ignorance did not vanish at the first glimmerings of the morning of science. Reason suffered a few

[12] Alfred E. Longueil, 'The Word "Gothic" in Eighteenth Century Criticism', *MLN* 38 (1923) 453–60.

[13] See the discussion in Lipking, pp. 396–401.

[14] Cited by James Ogden, *Isaac D'Israeli* (Oxford, 1969), p. 174.

demons still to linger, which she chose to retain in her service under the guidance of poetry.   (IV. 327)

And there is a still more plangent threnody for the poetic world which had been lost in the account of Henry VIII's reign (III. 284–5), where Warton describes the pageants and ceremonies of earlier times as 'friendly to imagery . . . and allegory'. His basic idea is that 'the customs, institutions, traditions, and religion, of the middle ages, were favorable to poetry'. What may strike us most today is not the truth or otherwise of the picture he draws, but the sheer fact of a period designated as 'middle ages' for Warton to dilate upon. The jargon of our schools owes an unsuspected debt to Thomas Warton.

Smart *Talk by Miss Austen*

MYRA STOKES

Many of the more significant items in Jane Austen's vocabulary have undergone shifts in meaning since her own day. Some knowledge of their semantic history is therefore necessary if the full implications of their selection by her in particular contexts are to be appreciated. Some of them convey much of the weight of her gravest judgements: there can scarcely have been any reader who has not sensed a more formidable seriousness in, for instance, the words *delicate, elegant, amiable*, as Jane Austen uses them, than they possess today. Discussion of such sober and portentous adjectives, however, would require much space and much solemnity. And remembering Mary Bennet, who, 'at the end of a long concerto', which merely overtaxed her own powers and her audience's patience, 'was glad to purchase praise and gratitude by Scotch and Irish airs', I offer instead something rather lighter: a divertimento on Jane Austen's use of the word *smart*.

Of the senses given by the *OED*, the one most relevant to her usage is (*adj.* 13) 'Fashionable; elegant' (the latter in the earlier sense of 'belonging to the social élite'). The first illustration given is, 'A Cluster of Smart Men, in tawdry Dresses, with little Rapiers' (1718). However, the sense of *tawdry* current at the time—'of the nature of cheap finery; showy or gaudy' (*adj.* 1)—suggests that *smart* was not an entirely complimentary word, and could connote a rather vulgar parade of modishness. This is certainly the case in Jane Austen, who prefers the words *fashionable* and *elegant* for the modernity and stylishness *smart* pretends to denote. *Smart* is used 'straight' only by her vulgar or uneducated characters; and is apparently rather a low, somewhat slangy word, which if used by the genteel suggests a sneer, either at the pretentious aping by inferiors of the fashions of their superiors, or at a rather ignorant and snobbish adherence to the more showy and superficial aspects of 'fashion'. In this, it seems to have been similar to such words as *posh, classy*, or *chic* today, which are (a) slightly slangy, and (b) used by the educated only with a hint of a sneer, or at the very least facetiously.

The distribution of the word in *Sense and Sensibility* confirms the element of vulgarity in it. It is used most frequently by and of the Miss Steeles, the deficiencies in whose background and upbringing the novel constantly emphasizes. They are a horrid pair, with an innate vulgarity of mind and manner (concealed behind a thin veneer of gentility a little more successfully by the shrewder Lucy than by her elder sister Anne). As they are also social climbers, it is appropriate that their attempts to appear qualified for the beau monde should be conveyed chiefly through the use of the word *smart*—itself a vulgar little upstart from slang, pretending to be conversant with the ways of gentility, but essentially rather a cheap word. It becomes practically a theme-word of the horribly common Anne Steele, who uses the word four times in the course of her first extended utterance, which takes the form of an enquiry as to whether Elinor had "a great many smart beaux" in Sussex; a reminiscence on the "smart beaux" she herself knew in Exeter; an expression of a liking for beaux, "provided they dress smart and behave civil"; and a recollection of one Mr Rose at Exeter, "a prodigious smart young man, quite a beau". (Here and throughout this essay I use double quotation marks to indicate direct speech.) The word *beau* itself is, of course, a vulgarism, one which Elinor professes not "perfectly to comprehend the meaning of"—with something of the air, one imagines, of Oscar Wilde's Gwendolen when she announces herself pleased to be able to say that *she* has never seen a *spade*. That Anne's preference for the word *smart* also gives her away is suggested by the hasty intervention of Lucy ('looking ashamed of her sister'), who substitutes a different word ("But why should you think . . . that there are not as many *genteel* young men in Devonshire as Sussex?"); and by the way the narrator gives it emphasis in an ironic piece of *erlebte rede* a few lines on: 'Elinor had not seen [the Miss Steeles] more than twice, before the eldest of them wished her joy on her sister's having been so lucky as to make a conquest of a very smart beau since she came to Barton' (pp. 123–5 in Volume I of R. W. Chapman's five-volume edition (London, 1933) of Jane Austen's novels). Miss Steele later announces proudly that she and her sister enjoyed the attendance of "a very smart beau" in their journey to London (p. 218); and during their stay there is in the habit of giving Marianne's evening dress a rude scrutiny generally terminating in a compliment which Marianne (hyper-sensitive to vulgarity) considered 'the greatest impertinence of all': Anne avowing that 'upon her word she looked vastly *smart*, and she dared to say would make a great many conquests' (p. 249).

The word is also used by Sir John Middleton, who, despite his title, is a pretty coarse (though warm-hearted) man, rather short on 'elegance' (i.e. genuine refinement of manners; p. 30). He is concerned 'at being unable to get any smart young men' to meet the Dashwood girls at Barton Park (p. 33). He is not referring to witty young men; Sir John has not much brain, and it would not occur to him that Elinor and Marianne might enjoy the society of livelier minds than he and Barton Park can provide; he is referring to fashionable young bucks, which, in his endearing vulgarity, he assumes is the sort of company such young girls would prefer to that of old squares like himself. Mrs Jennings, who shares Sir John's warmth of heart and coarseness of manner (she is the widow of a tradesman whose business had been conducted (p. 153) in a fairly down-market part of London), is another patronizer of the word. Miss Grey (the heiress for whom Willoughby jilts Marianne) is introduced to us by the narrator herself as 'a very fashionable looking young woman' (p. 176). But the word that comes more naturally to the less refined Mrs Jennings, answering Elinor's query about the lady, is *smart*: 'a smart, stilish girl they say, but not handsome' (p. 194). Similarly, Captain Tilney—the caddish, moustache-twirling elder brother of the hero in *Northanger Abbey*—is described at his first appearance in the narrative as 'a very fashionable-looking, handsome young man' (p. 131). But Isabella Thorpe (a cousin-in-fiction not many times removed from Anne Steele) revealingly uses the less elegant word: "being such a smart young fellow, I saw every eye was upon us" (p. 134). There is a strong family likeness between Isabella and her brother John, who likewise describes Elinor Tilney—previously introduced to us by the narrator as a 'fashionable' young lady and one possessed of 'elegance' (pp. 53, 56)—as a "smart-looking girl" (p. 85).

It is, then, Jane Austen's less genteel characters who tend to favour the word and the coxcomb brand of fashionableness it connotes. It is likewise *of* them that she most frequently uses it herself—presumably in mock imitation of their own term. Hence it is used in her *Verses to Rhyme with 'Rose'* (a friendly competition in which several of the Austen ladies participated) of a working-man in Sunday best:

> Happy the lab'rer in his Sunday clothes!
> In light-drab coat, smart waistcoat, well-darn'd hose,
> And hat upon his head, to church he goes.
> (*Minor Works*, ed. R. W. Chapman (London, 1954), p. 445)

This usage is really snobbish at worst, and condescending at best, though the context here is fairly trivial and non-malicious.

In *Sense and Sensibility*, Jane Austen uses the word in her own voice exclusively of the Steeles: and uses it in such a way as to suggest that their *smartness* is but a cheap imitation of real gentility. Lady Middleton (aware, no doubt, that her husband is not over-discerning in such matters) responds to his announcement of the invitation he has issued to them with some concern at an enforced association with 'two girls whom she had never seen in her life, and of whose elegance,—whose tolerable gentility even, she could have no proof' (p. 118). When she makes their acquaintance, their *exteriors* are sufficient to calm her fears; for 'their appearance was by no means ungenteel or unfashionable. Their dress was very smart, their manners very civil, they were delighted with the house, and in raptures with the furniture', etc.

(p. 119). And Lady Middleton, a very refeened but thoroughly lightweight and superficial woman, looks no deeper than the superficies, and is soon flattered into a partiality for the pair. But the prose here obviously hints that their social credentials may not be as unexceptionable as they appear: partly through the reserve of the phrasing ('their *appearance* was . . . their *manners* were . . .'); partly through the substitution of *smart* for '(not) unfashionable' in the second sentence, a word that here sounds a slight sniff; and partly through the withholding of the word *élegant* which Jane Austen customarily bestows on manners that evince the refinement, polish, and graceful poise of real good breeding. And despite the obsessive value placed on *elegance* by the rather precious Lady Middleton, it appears she is not very capable of distinguishing between the *smartness* that shams it and the real McCoy. For in the case of Anne, even that '(not) ungenteel' does not survive a second glance from the quick-eyed Elinor, who soon sees clearly that 'Lucy was certainly not elegant, and her sister not even genteel' (p. 231), and that Lady Middleton has been had. The *elegance* that distinguishes true good breeding is consistently differentiated from the fashionable *smartness* with which Lucy tries to pass herself off as a member of 'polite' society: 'her features were pretty, and she had a sharp quick eye, and a smartness of air, which though it did not give actual elegance or grace, gave distinction to her person' (p. 120).

This same distinction between the *elegance* of real gentility and the *smartness* of fake gentility again finds a parallel in *Northanger Abbey*: in the contrast between the gushy, affected cheapness of Isabella Thorpe, and the modest courtesy of Elinor Tilney. *Smart* is the word that heralds Isabella's entrance into the novel, as it does Lucy Steele's: ' "Here come my dear girls," cried Mrs. Thorpe, pointing at three smart looking females, who, arm in arm, were then moving towards her' (p. 32). Isabella's *smartness* denotes the 'fashionable air of her figure and dress' (p. 34), which the naïve Catherine is duly impressed by. But what the word connotes becomes clear when Elinor Tilney appears: '[Miss Tilney's] air, though it had not all *the decided pretension, the resolute stilishness* of Miss Thorpe's, had more real elegance. Her manners shewed good sense and good breeding' (pp. 55–6; my italics). The word *pretension* here is significant. *Smart* as applied to Lucy and Isabella is used to suggest a modish overlay of chic assumed by persons *not* really genteel in background, upbringing, manner or mind, but who nevertheless have social pretensions; and it is used to distinguish that voguish patina from the real good breeding or *elegance* of bona fide members of the polite society whose fashions are being aped by girls essentially vulgar and coarse.

'Upstart', then, can be part of what this potentially malicious little word may imply. Hence it could be used as a snub, and is so used in one of the funniest of Jane Austen's fictive letters, 'From a Young Lady in distressed Circumstances to her freind'. The writer, genteel but not wealthy, is the exasperated recipient of attentions from a local Ladyship given in a very insulting manner designed to keep the girl in her place. The young lady, for instance, gets a lift in her carriage to a ball:

> "So Miss Maria (said her Ladyship as she saw me advancing to the door of the Carriage) you seem very smart to night—*My* poor Girls will appear quite to disadvantage by *you*—I only hope your Mother may not have distressed herself to set *you* off. Have you got a new Gown on? . . . I dare say it is all very smart—But I must own, for you know I always speak my mind, that I think it was quite a needless piece of expence—Why could not you have worn your old striped one? It is not my way to find fault with people because they are poor, for I always think that they are more to be despised and pitied than blamed for it, especially if they cannot help it. . . ."

The next night, her Ladyship with equal graciousness forces Maria to leave her dinner to receive the following invitation delivered by her from her carriage:

> "Why I think Miss Maria you are not quite so smart as you were last night—But I did not come to examine your dress, but to tell you that you may dine with us the day after tomorrow. . . . There will be no occasion for your being very fine for I shant send the Carriage—If it rains you may take an umbrella—" I could hardly help laughing at hearing her give me leave to keep myself dry.   (*MW*, pp. 156–60)

Smart here is plainly a very ill-concealed and bitchy snub, intended to imply that Miss Maria is getting above herself in assuming stylish fashions she should not have the money for or the pretension to.

In the passages quoted above from *Sense and Sensibility* and *Northanger Abbey*, Jane Austen is, with a touch of sarcasm, using of Lucy and Isabella a word they might themselves use; and is using it to suggest defective or superficial notions on their part of what distinguishes polite society. The veiled sneer that can be heard in *chic* today is also audible in the only other use of *smart* in this novel by a genteel character. Edward Ferrars tells Mrs Dashwood that he himself had always inclined toward the Church as a profession, adding bitterly:

> "But that was not smart enough for my family. They recommended the army. That was a great deal too smart for me. The law was allowed to be genteel enough; many young men, who had chambers in the Temple, made a very good appearance in the first circles, and drove about town in very knowing gigs. . . . As for the navy, it had fashion on its side, but I was too old when the subject was first started to enter it—and, at length, as there was no necessity for my having any profession at all, as I might be as

191

dashing and expensive without a red coat on my back as with one,
idleness was pronounced on the whole to be the most advantageous
and honourable." (pp. 102–3)

Edward clearly intends by his use of the word *smart* to convey some sarcasm at
the very superficial notions of what are the 'honourable' 'fashions' of
'gentility' that his family entertain: they merely want him to cut a modish,
dashing, extravagant figure in the jet set. Again the word hints at a showy
stylishness that should not really be the hall-mark of true gentility.

There is a parallel in *Mansfield Park* for the contrast Edward here implies
between the truly honourable and respectable profession of the Church, on the
one hand, and, on the other, the voguish kudos of a career in the services—
which the more narrow-minded element of the beau monde might honour and
respect more. The comparison between the two vocations is drawn by Mary
Crawford, who does not, of course, intend it to be seen in those terms; but the
novel plainly does. She finds Edmund's choice of the church dull, tame,
unambitious; the forces have more glamour and style:

"The profession, either navy or army, is its own justification. It
has every thing in its favour; heroism, danger, bustle, fashion.
Soldiers and sailors are always acceptable in society." (p. 109)

The *fashion* that ensures officers their seats in the drawing-rooms of 'society'
Edward Ferrars refers to as *smartness*; Mary naturally uses the less barbedly
colloquial term *fashion*, because it is not her wish, as it is Edward's, to belittle
the criterion by which the profession is given preference over the Church.

The word makes its last appearance in *Sense and Sensibility* in connection,
once again, with Lucy Steele: Lucy as she figures in Elinor's imagination of
her as the wife of Edward:

She saw them in an instant in their parsonage-house; saw in Lucy,
the active, contriving manager, uniting at once a desire of smart
appearance, with the utmost frugality, and ashamed to be suspected
of half her economical practices. (p. 357)

Though the passage is in indirect speech, *smart* appears to be the word Elinor
is mentally applying to the figure Lucy would wish to cut; she is, then, with
resigned and ironic distaste, using the word Lucy herself would use, and the
one which best conveys the kind of gentility Lucy would aim at—a sort of
keep-up-with-Lady-Jones chicness of appearance and life-style.

The evidence from *Sense and Sensibility*, therefore, suggests that *smart* is a
lowish word, which tends to be used (1) by or of the less genteel characters,
who (2) may nevertheless have certain rather upstart social pretensions; and
(3) to suggest pretty vulgar, narrow notions of what constitutes social
distinction. The usage in the other novels confirms these conclusions: *smart*

has much the same sense, register, and often ironic/facetious tone that such words as *posh, classy, chic* or *modish* have today.

Jane Austen certainly does not use the word when she wishes to comment on the presence or absence of fashion and stylishness in a neutral or commendatory way (where a tone of slight slanginess and/or irony would be inappropriate). Nor, when her characters make the same observations in the same spirit, does it figure in their reported reactions. Mr Palmer, she tells us, had 'an air of more fashion and sense than his wife' (*SS*, p. 106): she does not want to suggest anything of the showily à la mode or pretentiously upstart in this gentleman. Similarly, the Bingley sisters 'were fine women, with an air of decided fashion' (*PP*, p. 10). Lady Middleton 'saw enough of fashion in [John Dashwood's] appearance, to think his acquaintance worth having' (*SS*, p. 228); Darcy sees in the Meryton assembly only 'a collection of people in whom there was little beauty and no fashion' (*PP*, p. 16); Caroline Bingley opines with jealous tartness of Elizabeth that "in her air altogether, there is a self-sufficiency without fashion, which is intolerable" (p. 271); Sir Walter Elliot 'did justice to [Mr Elliot's] very gentlemanlike appearance, his air of elegance and fashion, his good shaped face, his sensible eye' (*P*, p. 141). The contexts here would make the derogatory implications of *smart* out of place; it is not in the nature of Darcy, still less in that of the titled snobs Lady Middleton and Sir Walter Elliot, and not at all to Miss Bingley's purpose, to disparage the fashion of the polite world they all refer to in passing their judgements, as would be suggested if the word *smart* appeared in the record of them.

Smart is thus a marked word, which does not occur very often. It is most frequent in *Sense and Sensibility, Northanger Abbey*, and *The Watsons*. Lucy Steele and Isabella Thorpe account for most of the *smart* talk in the two former. The heroine of *The Watsons* lives in rather reduced circumstances; while her better-off and socially vain neighbours and in-laws anxiously maintain that 'resolute stilishness' predicated of Isabella Thorpe. And, as if in solidarity with her, *smart* tends to be used of all the voguish swishness of which the Watsons emerge as the poor relations. When Emma attends a local ball in the company of the wealthier Edwards family, the adjective is applied to the finery of those present: the ballroom starts to fill up with 'continual accessions of portly Chaperons, & strings of smartly-dressed girls', and the local grandee's daughter is engaged by 'the smartest officer of the sett' (*MW*, pp. 328, 330; officers were probably prime targets for the epithet). The word hints at strutting and parade, and conveys a rather dismissive attitude towards the determined modishness of the polite party-goers. Emma waits the next morning to be collected from the Edwards home by 'the convenient but very un-smart Family Equipage' run by her own house (p. 338). The anti-hero of the novel is a handsome, conceited young blood called Tom Musgrove, whose hobby is breaking all local female hearts, but who is saving himself for (he hopes) the very wealthy Miss Osborne. The fashionable and stylish air he cultivates exceeds even that of Lord Osborne, in the opinion of an old flame of his, Emma's eldest sister: "Tom Musgrove looks all to nothing, the smartest & most fashionable man of the two" (p. 347). The idiomatic 'all to nothing' sounds an informal note that does not make the colloquial word *smart* sound out of place or barbed; but it is interesting that Tom Musgrove, socially narcissistic and ambitious, is in fact much more the sort of person to whom the adjective *smart* would be applicable than is Lord Osborne, whose birth guarantees his social credentials, which therefore need no anxious parade.

Emma's sister-in-law Jane is a sister in spirit of Mrs Elton: of wealthy but not especially genteel origins, she is a stuck-up show-off, whose vulgar parade of genteel chic well deserves the contempt the word *smart* conveys: her manners are 'pert and conceited', conveying self-satisfaction at 'being now in possession of a very smart house in Croydon, where she gave genteel parties, & wore fine cloathes' (p. 349). Though she fussily insists, with horrid condescension, that she will not expect to be entertained with great magnificence at the Watson home, she comes down to dinner 'exactly as smart as she had been at her own party', but with 'apologies for her dress—"I would not make you wait, said she, so I put on the first thing I met with.—I am afraid I am a sad figure"' (p. 353). Tom Musgrove, not knowing of the visit of Robert and Jane, pays an unexpected call on the humble Watson abode, where he is surprised to find 'a circle of smart people whom he cd not immediately recognise arranged with all the honours of visiting round the fire, & Miss Watson sitting at the best Pembroke Table, with the best Tea things before her' (p. 355). Some jocular irreverence for the self-conscious poshness of the scene is here detectable in the choice of the informal Germanic monosyllable, which conveys the writer's amused relish of the momentary social disconcertion suffered by Tom.

Sanditon, the novel Jane Austen died before she could complete, looks as if it, too, might have had a relatively high incidence of *smartness*, as the word occurs three times in the mere twelve chapters that are as far as it got. One would certainly predict it from the plot, which mostly concerns the efforts of a crank called Mr Parker (labelled an 'Enthusiast' by the rather bemused Palmers) to turn the eponymous little town on the south coast into a fashionable and money-spinning resort for the beau monde. This is fertile ground for outcrops of *smart*, whose semantic range definitely includes efforts at classiness. Charlotte accordingly notices that the planned residential quarters include 'one short row of smart-looking Houses, called the Terrace, with a broad walk in front, aspiring to be the Mall of the Place'; and the village contains cottages 'smartened up with a white Curtain & "Lodgings to Let"' (*MW*, pp. 384, 383). The proposed amenities include a subscription library, which is to double as a gift-shop retailing all the usual trumpery of a fashionable tourist centre; here Charlotte makes some purchases, 'as soon as

Miss Whitby could be hurried down from her Toilette, with all her glossy curls & smart Trinkets to wait on her' (p. 390).

Since it is a lowish word (equivalent to *posh*), *smart* is not a word Jane Austen uses outside these rather specific contexts. Apart from the four instances relative to Isabella and John Thorpe which have already been cited, there is only one other occurrence of it in *Northanger Abbey*; *Pride and Prejudice* has two instances; *Catherine* (unfinished), *Mansfield Park* and *Emma* each include it only once; and *Persuasion* not at all. And there is no instance of it in any of the other minor short stories, such as *Lady Susan* or *Love and Freindship*.

The one remaining instance in *Northanger Abbey* concerns the heroine herself. Like most young girls, she has a tomboyish disregard for dirt—until an equally typical 'inclination for finery' awakens some pride in her personal appearance, and 'she grew clean as she grew smart' (p. 15). *Smart* here contributes to the pithy facetiousness of the comment, and to the objectively amused tone characteristic of the novel's unglamorizing treatment of its heroine.

The effect of its use in *Catherine* is rather different. The heroine is preparing to follow her relations to a ball when Stanley, the cousin she has never met, arrives unexpectedly at the house. He proves to have that brand of charm which Jane Austen shows elsewhere (in Charles Bingley, Frank Churchill and Frederick Wentworth, for instance) that she knew the power of: that is, an easy, open, lively manner—calculated to be peculiarly attractive to a girl like Catherine, who has spent all her life sedulously guarded from young men by a caring but very prim and proper aunt. Suddenly noticing that she is dressed for a ball, he breaks off to ask, "But tell me, where are you going to so smart?"; and, on being answered, proposes that he should escort her, adding a little cheekily that "this will be a most agreable surprize to everybody to see you enter the room with such a smart Young Fellow as I am" (*MW*, pp. 217–18). His use of the semi-colloquial word is part of the winning pleasantry and easy informality of his general manner.

It is not surprising to find the word (applied, again, to the military) in the mouth of Mrs Bennet in *Pride and Prejudice*, in her wistful reference to "a smart young Colonel" (p. 29). Kitty and Lydia are very much their mother's daughters, and it is in connection with them, predictably, that *smartness* makes its only other appearance in the novel. It occurs in the context of a wryly amused comment on the influences that operate most powerfully on their giddy young minds (beaux and clothes). The Bennet girls walk to Meryton, on reaching which the eyes of the youngest two 'were immediately wandering up in the street in quest of the officers, and nothing less than a very smart bonnet indeed, or a really new muslin in a shop window, could recal them' (p. 72).

The only person to use the word in *Mansfield Park* is William Price, whose background and social status are not of the highest gentility; so he does not feel inclined to visit the Rushworths at Brighton, as Mrs Norris suggests, for, "I could not expect to be welcome in such a smart place as that—poor scrubby midshipman as I am" (p. 245). Here, the word is probably intended to indicate something slightly sub-standard in William's speech; the Bertrams or Crawfords would certainly use the word *elegant* of the quality in question.

The single occurrence in *Emma* is particularly interesting, since the word appears here (as in one instance in *Sanditon*) as a verb—a verb which Jane Austen may well have been among the first to use, as this passage is the earliest cited for it by the *OED*. She is describing Mr Elton's house, the Vicarage, 'an old and not very good house, almost as close to the road as it could be. It had no advantage of situation; but had been very much smartened up by the present proprietor' (p. 83). This is almost certainly a case of the house reflecting the man. Mr Elton, despite his flowery talk and ways, is *not*, the novel makes clear, a true gentleman; he is, however, jealous of his social position, and determined to better it if he can (p. 66). When Mrs Dashwood in *Sense and Sensibility* contemplates improvements to her cottage, she speaks of supplying 'all that was wanted of greater elegance' (p. 29). One detects, therefore, in the selection of the less respectful phrase *smartened up*, a certain tartness of tone, a narrator not much impressed in general by Mr Elton's efforts at genteel fashion and style.

Where the word occurs in the novels, then, it is used by or of the ungenteel, or used in levity, irony, or disdain. The case seems to be different in the letters, where the more informal context apparently permits a word Jane Austen would avoid in literature intended for public consumption. In private chat to Cassandra, she uses it three times of head-dress: 'I still venture to retain the narrow silver round it, put twice round without any bow, & instead of the black military feather shall put in the Coquelicot one, as being smarter;—& besides Coquelicot is to be all the fashion this winter'; 'I find my straw bonnet looking very much like other people's, & quite as smart. Bonnets of cambric muslin on the plan of Lady Bridges' are a good deal worn, and some of them are very pretty'; 'I am glad she likes my cap so well.—I assure you my old one looked so smart yesterday that I was asked two or three times before I set off, whether it was not my new one' (*Jane Austen's Letters*, ed. R. W. Chapman, second edition (Oxford, 1952), pp. 37–8, 125, 335).

One remembers the 'smart bonnet' in *Pride and Prejudice*. But here there seems to be no ironic edge to the word. Some playful humour aimed at her own attempts to be stylish and fashionable is possible, but not strongly indicated by anything else in the phrasing. And she often writes at some length to Cassandra on the subject of gowns and head-dresses, which were matters the sisters took fairly seriously. The following item of news she likewise seems to be retailing pretty straight: 'I have not yet seen [Miss

Seymour's] face, but neither her dress nor air have anything of the Dash or Stilishness which the Browns talked of; quite the contrary indeed, her dress is not even smart, & her appearance very quiet' (p. 149). *Smart* here appears to be merely a fairly casual, colloquial word for *fashionable*, not one that is loaded in any way.

On only one occasion does she use the word with an audible playfulness, directed at letter-writing as one of the genteel accomplishments cultivated by polite females, and at her own epistolary performance. After an initial complaint that she has not sufficient matter for a letter, she finds trivia enough to fill up the paper, and ends by congratulating herself on having after all composed one tolerably up to the fashionable standard. Her concluding words form as fitting a closure as any to an academic paper:

> There, I flatter myself I have constructed you a smartish Letter, considering my want of Materials. But like my dear Dr. Johnson I beleive I have dealt more in Notions than Facts.   (p. 181)

Tabula Gratulatoria

Sebastian Anstruther: Clifton, Bristol.
Prof. Norman Blake: University of Sheffield.
Tony Boorman: University of Bristol.
Capt. Simon Burgess: Poxwell, Dorchester.
Dr J. D. Burnley: University of Sheffield.
Don Carleton: University of Bristol.
Mrs Freda Cottle: Teignmouth, Devon.
Thomas N. L. Custance: Deans Yard, London.
Det. Const. Dennis Cutter: Longwell Green, Bristol.
D. R. Davies: Sneyd Park, Bristol.
Professor Norman Davis: Merton College, Oxford.
Jon Donovan: Chapter & Verse Bookshop, Bristol.
Mr and Mrs J. R. Eachus: Westbury-on-Trym, Bristol.
Martin J. Crossley Evans: University of Bristol.
Miss Marion Fewell: 17 Poppleton Road, York.
Jean and John Flower: Mangotsfield, Bristol.
Ronald Gaskell: Penzance, Cornwall.
Dr Frederic A. Gaydon, OBE, VRD, FIMA: Bampton, Oxfordshire.
Prof. Johan Gerritsen: University of Groningen.
Prof. C. H. Gifford: University of Bristol.
Professor Douglas Gray: Lady Margaret Hall, Oxford.
Richard F. S. Hamer: Christ Church, Oxford.
Dr Alison Hanham: Massey University, New Zealand.
Dr T. G. B. Howe: University of Bristol.
Miss Lilian James: 20 Morgan Arcade, Cardiff.
J. P. M. Jansen: University of Groningen.
Peter January: Budapest, Hungary.
Mrs Judith Jefferson: Sommerville Road, Bristol.
Dr Deborah Johnson: University of Bristol.
Ian Johnson: University of St Andrews.
Sir John Kingman, FRS: University of Bristol.
Mr and Mrs E. Knopfler: Sneyd Park, Bristol.
Prof. Stephen Körner: University of Bristol.
Nicholas Lee: University of Bristol.
H. G. M. Leighton, MA, FSA: Bristol.
Miss Janice Lingley: Bedminster, Bristol.
Michael J. H. Liversidge: University of Bristol.

Mrs Joy Macdonald: Weston-Super-Mare, Avon.
Don M. Maltby: Bramcote Hills Comprehensive School, Nottingham.
Prof. Patrick McGrath: University of Bristol.
Stephen Medcalf: University of Sussex.
Dr Gerald Morgan: Trinity College, Dublin.
Mrs J. D. Morris: 29 St John's Road, Bristol.
Miss Bettina Nelemans: Utrecht, The Netherlands.
Prof. Wilhelm Nicolaisen: State University of New York, USA.
J. H. M. Parry: University of Bristol.
Prof. C. Bruce Perry: University of Bristol.
Mr and Mrs S. G. Phelps: Gloucestershire.
Mrs Ruth Pitman: University of Bristol.
Mr and Mrs D. G. Powell: Westbury-on-Trym, Bristol.
Miss Elizabeth Ralph: 9 Pembroke Road, Bristol.
Mrs Susan Rastetter: Cuddington, Cheshire.
Dr Alan B. Reynolds: 6 Richmond Terrace, Bristol.
Prof. Christopher B. Ricks: Boston University.
Charles A. J. Runacres: Eton, Berkshire.
Mrs Stephanie Roden Ryder: Henleaze, Bristol.
Miss Jennifer Scherr: University of Bristol.
Mrs Valerie Seeley: Clevedon, Avon.
Miss Marcia K. Segal: Maryland, USA.
James Sherborne: 26 Hanbury Road, Bristol.
Prof. Alan Simpson: University of Bristol.
Miss Celia Sisam: Isles of Scilly, Cornwall.
Tony Slade: University of Adelaide, Australia.
Michael and Maureen Smith: University of Bristol.
Mark N. Stuart-Smith: 2 Glenloch Road, London.
Prof. Eiichi Suzuki: Tohoku University, Japan.
Mrs Jan Tarling: University of Bristol.
Mrs Marjorie L. Taylor: University of Bristol.
William C. Tiffany: Memorial University of Newfoundland.
Peter Tomlinson: 3 Queen's Parade, Bristol.
George Turner: University of Adelaide, Australia.
Prof. John Vincent: University of Bristol.
Ronald A. Waldron: King's College London.
Alan Ward: Wadham College, Oxford.
Ass. Prof. Ruth Waterhouse: Macquarie University, Australia.
Evan Wright: University of Bristol.

Aberdeen University Library.
The Library, University of Bristol.
Bristol and Gloucestershire Archaeological Society.

Edinburgh University Library.
The Library, University of Lancaster.
The Library, University of London.
The Library, University of Nottingham.
Universitätsbibliothek Regensburg.
The Parochial Church Council of St Paul's Church, Clifton: Bristol.